SOCIOLOGICAL REVIEW MONOGRAPH 32

Power, Action and Belief

A New Sociology of Knowledge?

Edited by John Law

Routledge & Kegan Paul
London, Boston and Henley

First published in 1986
by Routledge & Kegan Paul plc

14 Leicester Square, London WC2H 7PH, England

9 Park Street, Boston, Mass. 02108, USA and

Broadway House, Newtown Road,
Henley on Thames, Oxon RG9 1EN, England

Set in Times
by Hope Services, Abingdon
and printed in Great Britain
by Billing & Sons, Worcester

Library of Congress Cataloging in Publication Data

Power, action and belief.
(Sociological review monograph; 32)
1. Knowledge, Sociology of—Addresses, essays,
lectures. I. Law, John. II. Series.
HM15.S545 no. 32 [BD175] 301 s [306'.42] 85–14273
British Library CIP data also available

ISBN 0-7102-0802-2

Power, Action and Belief

The Sociological Review

Managing Editors: John Eggleston, Ronald Frankenberg,
Gordon Fyfe

University of Keele

Contents

Contents

Cover picture Keele University library, Turner Collection

Contributors

Barry Barnes was trained in natural sciences and in sociology before moving to the Science Studies Unit, Edinburgh University. Among his publications are *Scientific Knowledge and Sociological Theory* (Routledge & Kegan Paul, 1974), *Interests and the Growth of Knowledge* (Routledge & Kegan Paul, 1977), and *T.S. Kuhn and Social Science* (Macmillan, 1981). He is the joint editor of two collections of readings in the sociology and social history of science: *Natural Order* (edited with S. Shapin, Sage, 1979) and *Science in Context* (edited with D.O. Edge, Open University Press, 1982). He has held visiting appointments at the University of Pennsylvania and at the Institute for Advanced Study, Princeton.

Michel Callon is Professor of Sociology at the Ecole Nationale Supérieure des Mines de Paris, and Director of the Centre de Sociologie de l'Innovation. He has written widely on the sociology of science and technology and on science policy, and is the editor (with John Law and Arie Rip) of *Mapping the Dynamics of Science and Technology* (Macmillan, forthcoming). His research, which is both quantitative and qualitative, is on the formation of economic markets, and he was directly involved in the development of policy for scientific research in France in the early 1980s.

Mark Cousins is Senior Lecturer in Sociology at Thames Polytechnic. He is joint author with Athar Hussain of *Michel Foucault* (Macmillan, 1984).

Mary Douglas has retired from the Avalon Foundation Chair in the Humanities, Northwestern University, Evanston, Illinois. She has been appointed Visiting Professor in Religion, Anthropology and Sociology in Princeton University. Most of her work has been consistently directed to developing a sociology of knowledge that is anchored in political and moral philosophy. Her recent books include: *The World of Goods; towards an anthropology of consumption,* co-author Baron Isherwood (Penguin Books, 1978); Introduction to the English language translation of *The Collective Memory* by Maurice Halbwachs (1980); *Edward Evans-Pritchard* (1982); editor, *Essays in the Sociology of Perception* (Routledge, 1982); *Risk and Culture, an Essay on the Selection of Technical and Environmental Dangers* (co-author, Aaron Wildavsky, 1982); editor, *Food in the Social Order* (Russell Sage Foundation, 1984); *Risk Acceptability According to the Social Sciences* (forthcoming).

Gordon Fyfe graduated at the University of Leicester in Social Sciences in 1967. Lecturer in Sociology at the University of Keele since 1971, he is the author of several papers on engraving and the nature of art markets.

Contributors

Barry Hindess is Professor of Sociology at Liverpool University. His books include: *The Decline of Working Class Politics, PreCapitalist Modes of Production* (with Paul Hirst), *Marx's Capital and Capitalism Today* (with Anthony Cutler, Paul Hirst and Athar Hussain) and *Parliamentary Democracy and Socialist Politics*.

Athar Hussain is Senior Lecturer in Economics at the University of Keele. He is joint author, with Mark Cousins, of *Michel Foucault* (Macmillan, 1984).

Bruno Latour was trained in philosophy and sociology. He occupies a research position at the Centre de Sociologie d'Innovation at the Ecole Nationale Supérieure des Mines de Paris, is the author of *Les Microbes: Guerre et Paix* (Métailié, 1984), and is currently preparing *Science in Action: Rules and Principles for the Study of Science in Society* (Open University, forthcoming).

Jean Lave, who obtained a PhD in Social Anthropology from Harvard University, is Professor of Anthropology in the School of Social Sciences at the University of California, Irvine. Her research is on the relationship between educational forms, everyday practice and cognitive theory, and is based on fieldwork undertaken in West Africa and the United States. She is the author of *Culture, Cognition and Practice: a Study of Arithmetic in Solution* (Cambridge University Press, forthcoming), the co-editor (with B. Rogoff) of *Everyday Cognition: Its Development in Social Context* (Harvard University Press, 1984), and is currently working on *Tailored Learning: Education and Everyday Practice among Craftsmen in West Africa.*

John Law is Senior Lecturer in Sociology and Social Anthropology at the University of Keele. He has written extensively on the sociology of knowledge, science and technology, is the co-author (with Peter Lodge) of *Science for Social Scientists* (Macmillan, 1984) and the co-editor (with Michel Callon and Arie Rip) of *Mapping the Dynamics of Science and Technology* (Macmillan, forthcoming).

Steve Rayner is a British social anthropologist specializing in the study of institutional and organizational cultures and public responses to technological risk. He received his first degree in Philosophy and Theology from the University of Kent at Canterbury and a PhD in Anthropology from University College London in 1979. He has conducted research on political movements for the past eight years, including two years intensive fieldwork in the UK and one year in the US. Since 1980 he has concentrated on both pro- and anti-nuclear campaigners as well as environmental groups in the United States. He is co-author (with Jonathan Gross) of *Measuring Culture* (Columbia University Press, 1985). Presently a research associate at Oak Ridge National Laboratory, he has also been a visiting scholar at Columbia University, Boston University School of Public Health, and the Russell Sage Foundation. He also holds an honorary research appointment at the Centre for Occupational and Community Research in the UK.

Steven Yearley is Lecturer in Sociology at the Queen's University, Belfast. He has published a number of articles on sociological theory and the sociology of science, and is author of *Science and Sociological Practice* (Open University Press, 1984).

Editor's introduction: Power/ Knowledge and the dissolution of the sociology of knowledge

John Law

(1) Introduction: Three phases in the sociology of knowledge

History, as we know, is a construction. Let me start, then, by constructing a three-part albeit schematic history of the sociology of knowledge. Its first phase was set in motion with the writing of Marx and Durkheim. They defined two traditions for the analysis of the relationship between social structure and belief. They also, though this is particularly true for Marx, sought to tease out the relationship between knowledge and social control. Yet the first phase foundered with the writings of Mannheim and Merton. Mannheim's analysis of the existential determinants of belief, while in one way a triumph, became entwined with a set of seemingly intractable epistemological problems. Merton's paradigm for the sociology of knowledge, whilst resolving Mannheim's epistemological problems by fiat, led to little work in what he called the European tradition of the discipline. The sociology of knowledge went into a quiet decline which lasted through the 1950s.

The second phase in the sociology of knowledge took the form of a number of largely independent lines of development which became visible in the 1960s. Some of these – for instance Berger and Luckman's phenomenologically informed dialectical analysis of the relationship between structure and knowledge, and the structuralism of Lévi Strauss – will not be discussed here. I want, instead, to draw attention to three themes that seem to me to have been of continuing importance within the mainstream of the sociology of knowledge. The first came out of, and contributed to, Marxist analysis of the relationship between infrastructure and superstructure. The role of ideology was re-examined and re-specified in the work of Althusser and his followers. The integral

1

relationship between practice and ideology, found in the writing of Marx but sometimes lost in that of his more enthusiastic followers, was reasserted. The epistemological problem posed by Mannheim was transcended by asymmetrical diktat, again in the robust manner of Marx.

The second tradition grew out of a renewal of interest in Durkheim's sociology of knowledge. In the hands of such writers as Basil Bernstein and Mary Douglas, an attempt was made to rescue Durkheim from a number of obvious difficulties and certain unwarranted complaints by his detractors. Like Durkheim, Douglas drew upon anthropological ethnography to analyse the striking homologies that are sometimes to be found between the form of a social structure and the form of its corresponding culture. Unlike Durkheim (but like the Marxists), her writing displayed an acute sensitivity to the importance of knowledge for social control. It culminated in the grid/group 'gadget' which a small but enthusiastic following have developed and applied to a range of empirical circumstances.

A third tradition, influenced by Marx, by Durkheim, by Douglas, but also by the historical work of Thomas Kuhn, developed within the sociology of science. Here again the focus was empirical and the epistemological problems upon which Mannheim's project foundered were dealt with by an overt acceptance of methodological relativism. Scientific knowledge was treated as a culture like any other form of knowledge, and was seen as being directed by social interests with the corresponding social control implications. A number of fine studies of esoteric knowledge showed that it might be profitably analysed in this way, and revealed that social interests may operate in arenas seemingly far from areas of class or political conflict.

The second phase of the sociology of knowledge is still with us. All three of the traditions that make it up have remained productive up to the present, and a number of the authors who have contributed to this volume have written in this spirit. Nevertheless, it is my suggestion that the second phase is in crisis. A third phase is upon us in the form of work that has gone some way to eroding the basis of the sociology of knowledge as this has traditionally been conceived. Some of this work has grown out of one or other of the three traditions mentioned above – there is, for instance, increasing uncertainty about what may be counted as social structure within both the post-Althusserian tradition of Marxism and the sociology of science. Some has come from elsewhere: the work of Michel Foucault, his followers and his interpreters has been important here. In current second and third phase work writers with diverse backgrounds and theoretical commitments are seeking to come to terms with at least three sets of difficult issues which have relevance for the relationship between knowledge and power. First, there is the problem of the reciprocal relationship between knowledge and structure as this is mediated through practice, and what this implies for an understanding of the latter. Second, and often closely linked with this, there is a problem about the relationship between discourse, structure and knowledge, and whether, indeed, the last two retain any status at all within the analysis of discourse. And third, there is a quite novel concern with what Foucault called the microphysics of power – the tools, so to speak, of social control.

The contributions to this volume depict some of the strategies adopted by writers in the face of such problems. They have been deliberately chosen in order to represent a wide spectrum of such positions. There has been no attempt to impose an editorial line, and the heterogeneity of the contributions will be obvious to the reader. Some, as I have already indicated, remain committed to one or other of the traditions of the second phase of the sociology of knowledge. Others are committed, to a greater or lesser extent, to one or more of the themes that seem to be emerging in this third phase of the 'sociology of knowledge'. In the remainder of this essay I briefly describe the way in which the phase-one problematic of the sociology of knowledge has been dissolved in the face of the problems mentioned above, and indicate how the contributing authors have attempted to cope with, or contribute to, this dissolution.

(2) Practice, structure and knowledge

On first inspection, the model of the sociology of knowledge is beguiling in its simplicity. There is social structure on the one hand. And there is knowledge on the other. Structure influences the form or the content of knowledge. The arrow of determination points in one direction.

If the initial model of the sociology of knowledge were sustainable then the relationship between structure and belief would be relatively easy to determine. But matters are not that simple because the relationship between these is two-way in character. Structure certainly influences belief but belief in turn acts upon structure, acting to sustain it or, indeed, to change it. Furthermore, structure and culture are not easily separable. They come, in the form of practice, rolled up together, and the sociologist who wishes to make claims about the way they influence one another is forced to tease them apart.

The notion that structure and belief are integrally related is not new. It is certainly, for instance, to be found in the writing of Marx. Marx starts by elaborating what may be treated as a materialist theory of interests. As is well known, the relations to the means of production are used to define the interests of classes. These interests account, at least in some measure, for people's beliefs. However, since (in capitalist society) it is in the immediate interests of the working class to alter the relations of production, it is also in the short term interests of the bourgeoisie that the true nature of the interests of the working class be concealed. Here, then, ideology enters the scene. Ideology distorts and conceals, but it is far more than mere dream. It must provide a basis for, or form a part of, a workable and sustainable working class practice which makes it possible to interact with both the natural and social worlds. Hence ideology is both interested and distorted, but also practical and lived.

Marx's analysis of ideology and its relationship to the reproduction of class relations is well known. His writing, with its stress on practice and its insistence on the existence of real class interests that are not recognised by those individuals interpellated in ideology, has defined an area within which much second phase work in the sociology of knowledge has taken place. For reasons that have, perhaps, nearly as much to do with politics as intellectual considerations, the writing of Durkheim has had less influence on the analysis of the relationship between structure and belief. This is not to deny that there are intellectual reasons for Durkheim's relative lack of popularity. First, his sociology makes it difficult, if not impossible, to think in terms of social interests – and in the context of the sociology of knowledge the notion that ideas have something to do with interests is obviously of great intrinsic appeal. Second, at least at first inspection, his sociology of religion appears to try to sustain the initial model of the sociology of knowledge mentioned above: it looks as if structure influences the form of belief, but that beliefs have no reciprocal influence on structure.

Though Durkheim's main argument is well known, it is

appropriate to rehearse it once again if only briefly, because it has offered and offers an alternative model to that of Marx for understanding the relationship between social structure and belief. The problem, as Durkheim conceives it, is to transcend the empiricism/*a priorism* debate about the origins of our categories of thought. Empiricism, he suggests, is unsatisfactory because it does not explain how our minds are capable of generating stable categories out of shifting appearances. *A priorism* is unsatisfactory because it solves this problem by mystical mentalistic means. His solution is to propose a kind of social *a priorism*. Categories of thought come from our social experience. Our social classifications provide, so to speak, a template upon which we build our structures of thought. The social, as always for Durkheim, describes a reality that is prior to individuals.

If this 'template thesis' is the nub of Durkheim's contribution to the sociology of knowledge, his position is more complex than it at first sight appears. Furthermore, these complexities go some way to undermining the second objection to his approach indicated above. Thus, though it is true that thinking and belief originate in collective action for Durkheim, they also function to sustain society. This is because a certain level of logical and moral conformity is essential if cooperative behaviour is to be achieved. As he notes in *The Elementary Forms,* societies 'feel the need' for the occasional reaffirmation of the collective sentiments and ideas that make their unity and personality (Durkheim 1915:427). Thus ideas may feed back into institutions and influence them – and here he cites the institution of French revolutionary holidays which failed because of the waning of revolutionary faith. In addition he suggests that ceremonies (which play a central role in sustaining belief) also require justification in terms of systems of ideas and theories if they are to be maintained or spread. Thus a society creates an ideal of itself, an ideal that may be 'pulled in different directions' either to the past or to the future (Durkheim 1915:423).

Interestingly, Durkheim is also drawn to a practical or pragmatic conception of belief. Categories, he notes, should be seen as tools – indeed he talks more than once of the 'intellectual capital' of a society (e.g, 1915:19), arguing that ideas are tested in practice over an extended period of time. In fact, science is simply a more systematic method for testing ideas, and there is no distinction in principal between the cognitive function of religion and that of science – they are both methods for making sense of the world.

Clearly, then, a detailed reading of Durkheim reveals that he was sensitive to the reciprocity of structure-belief relationship and he was also attracted to a pragmatism which implied that active subjects operated in a practical manner to solve the problems involved in social and physical action. Thus there is, perhaps, more than a grain of truth in the claim by Stone and Farberman (1967) that Durkheim, with his developing commitment to active agency and philosophical pragmatism, was moving towards something like the perspective of symbolic interactionism. At any rate, both Durkheimians and Marxists writing within the second stage of the sociology of knowledge have been concerned to explore and specify the three-way relationship between practice, knowledge (or ideology) and the context of social control that is central to the writing of Marx and is, as I have tried to suggest, of some importance to Durkheim.

The Marxists, and the writing of Althusser has been of particular importance in this context, have sought to explore the way in which ideology, while ultimately determined by the relations of production, is nevertheless sustained by, indeed constituted in, practice. Thus in Althusser's scheme (see, in particular, Althusser 1971), ideas are derivative. They, together with the knowing subject and the obviousness of experience, are generated by material actions that are inserted into practices which are in turn inserted into rituals. (Note, in passing, that there are more than superficial similarities between Althusser's theory of the subject and the social psychology of George Herbert Mead.) Taken together, these rituals (Althusser uses a musical metaphor) play more or less the same tune and accordingly function to reproduce the relations of production and generate a unitary sense of obviousness for the subject and his/her surroundings. As we shall see later, there are serious difficulties in this theory of interpellation.

It would be unfair on Gordon Fyfe, whose study of eighteenth and nineteenth century art markets is the first essay in this monograph, to suggest that he is Althusserian. His contribution, which owes something to Weber and more to Bourdieu, is a theoretically sophisticated empirical contribution to the analysis of practice and ideology within the 'superstructure' as these relate to the relations of production in art. None the less, his study lies within the territory defined by contemporary Marxist theory. In particular, it attends to that topic of burning concern – the nature of the knowing, or in the case of art, the creative subject. Fyfe's argument is that the creative artist was constituted by the developing relations of production in art. Indeed, the piece is attractive in part because it is thoroughly empirical in character. He sketches for us a backcloth of class relations in eighteenth and nineteenth century England, he considers how the Royal Academy was constituted in the context of those relations, and he shows how the RA (and subsequent galleries) in turn became the locus of a set of practices that constituted the artist as creator. As a contribution to the second phase of the sociology of knowledge his argument deserves careful consideration.

Arguably, as I have suggested above, Durkheim was also concerned with practice and social control. However, whether or not the argument may be sustained for Durkheim, in the second phase transformation of Durkheimian theory undertaken by Mary Douglas in the 1960s and 1970s these issues have come to the fore. Douglas makes some use of Durkheim's 'template' thesis. More important, however, she is concerned with the ways in which knowledge may be used to legitimate social structure. It is her argument (see, in particular, Douglas 1973a; 1982b) that Durkheim's claim about the existence of homology between structure and knowledge (a claim that has since been reinforced by much convincing ethnography, from both anthropology and the history of science – see, for instance, Bulmer 1973; Rudwick 1974) can be derived from an analysis of the different strategies available for social control and legitimation in different types of social structure. Her grid/group device is intended to make this possible by cutting through the confusion of anthropological ethnography with its 'bongo-bongoism'. It proposes that all social structures may be defined by a combination of greater or lesser control via '(a) personal pressure and (b) shared roles. This combination produces the characteristic grid/group four-way classification, where three of the available combinations represent relatively stable structures with characteristic social control problems and characteristic cosmologies for their solution.

Douglas's grid/group scheme remains controversial. Nevertheless, it has defined an area within which a number of suggestive studies have taken place. Steve Rayner has contributed to this tradition, and his piece in the present monograph is concerned with that most Marxist of topics, the relationship between belief, practice and power. Rayner's concerns are two-fold. First, he wants to resist the Weber/Michels thesis about the inevitability of hierarchisation in social movements. Second, he wishes to show that the critical claim which is sometimes made of the grid/group scheme that it cannot handle social change is without foundation. Like Fyfe's piece, his study is empirical – it is of the development of the International Socialists/Socialist Worker's Party from a relatively egalitarian amalgamation of tendencies to, first, a 'small group' in which conformity was maintained by expulsion, and second, an organisation with some of the hierarchy and control characteristic of bureaucracy. His argument is that Tony Cliff could not move in one step from the first to the last stage, because the creation of a strong inside/outside dichotomy was a necessary control prerequisite for the imposition of hierarchy.

Mary Douglas's own contribution to the monograph is concerned with the social genesis of radical scepticism. Her argument, which she makes in part by considering the position of radical sceptics both in the West and India, is that this becomes a particularly attractive option to those who find themselves in a position that combines privilege and powerlessness within a political system that is arbitrary and perpetuates visible injustice. Thus, it is through radical scepticism, the denial of the reality and importance of appearances, that the moral problems and contradictions of the privileged may be solved. This essay is of particular interest because the third phase of the sociology of knowledge (and perhaps, in particular, in its discourse analysis form) is clearly influenced, if not constituted by, a form of radical scepticism. Since this third phase of the sociology of knowledge appears to be eroding the presuppositions of the second phase and in particular its working distinction between structure and belief, it is especially appropriate that a writer located firmly within the second phase should have the chance to show that these intellectual developments are indeed susceptible to second phase analysis and explanation.

It would be wrong to suppose, however, that all second phase work on the relationship between practice, ideology and social structure lies within the Marxist and Durkheimian traditions. I shall return to developments within the sociology of science below. Here I want to note that there is a further relevant line of work that comes from the comparative social psychology of thought. In the United Kingdom it is perhaps the work of Sylvia Scribner and Michael Cole (1974) in this tradition that is best known. In the present monograph, however, this line of work is represented by the fourth paper, that of Jean Lave. Like the preceding papers, it is theorised with great care, yet develops in an empirical context. Lave's argument is of particular relevance to the sociology of knowledge since it is precisely about the relationship between social structure, ideology and practice or, as she puts it, the dialectical relationship between the person and his or her physical and social context.

In a study of Liberian tailors and Californians in their shopping and weight-watching, Lave and her co-workers have established that their arithmetical practice is situationally specific. In particular, she argues that if activities (of which arithmetical calculations form a part) are to be properly analysed then it has to be understood that aspects of the physical surroundings within which those activities take place are for all intents and purposes a part of the activity: that activity and its setting are mutually dependent upon one another. Practices, then, are an emergent property of people-acting-in-settings. Thus arithmetical practice does not normally take the linear place-holding form (as taught in schools), but makes use of aspects of the setting to generate, simultaneously, a puzzle and its solution.

Where, then, does this leave formal place-holding arithmetic as taught to Westerners? Lave's answer is that this is best seen as an ideology: shoppers are apologetic about their lack of formal arithmetical skills. Indeed, often they are not very good at this type of arithmetic, even though they almost always manage to get their situated calculations right. But, and this is perhaps the most interesting point in the context of the relationship between ideology and practice, Lave suggests that what she is observing, wherever she looks, is activity-oriented arithmetic rather than arithmetically-organised activity. It is *activity-in-setting* that is determinant, not generalised arithmetical ideology. One implication of her analysis is that commodities become decommoditised in settings. Where, one wonders, does this leave Marxist writing about commodity fetishism and the dominance of monetary relations? Another implication, though one that she does not discuss, is that those attempting social control would appear to be better advised to tinker with the physical environment than attempting to create ideological practices that cannot be transferred from the setting in which they are generated. Thus Lave's writing, while certainly not politically conservative in tone, stands in creative tension with some of the dominant themes in the Marxist theory of practice and ideology.

(3) Discourses, interests and subjects

As I have already indicated, the concept of social interest has played an important role in the sociology of knowledge. The Marxist analysis of real class interests is well known but it is not the only materialist theory of interests. Habermas's concept of knowledge constitutive interests has been influential, and in particular has influenced work on the sociology of scientific knowledge. The nature of this influence is perhaps most clearly seen in the work of Barry Barnes (1977). Barnes adopts the pragmatist position that all knowledge must be treated as culture and as such directed by social interests. This includes true scientific knowledge as well as belief that appears to be false or visibly ideological in character. Further, he cautions us against assuming that knowledge which is ideologically determined is necessarily false. The provenance of a belief system tells us nothing about its truth status. In a reworking of Habermas he argues that it is, however, possible to distinguish between knowledge that is ideologically determined and that which is not. Thus he suggests that knowledge develops as a function of the operation of two 'great interests' – an interest in prediction, manipulation and control on the one hand, and a concealed interest in rationalisation and persuasion on the other (Barnes 1977:38). He takes the first of these interests to be legitimate in character and the second to be illegitimate. Thus knowledge generated under the auspices of the second interest is 'ideologically determined' though, as I have indicated above, this tells us nothing about its falsity.

According to Barnes both interests operate to produce much of our knowledge. Thus, if one takes the case of beliefs that appear to be ideologically determined – i.e. directed by a covert interest in legitimation and persuasion – the effectiveness of such beliefs for their task is partly a function of how well it is possible to conceal the concern with persuasion. Knowledge that is simple rationalisation and nothing more will tend to appear implausible. Therefore, even those beliefs that are determined ideologically are normally presented as being implied by a well established and routinised body of knowledge that has been directed by a concern with prediction and control. This is one of the reasons why natural science or models of nature often get involved in political and social disputes. By contrast, Barnes suggests that there may be fields of inquiry, including some parts of the natural sciences, which are 'almost entirely dissociated from functions of legitimation and persuasion' (Barnes 1977:42) and may not necessarily be ideologically determined.

Though Barnes's work is primarily theoretical, a number of writers in the sociology of scientific knowledge have undertaken detailed empirical studies in order to tease out the interests that have directed the growth of branches of esoteric knowledge. Such studies have tended to organise their explanation in terms of the operation of two, empirically identifiable, classes of interests. First, working scientists are normally held to have a professional interest in making best use of the expertise that they have aquired. However, such professional interests are often held to be inadequate to explain the growth of knowledge. A second factor, that of class interests, is often seen to be operating. Thus in one well known and elegant study Mackenzie (1978) argues that the development of statistics in England in the late nineteenth and early twentieth century cannot be explained unless the political and class interests of its protagonists are taken into account. A number of studies in the sociology of science follow this pattern: local professional interests are set alongside broader class interests in order to offer an explanation (see, e.g., Shapin 1975). The latter are not necessarily conceptualised in a Marxist manner but it is interesting to note that such sociologists of science appear like Marx, or for that matter Weber, to work on the assumption that there is a relatively stable backcloth of social class interests that may be used in order to explain particular sets of beliefs.

Like their overtly Marxist analogues, such studies in the sociology of science lie within the second stage of the sociology of knowledge. This is because their explanations rely upon a distinction between structure and belief.However explanations posed in terms of structurally determined social interests have recently been questioned by those who, directly or indirectly, have been influenced by the work of Michel Foucault. It is beyond the scope of this essay to consider the overall significance of Foucault's *oeuvre*. Nevertheless, the implications of his *pouvoir/savoir* duo, as he explored them and as these have been assimilated by others, have had a range of profound implications for debate in the sociology of knowledge. Thus in the present context, it should be noted that Foucault leaves no room for a structure/ideology division. His attitude towards ideology is cautious in part because it implies a contrast with truth which is misleading – truths, he hypothesises, are systems of 'ordered procedures' for producing, distributing and operating statements which stand in a circular, indeed inseparable, relationship with systems of power (Foucault 1980:133). He is also cautious because it is in 'a secondary position' to some kind of material infrastructure (Foucault 1980: 118). With respect to power, his concern with concrete practices is well known. Here he notes that these were thought to be of little importance 'so long as the posing of the question of power was kept subordinate to the economic instance and the system of interests which this served' (Foucault 1980:116).

I shall return to the practices of power in the following section. Here I want to note that the idea that there is a backcloth of relatively stable social interests which directs knowledge or ideology is one that has been criticised in the English language literature by both Marxists and sociologists of science. In attacking the opposed reductionisms of theoretical humanism and structural causality, Hindess has argued that the explanatory form of most Marxism, with its dogma that the economy is determinant in the last instance, is vacuous with respect to the analysis of the outcome of political struggle since the precise relations between infra- and superstructure are not specified (Hindess 1983:40). Capacity-outcome theories of power are similarly untenable: 'power', he notes 'as *capacity* to secure . . . disappears, for outcomes are not "predictable and unvarying" in the way this conception requires' (Hindess 1982:501). In part this is because social interests, whether subjective or objective, are not determined by a stable structure which thereby influences and conditions struggle. Rather they are a function of the discursive conditions and outcomes of struggle. Thus though they are important in social analysis, they cannot play the reductionist explanatory role that they are given in many of the studies of power.

A parallel line of argument has developed in the sociology of science in response to the type of interest explanation outlined above. Here, however, the roots of the critique lie in another kind of discourse analysis – that of ethnomethodology. The argument here is posed in terms of the problem of imputation: how it is that an analyst has the right to impute interests to a given social group or individual, and thus make the interest/knowledge link necessary for explanation. Though the sociologists of science who pose explanations in terms of imputed interests concede that there is an explanatory leap here and note that their imputations are provisional and revisable (see, e.g., Barnes 1981), Steve Woolgar (1981) has argued that they introduce an unacceptable explanatory asymmetry: while they make no judgements about the truth of the scientific knowledge in question, rather seeing this as the outcome of a negotiation between the relevant scientists, they do not subject the 'interest-work' of the latter to the same scrutiny. In fact, says Woolgar, there is no need to introduce this asymmetry: the imputation of interests may be analysed in the same terms as the construction of knowledge. Here again, then, though from rather different intellectual roots, we see a concern with discourse and the discursive conditions in which interests are generated eroding the structure/knowledge reciprocity that underlies the second phase of the sociology of knowledge.

The first two papers in the second section of the monograph extend this debate about the relationship between interests and discourse. Barry Hindess, in a theoretical piece, argues that interests have explanatory significance only in so far as they offer actors reasons for action. It is necessary, he suggests, to study the conditions in which political interests and other concerns are formed, and in particular to note that they are routinely open to dispute. Thus it is important to consider the discursive conditions which make possible the formulation of interests and other politically relevant categories. Steven Yearley contributes to the argument as this has developed in the sociology of science by considering the structure of James Hutton's 1788 paper on the origins of the earth. By drawing upon conversational analysis, he shows how texts operate on the imputed interests of readers to persuade the latter that the argument is valid. His argument is that texts display some of the persuasive features of conversations – notably formulations (he focuses on philosophical formulations) – and are thus able to influence readers without dominating them. In so far as Yearley is writing about *methods* of domination his contribution might equally well have come in the third section of the monograph.

The paper by Mark Cousins and Athar Hussain is the final contribution to this section. This too, is concerned with an exploration of the corrosive effects of discourse analysis on the structure/ideology duality. The authors note that for Althusser the subject is an effect of a general mechanism of mutual recognition – called interpellation – but, with the exception of a few homely examples, he leaves this unelaborated. Their paper draws attention to Pecheux's innovative attempt to deal with the question of how interpellation is, in fact, achieved. Pecheux's starting point is the recognition that interpellation, although (as Althusser would have it) experienced as recognition, really concerns identification. It is by identifying with something that is preconstructed that individuals constitute themselves as subjects. Pecheux develops this notion of identification with respect to the old philosophical problem of the production of meaning but changes the shape of the latter. Thus he argues that meaning is not a natural property of language but an effect of the mechanisms (termed articulation) by which individual utterances become part of what, following Foucault, may be called discursive formations.

After considering Pecheux's attempt to develop the Althusserian theory of ideology, the authors next sketch the path taken by Michel Foucault. Rather than develop the analysis of ideology or pronounce upon the vexed question of the subject, Foucault circumvents them altogether. Thus, though Foucault nowhere talks of Althusser's essay, it could well be regarded as the exemplar of the path which he resolutely refuses to take. Foucault questions the Althusserian assumption that all social practices are 'through ideology and in ideology' by emphasising that the target of many social practices characteristic of modernity is neither ideas nor signification, but the body. Cousins and Hussain thus draw attention to the implications of the Foucauldian notion of *assujettisement* and his attempt to turn the general questions of ideology and subjects into the specific question of 'how are humans made in our culture?'

(4) The techniques of power

If the discovery of discourse has eroded the distinction between social structure and knowledge then analysis of the modes of operation of power have shown that it is scarcely possible to talk about power without at the same time talking of knowledge. The result has been the rapid growth of interest in what might be called the *techniques* of power/knowledge – methods, if one might put it this way, for the reduction of discretion. The first contribution to the last section of this monograph is precisely on the reduction of discretion. Barry Barnes reviews the distinction between power and authority and advances a proposal that reverses the standard view of their relationship. The received view of authority is a 'power plus' view: for instance power plus legitimacy. The 'plus' is normally held to increase the efficacy of power. His view is the converse: that authority is 'power minus' – power minus discretion. Power is, he argues, more expedient than mere authority. For an authority is one who directs a routine in response to external signs and signals – it has no discretion, no capacity to make decisions. By contrast, powers are those that are able to retain discretion – they are able to make their own judgements and exercise choice between options. To maximise power it is, however, necessary to delegate to authorities which must know what is to be done. Furthermore, the power must know what the authorities know. This implies a distribution of knowledge or instructions.

This conclusion leads Barnes to consider how definite a text or a set of instructions can be made. The problem, as he notes, is that there are two views of rule-following in sociology. One, which is normally found in macro-sociology, assumes that rules can be made definite in their sense and that agents can be made passive. The other, more usual in micro-sociology, suggests that meanings are always at the discretion of agents. He notes that the first view is consistent with the notion of authority as he has defined it, while the second view leaves room only for powers since everyone retains complete discretion. Barnes is unwilling to make a judgement between them, but suggests that the second view is right about rules and verbal formulations but not for behaviour. Acquisition of shared culture can, he suggests, lead to the acquisition of immediate responses to verbal formulations. Powers may, indeed, create authorities.

The other contributions to the final section of the monograph are also concerned with methods for the production of passive agents. The difference between their position and that of Barnes lies in part in the fact that Barnes appears to be concerned only with the creation of passive *human* agents, whereas Michel Callon and John Law, at least, are both concerned with the reduction of discretion amongst both human and non-human agents. Callon's piece presents in concise form an approach to social analysis – the so called theory of the 'actor-network' – that has hitherto been relatively inaccessible to English-speaking sociologists. The approach is based on the assumption that as actors struggle with one another they first determine their existence and then (if that existence is secured) define their characteristics. An actor that exists is thus one that is able to exert itself upon others. It attempts the latter by borrowing the force of others in a process that Callon calls 'translation'. This process involves four stages. First, an actor tries to make itself indispensable to others – to force them to come to it. Having done so, it moves to a second stage – called by Callon 'interessement' – in which it attempts to lock these others into place by coming between them and their alternatives. It is at this stage that discretion is removed and the actors so trapped become authorities in the sense defined by Barnes. The third step involves both the definition of the roles that are to be played by these 'authorities' and the way in which they are to relate to one another in the scheme devised by the principal actor. This process, which Callon calls enrolment, thus involves the generation of a network of passive agents that may, for all intents and purposes, be seen as forming part of the actor in question (hence the term 'actor-network'). Finally the actor borrows the force of the passive agents that it has enrolled by turning itself into their spokesman and talking on their behalf. Callon calls this part of the process mobilisation, and develops his argument throughout in an empirical context – that of the struggles by marine biologists to understand and regulate the activities of fishermen and scallops in Brittany's St. Brieuc Bay.

Callon's contribution is thus a major contribution to the analysis of methods for creating passive authorities, albeit one that is very different in character to that of Barnes. It is noteworthy that he treats with many of the themes touched upon by Hindess in a way that is broadly consistent with the position of the latter. This is particularly obvious when he talks about mobilisation. Thus, as Hindess has noted, there are various competing ways of formulating the boundaries of groups and characterising their interests. The outcome of struggles are both influenced by and influence the discursive conditions that make it possible to talk of interests and groups. Neither Hindess nor Callon have recourse to a determinant background social structure. Both assume that this is generated in the course of struggle. Again, neither assume that actors or agents are necessarily individual people. For Hindess an agent is a locus of decision and action. Callon does not even assume this: an actor is anything/anyone that acts upon others. Finally, both assume that the outcomes of struggles depend upon the particular combination of elements in play. Thus, neither hold that power is a latent capacity – something that an actor or agent may possess. In this, of course, they are in agreement with Foucault who warns us that power is not a property or a possession, but a strategy or something exercised, the overall effect of a set of a strategies. Hence the operation of power is specific to its instances.

My piece, which is consistent with that of Callon, makes more explicit reference to the work of Foucault. Again, the theme is the way in which power is exercised via a set of strategies that have the effect of reducing discretion amongst a network of agents. My particular concern is with the methods that actors may use to create passive agents at a distance. The argument is that the network which is generated must make it possible for envoys to move in safety from the centre to the periphery, exercise force upon their surroundings, retain their shape, and return unscathed once more to the centre. It is, then, an essay about the techniques of undistorted communication. Like Callon, I choose to write via an empirical example – the fifteenth and sixteenth century Portugese imperialist expansion. I argue that in order to ensure the forcefulness, durability and mobility of their vessels the Portuguese were forced to reconstruct the navigational context within which such vessels moved. This context, with its charts and tables, its instruments and its trained navigators may be seen as an important part of the Portuguese imperial network. I suggest that the Portuguese navigational innovation depended upon three parallel but interrelated techniques: one, after Foucault (1979), for the creation of docile bodies (here navigators); a second, after recent work by Latour (1985), for the creation of powerful yet passive and transportable documents (here astronomical tables); and a third for the generation of docile devices (for instance astrolabes). If the West achieved hegemony then, so runs the argument, this may be explained by referring to revolutions in these three related methods for creating loyal, mobile, yet otherwise passive agents.

The last essay in the monograph is by Bruno Latour who is also concerned with methods for the reduction of discretion. He starts by noting that it is not possible to possess or store power – that it is something that is better seen as a consequence rather than as a cause of action. This leads him to a brief exposition of two approaches to the analysis of power, one the standard 'diffusion' model and the other a 'translation' model which bears many resemblances to the perspectives adopted in the two preceding pieces. In the diffusion model commands are seen as being obeyed and disseminated because they obtain an initial impetus from their powerful source. By contrast, in the translation model commands are respected, if they are respected, because they are passed from hand to hand by (translating) agents who do so for reasons of their own. In this model, then, power is a composition, the composition of a set of actors who are temporarily enrolled in the schemes of the powerful and who accordingly lend their efforts to his/her project. Latour thus rejects the idea that there is a background, determinant, social structure. Rather, what may be observed are sets of different people trying to define the nature of social structure, and then trying to persuade others to subscribe to that definition. This claim has a methodological corollary: social scientists should stop trying to determine the *nature* of the social structure that they believe generates these conflicts, and instead treat the latter as data. In other words, society should not be seen as the referent of an ostensive definition, but rather seen as being *performed* through the various efforts to define it.

Latour next considers the various methods by which actors may enrol others. Thus human society differs, he suggests, from that of non-human primates because the latter are obliged to solve their problems of social organisation without most of the physically durable resources that are available to people. They cannot label, they have no materials with which to simplify and codify as they attempt to impose an order upon themselves. Thus, in an argument that has its parallels with mine on the methods of long-distance control, he suggests that it is only via technologies of simplification that it becomes possible to consolidate particular versions of social structure. He also finds that (of all people!) Durkheim has recourse to a similar dependence on material forms in order to maintain the social coherence of the clan at certain points in *The Elementary Forms*. The sociologist should, he suggests, abandon study of the 'social' as this is usually conceived – the social is not strong enough to link us all together – and instead focus on a much more general problem, that of the forms and in particular the methods of association used by those who seek to enrol others.

The papers in the last section of the monograph are all, therefore, essays on the techniques of power/knowledge and most owe more than a little to the writing of Foucault. Though they differ greatly between themselves, when taken in conjunction with the discourse analyses of the second section, they show how far many writings have moved outside the assumptions of the second phase of the sociology of knowledge. Structure has collapsed into knowledge in the form of discourse, and the sociology of knowledge (if this is still an acceptable title for an inquiry that has so extensively chopped away at its own foundations) has been refocused upon methods for the reduction of discretion and the constitution of power.

References

Althusser, Louis (1971), 'Ideology and Ideological State Apparatuses', pp. 242–80 in B. R. Cosin (ed.) (1971).

Barnes, Barry (1977), *Interests and the Growth of Knowledge*, London, Routledge & Kegan Paul.

Barnes, Barry (1981), 'On the "Hows" and "Whys" of Cultural Change', *Social Studies of Science*, 11 (1981), pp. 481–98.

Bulmer, R. (1973), 'Why the Cassowary is not a Bird', pp. 167–93 in Mary Douglas (1973b).

Cole, Michael and Sylvia Scribner (1974), *Culture and Thought: a Psychological Introduction*, New York, Wiley.

Cosin, B.R. (ed.) (1971), *Education, Structure and Society*, Harmondsworth, Penguin.

Douglas, Mary (1973a), *Natural Symbols, Explorations in Cosmology*, Harmondsworth, Penguin.

Douglas, Mary (ed.) (1973b), *Rules and Meanings: the Anthropology of Everyday Knowledge*, Harmondsworth, Penguin.

Douglas, Mary (1982a), *In the Active Voice*, London, Routledge & Kegan Paul.

Douglas, Mary (1982b), 'Cultural Bias', pp. 183–254 in Mary Douglas (1982a).

Durkheim, Emile (1915), *The Elementary Forms of the Religious Life*, London, George Allen & Unwin.

Foucault, Michel (1979), *Discipline and Punish: the Birth of the Prison*, Harmondsworth, Penguin.

Foucault, Michel (1980), *Power/Knowledge: Selected Interviews and Other Writings, 1972–1977*, edited by Colin Gordon, Brighton, Harvester.

Hindess, Barry (1982), 'Power, Interests and the Outcomes of Struggles', *Sociology*, 16, pp. 498–511.

Hindess, Barry (1983), *Parliamentary Democracy and Socialist Politics*, London, Routledge & Kegan Paul.

Latour, Bruno (1985), 'Visualisation and Cognition', *Knowledge and Society*, 6, forthcoming.

Mackenzie, Donald A. (1978), 'Statistical Theory and Social Interests: a Case Study', *Social Studies of Science*, 8, pp. 35–83.

Rudwick, Martin (1974), 'Poulett Scrope and the Volcanoes of the Auvergne: Lyellian Time and Political Economy', *British Journal for the History of Science*, 7, pp. 205–42.

Shapin, Steven (1975), 'Phrenological Knowledge and the Social Structure of Early Nineteenth Century Edinburgh', *Annals of Science*, 32, pp. 219–43.

Stone, G.P. and H. A. Farberman (1967), 'On the Edge of Rapprochement: was Durkheim moving toward the Perspective of Symbolic Interaction?' *Sociological Quarterly*, 8, pp. 149–64.

Woolgar, Steve (1981), 'Interests and Explanation in the Social Study of Science', *Social Studies of Science*, 11 (1981), pp. 365–94.

Art exhibitions and power during the nineteenth century

Gordon J. Fyfe

Abstract

This paper concerns the relationship between nineteenth century art exhibitions and the social construction of the artist. Attention is focused on the institutional conditions which endorsed the fine artist in the role of an individuated creator within the context of the changing social relations of artistic production. In this way art exhibitions are considered as sites of cultural production and it is argued that matters of their organization relate fundamentally to both questions of power and the production of the artist's pictorial authority. An assessment of the problems that faced the powerful Royal Academy of Arts and its Exhibition points to the way in which such questions took on political and class hues in the context of a developing capitalist society. It is suggested that what is at stake here is the way in which the institution of the art exhibition relates to the emergence of a dominant tradition of creativity – symbolically restating the class situation of the bourgeoisie.

I

This article assesses the relationship between art exhibitions and the social construction of the artist in the nineteenth-century London art world. From the eighteenth century the institution of the public exhibition had been *one* site at which certain image-makers, particularly painters, had struggled to regulate their relationship to aristocratic cultural power and articulated their claim to be 'original' artists within an art world defined by the interplay of patronage and the market. I am concerned with the institution of the exhibition as a site of cultural production, as a medium through which the notion of the 'artist-as-creator' was constituted. I am not arguing that the period under consideration witnessed the genesis of the artist – the Renaissance had, of course, ushered in the difference between the artist and the craftsman. Rather, the concern is with the way in which the exhibition endorsed the fine artist in the role of an individuated creator.

Giddens (1979:44) has argued that to study the production of texts is at the same time to study the production of their authors. I suggest that we treat art exhibitions as texts, that we focus on their relationship to the production of authorship, and that we consider the exhibition as a locus of cooperation, collusion, tension, conflict and struggle over the determination of pictorial meaning. Central to the thesis advanced here is the identification of a growing pre-occupation amongst nineteenth-century artists, exhibition directors and others, with gallery arrangements that would secure the public's recognition of the *complete* pictorial authority of the artist in relation to his or her works. Here we have the growing emphasis on the idea that art was most satisfactorily displayed when the works of an artist were grouped together – the privileging of the artist as the single, monadic, source of pictorial meaning.

These developments were intimately associated with the changing situation of the London Royal Academy of Arts (RA). During the nineteenth century the RA, with its prestigious and hegemonic annual Exhibition, was the focus for politico-cultural power plays which had profound consequences for many aspects of the structuring of creativity – e.g. in relation to industrial design, reproductive engraving, the genesis of national art collections and the organization of professional art exhibitions. Such matters were the very stuff of nineteenth century art politics, a politics whose possibilities were increasingly mediated through the extension of state cultural power, the commodification of art and the growing weight of certain cultural agents – critics, art dealers, museums/galleries, art bureaucracies and an art officialdom. In what follows I assess the link between the situation of the RA in the nineteenth century and the production of the fine artist's authorship through the medium of the exhibition.

From the late eighteenth century European Romantic artists had been expressing their antipathy of the 'rules' and the 'universalism' of the Academic system (Pevsner 1973:190–242). By the second half of the last century the conditions of public exhibition had become the focus of artistic concern and discontent and were increasingly constituted as a 'problem' within the public realm. From the 1830s the London Royal Academy was the subject of successive official inquiries with respect to its public 'accountability' and the organization of its annual Exhibition. What was at stake was the autonomy of the RA in relation to the bourgeois state and it was a relative autonomy whose political significance was partly worked out in relation to fissures within the art profession. The growth of a fine art profession and the fine art market placed ever-increasing strains on a centralized, congested and successful Exhibition that was controlled by a privileged professional elite – the forty full members of the Royal Academy of Arts. The difficulties encountered by particular nineteenth century artists (e.g. Whistler and the Impressionists) in relation to exhibitions have, of course, passed into twentieth century myth of what it *means* to be an artist.

Two aspects of the structuring of creativity warrant attention here – the *collective* action (including that of the situated consumer) presupposed by the making-interpretation of art-objects *and* the genesis of ideologies of creation which elide and mystify the social production of art. What is at issue here is not some contrast between the 'real' relations of art's (collective) production and the fiction or 'label' of the 'artist-as-creator'. Rather, what requires our attention are: (1) the modes of creative intervention that are claimed, secured and authorized through the medium of the label 'artist'; (2) the constitution of the artist, not prior to, but within determinate (not determining) relations of production; (3) the contingencies that may arise from the interdependence of the 'artist-as-creator' with other cultural agents (e.g. craftsmen, critics, art dealers, museum directors, reproductive engravers/ photographers etc.) and (4) the extent to which an individuated authorship may be contested, asserted or extended through association with other agents operating within the cultural field.

II

In London, art exhibitions first took place in the middle of the eighteenth century – somewhat later than in the cases of other European cities. Their development was associated with the emergence of an art profession which was struggling to regulate its relationship to patronage and to exploit the advantages offered by the growth of a consumer society. The functional ties between the augmentation of agrarian capitalism and the legal/financial apparatus of a London which was the centre of the land market had, by the end of the eighteenth century, spawned the distinct cultural style of the English landed gentleman (programmes of house-building, decoration, the Grand Tour etc.) along with the expansion of the cultural/entertainment world responding to the needs of Seasonal migrants and a growing urban gentry (Fisher 1947). Recent research (McKendrick 1982) has suggested that the eighteenth century marks a 'take-off' with respect to English consumption – the pursuit of the novel, the proliferation of new styles of dress, the compulsion of fashion and the emergence of new strategies of commerce and salesmanship. Entrepreneurship made novel use of artists' pictorial skills (e.g. Wedgwood) and it is now abundantly clear from the work of Lippincott (1983) that mid-eighteenth century London artists – and not just Hogarth – were pioneering the development of a commercial/artistic infrastructure. The artistic and entrepreneurial projects of people like William Hogarth, Arthur Pond, J. B. Jackson, John Boydell and many others, are symptomatic of the shift away from old patronage to a nexus of urban institutions that were the bases for new creative possibilities and opportunities of professional contact – coffee houses, taverns, clubs, learned societies and, of course, print making, academies and exhibiting societies. Art exhibitions were being held from the mid-eighteenth century – at the Foundling Hospital, at the Society of Arts, the Free Society of Artists and the Society of Artists of Great Britain.

The development of metropolitan art institutions in the second half of the eighteenth century was accompanied by power struggles among artists and the consolidation of the power of fine artists. The Society of Artists was a key site of these struggles and its politics were marked by the institution's differentiation into a controlling elite and a group of rank and file members increasingly excluded from the decision making process. The incorporation of the Society of Artists in 1765 created two types of member – fellows and directors. In 1768 the fellows made an attempt, through the attorney-general, to contain the power of the directors. They were successful but the manoeuvring of Court artists drew George III into the affair, shifting the centre of gravity of the power struggle away from the market and towards patronage. The establishment of the RA in 1768 resolved the power struggle between patronized/Court artists and a larger body of more market-oriented artists and craftsmen in favour of the former who determined policy in relation to the Exhibition and secured important privileges for themselves. These privileges included the right, indeed the obligation, to exhibit annually at the RA and (from 1809) the so-called 'varnishing days' which enabled members to retouch their paintings *in situ* after they had been hung at the Exhibition.

The RA was a self-elected artistic oligarchy and was composed of two strata. There were forty full members who, with the exception of the first generation were elected from amongst a subordinate body of Associates (a maximum of twenty). The Associates were in turn elected from amongst the body of exhibitors at the annual Exhibition to which all artists were invited to submit their work. Control over selection for the Exhibition was in the hands of the Academy's governing Council (a rotating body of eight RAs plus the President) and the hanging of works was executed by five RAs making up the 'hanging-committee'. The uncertainties of submission, selection and hanging were key facets of an artist's career in the nineteenth century and were subjects of much discussion and controversy in the art press. The Academy's association with the monarchy was of enormous importance. Not only did George III provide a location at Somerset House and give the new institution much needed financial support in its early years,[1] but the very association with the monarchy though not without its dangers was to be a strategic ideological resource in the context of radical bourgeois attacks after 1830. In competition with the RA the financial situation of other exhibiting societies weakened as they lost revenue, the support of talented artists and were marginalized. In due course the Exhibition, firmly embedded in the ritual cycle of the Season, took on a singular meaning that was only lost with the Great Exhibition of 1851.

The cultural dominance achieved by the Academy towards the end of the eighteenth century in the art market expressed the hegemonic association between a patronage rooted in agrarian capitalism and a developing bourgeois art market. In this context it will not do to treat the art market as evidence of the percolation of elite values, of Art, down some kind of 'social scale' or prestige hierarchy. Changes in art institutions and the social distribution of visual habits were *contested* changes and involved power struggles over the control of metropolitan fine art institutions. The Academicians (defined through their association with the residues of pre-capitalist patronage, agrarian capitalism and the market) asserted their professional identity as artists *against* other, co-existing, cultural identities (water-colourists, women's needlework, reproductive engravers and others). The RA's Exhibition was a strategic medium for the projection of that identity.

The RA was no reflex of patronage and its members fought off attempts by the monarchy/artistocracy to increase their influence over its affairs. The impact of patronage and the attempts of wealthy connoisseurs to extend their power in relation to developing metropolitan art institutions were recurring features of nineteenth-century art-politics.[2] In 1806 the British Institution, backed by wealthy amateurs/connoisseurs was founded, clearly a threat to the Academy in that it too promoted an annual exhibition of living artists' works. Individual artists may have been prepared to show their work there, but they retained a collective anxiety in a period that 'witnesses a barely concealed struggle for power between the Academy, representing the profession, and the main body of connoisseurs and patrons' (Hardie 1968: vol. 3, 270).

III

The exhibition, *pace* Benjamin (1970), takes us away from the aura of a cult (with a specific religious/physical location), away from the palace where authorship retains the sign of the contract and the preference of princely patronage. Patronage displays art as a 'spectacle of treasures which the public is allowed to invade and marvel at' (Grana 1971:100) and inevitably locates the eye of the visitor within the ambience of the patron's cultural power. Visitors are presented with the viewpoint of the patron. They are likely to encounter signs of the patron's presence even in his or her absence – the very conditions of access, the patrimony of family portraits, the pre-occupations, perhaps the obsessions of the collector, the prince's private study and an architecture which is tribute to the patron's authority/authorship.

The emergence of the public exhibition is linked to a re-organization of the eye's relationship to art-objects. The more attenuated, impersonal, relationship of artist to exhibition con-sumer/visitor is (like that of patronage) one of *power* and persuasion for it is associated with a growing pre-occupation with the requisite strategies (gallery arrangement, decor, lighting etc.) for determining the encounter between pictures and the public gaze. The visitor's eye is now constituted in relation to the authority of the artist: an eye which is socialized in this mode is disturbed and confused when it confronts paintings 'exhibited or stored up like merchandise in a hall' and struggles 'to contemplate each picture separately without having to see at the same time half of four other ones' (Casper David Friedrich, *circa* 1830; quoted in the Tate Gallery 1972). At the same time the public exhibition is constitutive of what it is to be an artist, of how works may be judged – something that has consequences for what it *means* to have one's art purchased.

John Constable's response to public exhibition was intimately bound up with his view of himself as an artist and indexes the possibilities opened up by the shift from patronage to bourgeois art market. The world of patronage is a world of 'friends' (Perkins 1972:44–8). In its purest form it embodies the artist as a houseman/servant or perhaps, courtier; it enmeshes the artist in a network of reciprocal ties and obligations and connects the artist's 'career' to the economic and political fates of patrons, to matters of their personal favour, recommendation etc. Constable had his friends, his patrons, but he records the impact of the contrasting impersonality of the market on his sensibility as an artist: 'I . . . felt flattered that an application should be made to me from an entire stranger without interest or affection or favor, but I am led to hope for the pictures' sake alone' (Beckett 1966: vol. 4, 98). In 1825 Constable writes with pleasure about the sale of one of his pictures in Paris; 'purchased by a nobleman (a great collector, *I know not whom*) for twice or three times what I sold it for' (Beckett 1966: vol. 4, 99–100, my emphasis).

Exhibitions are sites of cultural production as well as consumption in that they sustain an 'argument' about creativity through the terms of their selection and organization (here see Brighton 1977 and Duncan and Wallach 1980 on official art). The development of art exhibitions in eighteenth and nineteenth-century England (as elsewhere) was related to new forms of authorial *intervention* and *experience* for artists. I stress *experience* because there is evidence that artists could, as it were, be caught by surprise (*Is this what I'm saying?*) – evidence that the exhibition, and the process of organizing it, was a medium through which artist, gallery-owner and visitor collaborated in the production of author as 'original' artist. I stress *intervention* because the exhibition also relates to questions of power and control over the organization and transmission of aesthetic principles – those governing the inclusion/exclusion of art-objects, their 'naturalization' as Art, as well as the way in which the visitor's eye is captured, situated and manoeuvred. This is a matter of *power* in that the agency of the image-maker as fine artist is constituted in relation to encounters with gallery visitors/consumers and relates fundamentally to questions of control over the conditions of exhibition – e.g. does the exhibitor compete for attention within a mixed exhibition of juxtaposed canvases or is it a 'one-man' show with the artist determining the sequence, spacing etc. of a number of canvases within a 'sympathetic' ambience?

Though not unknown the one-man show was a relatively untried formula during the first three quarters of the last century. Its development endorsed what Sloane (1961) identifies as the shift from the 'masterpiece' as the object of aesthetic contemplation to the 'master-sequence': 'The individuality of the new picture is the individuality of the artist who painted it, but it is less sharply differentiated from the canvases just before and just after it. The more the work is solely the artist's own creation, the more each one will blend into the sequence of what he has done to form the larger whole which is *his universe of forms*' (Sloane 1961:424, my emphasis). What is crucial here is the opportunity to *articulate* that universe of forms, an opportunity not created by the Academy's annual Exhibition which dealt with thousands of submissions and was always struggling to accommodate those works that were judged fit for display – an increasingly hopeless struggle which, by the 1880s, seemed to be losing the Academy something of its public credibility and was fuelling attempts by disaffected artists to establish an alternative exhibition. For some exhibitors, as we shall see, this crisis was experienced in terms of the question: what does it mean to be an artist and to have one's works publicly displayed?

White and White (1965) have presented a systematic account of the crisis that faced the Paris Salon in the second half of the last century – a crisis that expressed itself most visibly in the problems of congested exhibitions and the ever growing number of canvases that were submitted by aspiring artists for consideration by the presiding jury. The relevance of the Whites' analysis for my argument resides in its exploration of the relationship between the dynamics of institutional change and the gestation of a new concept of pictorial authority. They identify a fundamental shift in emphasis away from the canvas as the locus of institutional transactions governing artistic success and failure (judging the merits of individual paintings, selecting and hanging them in the Salon, awarding prizes). Instead there is a growing pre-occupation with the artist's career, with his or her total *oeuvre* and the means by which it might be publicly constituted. This shift was facilitated by the emergence of what the Whites call the 'dealer-critic system': a configuration of institutions that was born out of the problems thrown up by the contradiction between a 'successful' centralized academic system and the growth of a dispersed bourgeois art public. As the academic system threatened to choke on its diet of canvas it struggled to regulate the process of selection and exhibition, attracting accusations of bias, inefficiency and corruption and was occasionally nudged into reform by the state. With the crystallization of the dealer-critic system, particularly around the careers of the Impressionists, the one-man exhibition took on a decisive role as a basis for validating art and publicly presenting an account of artists' achievements. The individual canvas now became a 'piece of a meaning' (White and White 1965:117–18); its point of reference was the artist as a creative subject.

IV

Can the Whites' thesis be generalized to include the case of the English art world? Certainly, there is evidence in the second half of the nineteenth century, particularly in the last quarter, of an Academy that is on the defensive and that the organization of the annual Exhibition was at issue. In 1863 the affairs of the RA were, not for the first time, publicly scrutinized – this time by a Royal Commission inquiring 'into the present position of the Royal Academy in relation to the Fine Arts'. The Commission judged that 'want of adequate space' was the most 'unanimous' and 'justly founded' subject of complaint about the Academy (*Report:* xiv). The testimonies of the witnesses (including those of Academicians) along with other contemporary evidence – press reports, attacks by disaffected artists and statistics concerning submission/rejection/ exhibition at the RA – convey the sense of a widely diffused feeling that something was wrong.[3] In order to make sense of this it is necessary to locate the RA within the context of class and state formation. The Academy was frequently the site of power plays during the nineteenth century and these were not neutral with respect to the political and economic domains. The question of an overcrowded Exhibition was both an aesthetic problem and a problem of art-politics coloured by the Academy's close connection with aristocratic patronage. What was at stake was the role of the RA (and its Exhibition) within the context of a developing state cultural apparatus. (Was the Academy a private institution? Should its affairs be subject to Parliamentary scrutiny? What was the role of the RA in relation to a *national* art collection? In relation to industrial design? Did the RA abuse its powers in relation to the Exhibition? Should the RA be made more answerable to the artistic community as a whole?) Throughout the last century successive official inquiries into the state of the Arts probed the affairs of a far from supine RA and threatened to breach the institutional autonomy that (increasingly) seemed to be encoded in the *Royal* of Royal Academy.[4]

The key here is the tension between the ascriptive privileges of aristocratic cultural power (adapting to the terms of metropolitan/ professional art institutions) *and* the ideological weight of the bourgeoisie as a *public* – corralling Art and its institutions into the public domain, preaching the Word, translating Art into 'cultural capital' (exhibition visiting, reproductive prints, art journalism etc.).[5] This tension was the locus of production of a whole political economy of art. (See e.g. Edward Edwards, *The Administrative Economy of the Fine Arts in England,* 1840 and the published responses of M. A. Shee, president of the RA, to demands that admission to the Exhibition be free and to the charge that the RA had refused co-operation in supplying information required by the 1836 Select Committee).[6]

The annual Exhibition, with its exclusive Dinner[7] and Private View day, was an integral part of the Season, part of the institutional fabric through which the cohesive identity of 'Society' was reproduced within a developing capitalist society (Davidoff 1973). But by the late nineteenth century it is a Society that is manifestly being divested of direct political and administrative control (Northcote-Trevelyan reforms) and with the push towards an accountable expertise in Art, as elsewhere, the RA's prerogatives are under direct assault. By the 1880s Society's contours were becoming increasingly difficult to discern: 'English society has grown too large for its representatives to be contained within the limits of a single drawing room' (Escott 1880). The political power of the salon, with its emphasis on personal invitation and knowledge is, Escott tells us, now replaced by the club (1880: Vol. 2, 64–5). Through more junior eyes 'London appeared as a shifting mass of miscellaneous and uncertain membership' (Webb 1929:46). Webb writes:

> The bulk of the shifting mass of wealthy persons who were conscious of belonging to London Society, . . . were, in the last quarter of the nineteenth century, professional profit makers: the old established families of bankers and brewers, often of Quaker descent, coming easily first in social precedence; then one or two great publishers and, at a distance, shipowners, the chairmen of railway and some other great corporations, the largest of the merchant bankers – but as yet no retailers. (Webb 1929:47)

At the same time that bulwark of the Academy, agrarian capitalism, was itself in crisis with the agricultural depression of the 1870s. It has been argued (Morgan 1969) that by the 1870s the RA had 'lost an opportunity' to retain its earlier dominance in matters of Art. Of course, Academies, like people, do not make history in circumstances of their own choosing.

The situation of the RA was profoundly and irreversibly affected by the agrarian crisis of the last quarter century (with the decline in housebuilding[8] and what has been characterized as the increasingly 'caste-like' attributes of the landed aristocracy – 'distancing itself from, and distanced from the newer business magnates. . .' (Rubinstein 1981:219)). What was the fate of the Academy within the context of this shift from 'elitism to electoralism' (Scott 1982:96–110), and these changes in the class contours of cultural power? If, (Dimaggio 1980), art exhibitions function as 'differentiating rituals' what were the effects on the Exhibition's role as as ritual form reproducing the cohesion and separation of an elite culture? Some of the effects are perhaps evident in the opening of more exclusive exhibition venues in the 1870s, 1880s and 1890s – the Grosvenor 1877, the New Gallery 1888, and the Grafton 1893.

Other effects show through in observations and anxieties emanating from that distinct literary genre – late Victorian/ Edwardian art memoirs, diaries and reminiscences. These chatty, gossipy narratives of a life's art are themselves outgrowths of a Society art world that is under siege, sometimes symptomatic of a cultural occlusion and sometimes articulating the sense of an emerging aesthetic.[9] Take H. S. Marks's account of the fate of 'Picture Sunday'. Once it had been a relatively intimate affair with painters opening their studios to a few 'friends' (also the odd dealer and potential buyer) just prior to the Academy's 'sending in day'. Now (early 1890s) it 'has degenerated from a simple friendly meeting into a crowded over-grown abuse' (Marks 1894: vol. 2, 83). Take Lady Butler's response to a private view at the Grosvenor Gallery in 1879 as 'more and more annoyed', she escapes into 'the honest air of Bond Street' and catches a hansom to her studio: 'There I pinned a seven foot sheet of brown paper on an old canvas and, flung the charge of "The Greys" upon it' (quoted in Clive 1965:103).

Lady Butler was abandoning a Grosvenor (established in 1877) that was pivotal with respect to the emergence of an artistic opposition to the Academy – but the terms of that opposition require setting within the context of class structuration as it manifests itself on the aesthetic terrain. Contemporary accounts of the Grosvenor give us a sense of aristocratic retrenchment and of a 'habitus' that contrasts with the more 'public' aesthetic of the Academy:

> Pottery and china, and groups of plants disposed about the rooms, serve to heighten the impression that this is not a public picture exhibition, but rather a patrician's private gallery shown by courtesy of its owner; indeed so studiously are the business arrangements kept out of sight, that but for the inevitable turnstiles and catalogue-keepers the illusion would be complete. (*The Portfolio* 1877:98)[10]

What was on the agenda, however, was not the proliferation of a landed artistocratic 'caste's' aesthetic but the institutionalization of aesthetic attitudes associated with the 'reforming' and bureaucratizing strategies of an elite professional and administrative stratum – the intellectual aristocracy (here see Williams 1981:79–81). Important here is the transformation of elite culture and the power struggles through which new cultural fissures are constituted – the production and reproduction of the *social* difference between a 'popular' aesthetic (as expressed in the Victorian 'subject' painting) and the 'pure', disinterested aesthetic of the bourgeoisie (Bourdieu 1968, 1980a). Measured in terms of exhibition visitors the late nineteenth century Academy was successful, numbering hundreds of thousands per year. Part of the key here is the popularity of the 'block-busting' sensational narrative works (W. P. Frith: *The Railway Station;* Luke Fildes: *The Doctor,* W. F. Yeames: *And When Did You Last See Your Father?*) whose 'subjects' were so often the process of state formation itself. It was the aesthetic status of such *popular* successes that was increasingly called into question by an argument about art that directs attention away from the 'subject' and towards the pertinences of *style* and a 'universal' art history. Indeed, 'popularity' begins to be assimilated into the language of critical opprobrium.[11] The developing cultural apparatus of the bourgeois state and the emergence of inter-national, 'universalizing' bourgeois art locked the RA into a posture that was increasingly particularistic.[12]

Bourdieu has argued that the 'cultivation' of 'art' by the bourgeoisie relates to its historical situation as a class. On the one hand the bourgeoisie cannot legitimate its privilege through an appeal to birth for this is precisely what it has 'refused to the aristocracy'. And on the other hand it is not possible to invoke Nature because this is 'the ground on which all distinctions are abolished'. So, this dilemma is resolved as a charismatic ideology which elides and mystifies the relationship between nature and culture:

the sacralizating of culture and art fulfils a vital function by contributing to the consecration of the social order: to enable educated men to believe in barbarism and persuade their barbarians within the gates of their own barbarity, all they must and need do is to manage to conceal themselves and to conceal the social conditions which render possible not only culture as second nature in which society recognizes human excellence or 'good form' as the 'realization' in a *habitus* of the aesthetics of the ruling classes, but also the legitimized predominance (or, if you like, the legitimacy) of a particular definition of culture. (Bourdieu 1968:610)

Notions of art and artists can be seen as essentialist representations of 'the bipartition of society into barbarians and civilized people' (Bourdieu 1968:610).

The ideological (re)presentation of the relationship between nature and culture is secured partly through the institutional practices of 'modern' art worlds (e.g. those associated with the 'one-man' exhibition and the 'original' print). The 'creation' of these practices *is* the artist as a creative subject. The 'problems' faced by the late nineteenth-century RA were crucially bound up with the elaboration of this ideology of creation, an ideology that it had nurtured in the early part of the century but whose elaboration now seemed inhibited by the conditions imposed at the annual Exhibition. It is not a question of treating the *artist* as a kind of 'label'. The object of attention is an ideology of creation both as it conceals the social and as it informs the realization of individuated modes of pictorial intervention, control and authority. What is also a matter of concern is the way in which relations of power in a society are symbolically reworked as the dominant traditions of creativity. The nineteenth century art exhibition was one site at which conceptions of creativity were nurtured and in the next section I turn to a more detailed discussion of the public exhibition as a locus of cultural power.

V

Like the organizers of earlier eighteenth-century exhibitions, Royal Academicians found means for ensuring the exclusion of 'improper Persons' (Hutchison 1968:55) and this, along with other evidence, indicates the felt need to secure a distinction between the Exhibition and the popular forms of showmanship with which it co-existed. (E.g. in 1788 the Academy found itself next door to a display of 'Automaton Figures which move in a great variety of descriptions, by clockwork, with the Diamond Beetle, scarce and valuable paintings, Needlework, Shells, Flies, Water Fall, etc., etc. . . .' Whitley 1928, vol. 2:104; also see Altick 1978:99.) The early records of the Academy show that this kind of thing obtruded into its proceedings and it is also clear that the Exhibition was a medium for establishing the *difference* between the aesthetic domain and what Altick identifies as the documentary representations and historical *realia* of gentleman's cabinets (100). In 1772 the Academy is refusing application by a Mr. Malton to exhibit his 'Perspective Machine' (*Council Minutes*, vol. 1:130–1). Ten years later the Academy was approached by a G. P. Towry seeking endorsement for a proposed 'Mart or Court Fair'. The Academy refused to cooperate, replying that the proposed show 'must weaken the Effect of Exhibitions, divert the Attention of the Public from that of the Royal Academy, and by a multiplication of such Shows render them disgusting' (*Council Minutes*, vol. 1:317–18).

The organization of the Exhibition was always a matter of

concern to the Royal Academicians and its principles of organization encoded their sense of themselves as *original* professional fine artists. Certain objects were explicitly excluded under the laws of the Academy and others (e.g. reproductive engravings and watercolours) were admitted but discriminated against. In January 1769 Council, the governing body of the Academy, ruled that no copies could be admitted: 'No Picture copied from a Picture or Print, a Drawing from a Drawing; a Medal from a Medal; a Chasing from a Chasing; a Model from a Model, or any other Species of Sculpture, or any Copy. . .' (*Council Minutes*, vol. 1:8). From the early 1770s: '. . . no Needle-Work, artificial Flowers, cut Papers, shell-work, or any such Baubles shall be admitted into the Exhibition' (*Council Minutes*, vol. 1:75–6); '. . . no models in coloured Wax shall be admitted' (*Council Minutes*, vol. 1:101). In 1813 the rules concerning the exhibition of copies were amended as follows 'No Copies from any other Works of Art, with the exception of Paintings in Enamel, and the Prints of Associate Engravers, shall be admitted. . .' (*Council Minutes*, vol. 5:94; also p. 151).

The evidence of legislation concerning copies suggests that the Academy was operating within a cultural terrain where the distinction between 'originals' and 'reproductions' was not always clear, or at least, not clear to everyone. Certainly the conditions of mass reproduction in the fine arts, based as they were on the 'interpretive' work of craftsmen (work that was largely shunned by painters as the province of an inferior caste) represented a context in which the distinction was blurred.[13] Here the Academy conceded the exhibition of copies (were they really *translations?*) but resisted repeated attempts to improve the restricted and junior status of engravers within the institution.

More generally, the exhibition policy of the Academy should be set in the context of changes in the conditions of creativity and the long term gestation of a 'habitus' that displaces older and more sanguine attitudes towards copies and even 'forgeries'.[14] The Exhibition endorses the artist in the role of *creator* and celebrates the possessive individualism of one who has the attributes of creativity. Crucial here are changes in the meaning of 'originality' and the seventeenth/eighteenth century semantic shifts which *interiorized* creation (Williams, 1976:192–3 and Shils 1981:152–6). As Shils explains, 'originality' was once conceived as prior to or external to human beings: 'a reminder of the ineluctable dominion of the past over the present' – original sin, the burden of a scribal culture that must seek out the authentic in the confusion of past sources. Now, originality refers to one who makes a new cultural statement, someone whose art can be displayed in the Exhibition as 'supplying sufficient novelty, and interest to excite public attention. . .' (*Council Minutes,* vol 4:395–6).

Nevertheless, we are still a long way from the bourgeois 'monad' of high Modernism and the unique style of the artist (Jameson 1984:63). Creativity still appears to have transactions with a pre-existing symbolic order (Nature, the Antique, narrative history, literature). Nineteenth-century painting had a marked narrative/ 'subject' orientation, trading on a shared 'iconography' – a medium through which the limits of pictorial authorship were constructed ('the artist has recorded an historical event that never occurred, got the technical details of costume wrong, misrepresented the literary account' *etc.*).[15] By the end of nineteenth century such 'limits' were increasingly seen by *some* artists as obstacles to a proper individuation of creation and, moreover, as limits that were institutionalized in the powerful Academy and its annual Exhibition. I now turn to a consideration of what those limits were perceived to be and the terms within which the Exhibition became a focus of public controversy.

The Report of the 1863 Royal Commission had made an assessment that the Exhibition was 'fairly conducted so far as is consistent with the existing rules, and . . . present space' (p. xv). It went on to recommend a package of reforms which were tied to the judgment that some way of increasing the exhibition space was required.

One theme that the Commissioners and witnesses touched upon was the kind of participation that might be allowed to Associate Academicians and to exhibitors who were not members of the Academy. Should the Academy be elected from a constituency of exhibitors? (q.199). Should Associates be given a voice in the government of the Academy? (q.3). And, echoing the (more hostile) Select Committee of 1836, there was the question as to whether or not the Academy was a *public* institution that was failing to discharge its responsibilities – should it be accountable to British artists as a whole? (q.895).

Although there seems to have been some anxiety at the time the overall tenor of the Commission's *Report* was not hostile and the Academy rode out the attendant criticism. However, by the 1880s criticism of the Academy and complaints about the Exhibition were becoming more shrill.[16] As the correspondence columns of

The Times suggest, overcrowded exhibition rooms and disappointed artists made up the stock of common knowledge about the fine arts (see *The Times,* Monday, April 26th 1880, p.8, col.6). Could room be found at the Horticultural Gardens for the 'great unhung' to show their work (*The Times,* Friday, April 23rd 1880, p.8, col.2). And 'Rejected-Dejected-Neglected' writes: 'How many hearts would be glad and crushed hopes revived if the suggestion . . . relative to the opening of a "Supplementary Exhibition" were to assume a practical shape! The wolf is at many a studio door. . .' (*The Times,* Saturday, April 24th 1880, p.8, col.3).

The Academy's Exhibition was increasingly perceived as a 'problem', as an unfortunate crowding of canvases many of which were condemned to comparative obscurity even though they were selected (perhaps accepted but still unhung, or else hung without the advantage of being 'on the line') and perhaps juxtaposed with unsympathetic neighbours. In the last quarter of the century what amounted to a crisis in the Exhibition was fuelled by changes in the imagery and vocabulary of creativity as they were determined within a developing fine art market. A central image here is that of the artist's studio and a sense of the studio as the locus of a creative life. Symptomatic is the popularity of such imagery in nineteenth-century paintings and its exploitation by art journalism (illustrated accounts of visits to contemporary artists' homes and studios).

The kind of aesthetic control that the artist can exert in the intimacy of his/her studio becomes more clearly seen as the basis for judging how art works ought to be displayed: 'When you go to a painter's studio and ask him to show you a picture, he does not run upstairs with it and hang it out at the window of the third storey and tell you to go out into the street and look up at it; he puts it on an easel, level with your eye, wheels the easel into the best light, and you really *see* the work. Now in a rationally contrived gallery. . .' (Hamerton 1889:243). Moreover, the studio of the working artist was the site of aesthetic effects that could not be obtained through encountering works that were distributed between collections (public and private) or dispersed within a large mixed exhibition. In the early 1830s Constable comments on the effects to be gained from seeing his pictures at his studio: 'It is much to my advantage that several of my pictures should be seen together, as it displays to advantage their varieties of conception and also of execution. . .' (Beckett 1965: vol. 4:129). What Constable was signalling, as Turner had already done at Queen Anne Street, as Delacroix and Ingres were to at the 1855 Paris

World Fair and Manet was to in 1867, was the importance of the 'one-man' show or exhibition.

In 1877 Sir Coutts Lindsay (the wealthy dilettante) with his wife and C. E. Hallé had launched the Grosvenor Gallery ('greenery-yallery') on an aesthetic programme that would avoid the 'annoyances .incidental to Exhibition at the Royal Academy' as well as 'the juxtaposition and crowding together of ill-assorted canvases' (Hallé 1909:99). Here the works of individuals were grouped together within a physical setting that was designed to harmonize. M. S. Watts (1912) gives a particularly coherent and explicit account of what she perceived as the effects of the Grosvenor's arrangements and it is worth quoting at length.

> Afterwards came the consciousness that the work of some
> English painters of the day was being revealed to the public for
> the first time . . . in the setting of this well conceived building
> each was being allowed to deliver his message consecutively,
> and the visitor was not called upon to listen to him between
> other and conflicting voices, or to hear from him nothing but a
> broken sentence. The works of each artist, grouped together
> and divided by blank spaces, allowed the spectator's eye and
> mind to be absorbed entirely by what the painter had to give
> them . . . those who had cared to search the Academy walls,
> season after season, for the work of George Frederic Watts . . .
> stood before the end of the West Gallery wall, and hailed their
> master. . . It was not too much to say that now to a larger
> public, beyond the circle of his friends, *the mind of the painter
> was speaking for the first time*. . . (M. S. Watts, 1912:
> vol. 1:323–4, my emphasis)

Sennett (1976:205–9) plots the nineteenth-century changes in the theatre that redefine the prerogatives of an audience, constituting it as a silent, self-policing aggregate shrouded in darkness with its attention commanded by the stage. There were parallel developments in the organization of art exhibitions with artists, gallery owners/directors and dealers collaborating to produce the physical conditions and the arrangements that would guarantee the artist's 'visibility' presenting her or him as *the* locus of creation. The requisite techniques were pioneered by Whistler, Hallé and others in the 1870s who used lighting, decor and the arrangement of pictures as a means of establishing the pictorial authority of the artist and securing the gaze of the visitor. There are many accounts of the strategies and techniques adopted by Whistler: his use of controlled lighting (by means of a velarium) to ensure that the spectators remained in shadow whilst the pictures were bathed in soft light, the choosing of colours and tones for gallery decoration that would not compete with the pictures for attention, the careful arrangement and spacing-out of the pictures by the artist and a scrupulous attention to other matters of detail (see Menpes 1904:104; Eddy 1904:132–9; Pennell 1921:304–5). The effects that Whistler and others sought were intimately bound up with questions of power: control of the physical environment within which pictures were encountered, securing the artist's point of view, establishing the artist as the single source of pictorial meaning.[17]

The Academy dispersed the artist's art across its walls; the visitor 'heard' a fragmented 'message', a 'broken sentence' whose meaning had to be sorted out from that of 'other and conflicting voices' (Watts 1912: vol. 1: 32). In so far as the experience of what it 'meant' to be an artist who structured through the medium of the exhibition the one-man show was the means by which some artists found themselves, or were encouraged to see themselves, as *creators*. It was clear that although he was persuaded to engage in the project, Millais had considerable misgivings about putting on a one-man show: 'It is the kind of thing that should never be done till a man is dead. . . I feel a little as if a line was drawn across my life now and the future won't be the same thing I meant it to be. . .' (Burne-Jones, 1906/12: vol.2: 230). Hallé (1909) tells how he inveigled Millais into the idea of an exhibition and gives us an account of difficulties that were encountered in arranging the pictures. Having decided that he would arrange them himself, Millais adopted the principle that the most 'popular' and highly priced pictures should be placed prominently. However, 'the result was deplorable' and a disappointed, unhappy Millais came to the conclusion 'that he was not an artist at all'. Hallé's response was to organize the rehanging of the pictures himself, this time on the principle of 'their artistic merit alone', giving 'the *merely popular* pictures less prominent places'. Millais was jubilant at the effect: 'Charlie, my boy, Van Dyck wasn't in it!' His next response was to set about retouching the pictures; 'strengthening the colour in one place, glazing in another, toning in a third' (Hallé, 1909:155–6). Another case worth citing is that of the Alma-Tadema exhibition put on by the Grosvenor Gallery in 1882–3. Against the advice of others, the artist had wanted to hang his pictures – some of which he had not seen in years – in a strict chronological order. However, coming across 'one of his best pictures', he decided, irrespective of chronology, that it warranted hanging in the best light.

'How about chronology?' said Carr. 'The picture's place is in that dark corner.' 'Chronology be d----d!' said Tadema, and we heard no more about chronological arrangements at that or any other exhibitions.

What are we to make of these anecdotes? I suggest that the institution of the exhibition did not translate or encode a pre-established authorship and that they give us some clues as to how the artist's identity as a *creator* was constructed. The one-man exhibition was a site at which the artist's 'universe of forms' could be explored. It was the site of aesthetic effects that could not be obtained through encountering the works of an artist which were scattered around in different collections or within a large mixed exhibition. The Academy dispersed an artist's art across its walls: the visitor 'heard' a fragmented 'message', a 'broken sentence' whose meaning had to be sorted out from that of 'other and conflicting voices' (Watts 1912: vol. 1: 32). In so far as the experience of what it 'meant' to be an artist was structured through the medium of the exhibition the one-man show was the means by which some artists found themselves, or were encouraged to discover themselves as *creators*. At the same time the spectator approached pictures whose very arrangement was an 'argument' for the primacy of the creative subject, an arrangement which broke with the common-sense principles that might have dictated to it – thus, neither chronology (Alma-Tadema) nor mere popularity (Millais). What is at issue here is the production of a distinct authorship, the establishment of an aesthetic that meta-morphizes the terms of the spectator's participation and denies the relevance of certain kinds of knowledge. Why, asks Whistler, should you be concerned to know that a portrait I exhibit at the Royal Academy is of my mother?

It is clear that this 'way of seeing' was at variance with the central thrust of Victorian art criticism with its literary and narrative emphasis (Roberts 1973) and that there were obstacles to its production and dissemination – not least in the aesthetic effects generated by mass produced reproductive engravings. Nonethe-less, the 'news' was being spread, the key to the cultural code was in the process of transmission. Why not, asked the influential *Art Journal* in 1860, reviewing a posthumous show of the works of Thomas Faed, mount a one-man exhibition of the works of a *living* artist? In 1875, 1876 and 1877 *The Art Journal* was preaching, through a series of illustrated articles on Edwin Landseer, the merits of the 'original' sketch and the possibility of watching 'the growth of the painter's mind as developed in his works' (*The Art Journal* 1875:1) By 1889 we hear, not altogether favourably, of 'the modern fashion of "one-man" exhibitions' (*The Art Journal* 1889:53).[18]

It is also clear that the institution of the exhibition was not the only context in which authorship was at issue. There was the long drawn-out struggle to determine the aesthetic possibilities created by nineteenth century print making and the debate about the artistic status of reproductive engravers. There was the campaign, fought by Haden, Hamerton and others in publicising the difference between an *original* etching and a reproductive engraving. There was the appropriation of French Impressionism through a displacement of criticism onto the terrain of the quality of the medium, comparative technique and the formal properties of an artist's style. What I have discussed here is the importance of the exhibition as one site at which the encounter between image-maker and exhibition visitor was constituted as the charismatic power of the artist-as-creator.

Notes

1 See Royal Academy Council Minutes, vol. 4, p. 351 (March 25, 1912). Also see Farington's Diary (Greig edition) vol. 6, p. 337 (Jan 29, 1823).

2 The association between the monarchy and the Academy was sometimes the site of suspicion, distrust and power struggles. There was always the latent possibility that disputes within the RA might be resolved by one party drawing the monarch into the fray – but at what cost? Such was the concern of Joseph Farington (RA) in 1804 when the deteriorating relationship between Benjamin West (President) and George III threatened to draw the King *directly* into the Academy's affairs. See Farington's Diary (Garlick & MacIntyre edition) vol. 6, p. 2403. Also see Whitley 1928: vol. 1, chapters 3 and 4. What is central here is the contradiction between the 'arbitrary' nature of patronage and the institutional autonomy secured through the democractic election of Academic officers. A quarter of a century later George IV is reported as considering the idea of changing the constitution of the RA with a view to installing a nobleman as President. Home-secretary Peel adroitly flattered the King out of the idea. As Peel pointed out: there were artistic appointments that fell within the King's

gift – but the RA, although *Royal* was self-elected (see Whitley 1930: 186–7).

3 See the partisan John Pye (1845), Thomas Skaife (1854) and Laidlay (1898). In the 1880s and '90s there was a considerable growth in the number of works being submitted to the RA Summer Exhibition – 6,415 in 1879, 8,686 in 1887 and 12,408 in 1896 (see Hutchison 1968: 139). At the end of the century there were about 5,000 artists annually submitting works with not more than two-fifths gaining a place in the Exhibition (Hutchison:150).

4 There was even talk of the Queen being prepared to support a new Academy: '. . . she will not appoint the members of the 1863 Commission, until she knows whom he [the President] approves. . . But should Lord Elcho succeed in altering the Constitution of the Academy, the principal members, with Sir Charles (the President) at their head, would instantly leave it' (Charles Eastlake Smith (ed), *Journals & Correspondence of Lady Eastlake* 1895: vol. 2, 167).

5 It was not until 1871, after years of petitioning, that the Press was officially given access to the Exhibition. Improved conditions of access were granted to the Press in 1892. See M. H. Spielmann, *The Magazine of Art 1892:* 186–8 and 222–8.

6 Martin Archer Shee, *A Letter to Lord John Russell . . . on the Alleged Claims of the Public to be Admitted Gratis to the Exhibition of the Royal Academy* (1837) and Martin Archer Shee, *A Letter to Joseph Hume Esq M.P.* (1838): 'The Royal Academy, my Lord, owe much to their Sovereign, but nothing to their country' (13).

7 Its exclusiveness appears to have been in question in the early 1800s: 'It should never be forgotten that the original intention of this entertainment was calculated to bring together at the opening of the Exhibition the highest orders of Society and the most distinguished characters of the age; but unfortunately, by degrees, the purity of selection has given way to the influence of private friendships and the importunity of acquaintances. . .' (Royal Academy, Council Minutes: vol. 4, p. 111, 1st April 1809).

8 See Girouard 1979: 8–9; Clemenson 1982: 48–50)

9 See Hallé (1909); J. Comyns Carr (1908) and Mrs J. Comyns Carr (1925).

10 See also Mrs. J. Comyns Carr (1925): 'Lady Lindsay's Sunday afternoon parties at the Grosvenor were among the social events of the 'eighties. . . Admissions by ticket to the private-view days had always been in great demand, but the Sunday afternoon receptions were entirely confined to personal invitations, and Sir Coutts and Lady Lindsay took a certain pride in being the first members of Society to bring the people of their own set into friendly contact with the distinguished folk of art and literature. In these fine rooms hung with crimson damask they certainly gathered together the elite of the great world as well as all the brilliance of a select Bohemia' (54). Of course it *was* an illusion. By 1887 the patrician Sir Coutts Lindsay's associates (Charles Hallé and J. Comyns Carr) have fallen out with him, resigned their directorships and are busily establishing the New Gallery – taking with them the star of the Grosvenor, Edward Burne-Jones. Thompson's metaphor (1978:55) characterizing the aristocracy as presiding, like the staff of an expensive hotel over the comings and goings of guests who may choose to do what they want is entirely apposite here. Worth noting here is the growing importance of the commercial directorship as a mode of aristocratic participation in the affairs of exhibition galleries – see *The Magazine of Art* (1892:348–50) for a description of the Grafton Gallery and the composition of its board of directors.

11 This is particularly noticeable in the case of the assault mounted on the RA's control of the Chantrey Bequest in the years c.1880–1915. The Report of the 1904 Select Committee on the Chantrey Trust asserts that the Chantrey selection 'contains too many pictures of a purely popular character, and too few which reach the degree of artistic distinction evidently aimed at by Sir Francis Chantrey. . .' (*Report:* 498, para 7).

12 On the other hand there is the emergence of an increasingly evident reforming tendency within the RA in the 1880s and '90s. See Hutchison 1968: chapter 13. By 1894 the Academy is being congratulated on its reforms – see *The Magazine of Art* 1894:217–220.

13 Elsewhere I have argued that in the case of the pre-photographic reproduction of paintings the *social* production of authorship, within the context of the contested relations of pictorial mass production, is evident. Within the world of handicraft reproduction, craftsmen engravers laboured to extend the reputations of fine artists. The means of fine art reproduction (line engraving, wood engraving, chromolithography and a host of other, often hybridized techniques) were the site of an aesthetic tension which threatened the complete pictorial control of the artist – the 'hand' of the reproductive engraver breaking through, perhaps challenging and obscuring the pictorial intentions of the artist.

14 See John Barrell (1972) *The Idea of Landscape and the Sense of Place 1730–1840.* p.4. Important in this connection is the campaigning journalism of S. C. Hall, lawyer and editor of the *Art Journal.* Throughout the 1840s and 1850s Hall used the *Art Journal* to expose dealers in forged pictures.

15 See e.g. 'Some Anachronisms of Art', *The Magazine of Art* (1880:39–40). Crucial here is the ideological role of narrative painting in elaborating historical 'knowledge' within the class context of state formation.

16 Within the profession disaffected artists, amongst them French trained dissidents, were given much publicity to schemes for a broadly based exhibiting society. There was considerable discussion and debate about the principles upon which a new society might be organized and proposals that universal suffrage – the participation of all British artists – should be the keynote. The major outcome was the foundation of the New English Art Club in 1886: 'the outcome of a movement or feeling expressed at divers little meetings held in Paris and London between the years 1880 and 1886, with a view to protesting against the narrowness of the Royal Academy. . .' (Laidlay 1907:3). What particularly distinguished it from the Academy was that the 15 strong jury (selecting exhibits) was 'elected by and from members and exhibitors of the previous year' (Laidlay 1907:202). Resentment within the profession continued to fuel a campaign for 'a really national exhibition . . . conducted by artists on the broadest and fairest lines' (*The Times,* August 7th 1886, p.6) but this seems to have disintegrated.

17 Also see *The Portfolio* (1893: v) for an account of the newly opened Grafton gallery and the problems of its lighting: 'Each wall is . . . lighted by the skylight opposite it. The result is that when the pictures are looked at from exactly the right spot they are seen very well. On the other hand, the system limits the choice of point of view, for when the spectator stands too close he is bothered by reflections. . .'.

18 The kind of misgivings that Millais had had appear to have persisted. The art dealer Oliver Brown recalls that in the early years of the present century there were many successful artists who had reached the end of their careers without

ever having had a one man show 'and were by no means convinced that they would be of any benefit' (Brown 1968:139).

Acknowledgment

I am grateful to the Royal Academy of Arts for permission to consult the Council Minute Books.

References

Altick, R. (1978), *The Shows of London*, Cambridge, Mass: Harvard University Press.
Becker, H. (1982), *Art Worlds*. Berkeley: University of California Press.
Beckett, R.B. (ed.) (1966), 'Patrons, Dealers and Fellow Artists', in *John Constable's Correspondence*, vol. 4, Ipswich: Suffolk Records Society.
Benjamin, W. (1970), *Illuminations*, London: Jonathan Cape.
Bourdieu, P. (1968), 'Outline of a Sociological Theory of Art Perception', *International Social Science Journal*, vol. 20.
Bourdieu, P. (1980a), 'The Aristocracy of Culture', *Media, Culture and Society*, vol. 2, no. 3.
Bourdieu, P. (1980b), 'The Production of Belief: contribution to an economy of symbolic goods', *Media, Culture and Society*, vol. 2, no. 3.
Brighton, A. (1977), 'Official Art and the Tate Gallery', *Studio International*, vol. 193.
Brown, Oliver (1968), *Exhibition: The Memoirs of Oliver Brown*, London: Evelyn, Adams & Mackay.
Burne-Jones, Lady Georgiana (1906 and 1912), *Memorials of Burne-Jones*, (two vols) 2nd edn, London: Macmillan.
Carr, J. Comyns (1908), *Some Eminent Victorians: Personal Recollections in the World of Art and Letters*, London: Duckworth.
Carr, Mrs. J. Comyns [1925], *Reminiscences* (edited by E. Adam), London: Hutchinson.
Clemenson, H.A. (1982), *English Country Houses and Landed Estates*, London: Croom Helm.
Clive, Mary (1965) *The Day of Reckoning*, London: the Reprint Society.
Davidoff, L. (1973) *The Best Circles*, London: Croom Helm.
Dimaggio, P. (1982) 'Cultural Entrepreneurship in Nineteenth-century Boston', *Media, Culture and Society*, 2 pts, vol. 4, nos. 1 and 4.
Duncan, C. and Wallach, A. (1980), 'The Universal Survey Museum', *Art History*, vol. 3, No. 4.
Eddy, A.J. (1904), *Recollections and Impressions of James A. McNeill Whistler* (2nd edn), Philadelphia: J.B. Lippincott.
Escott, T.H.S. (1880), *England: Its People, Polity and Pursuits* (2 vols), London: Cassell, Petter, Galpin.
Fisher, F.J. (1947), 'The Development of London as a Centre of Conspicuous Consumption in the Sixteenth and Seventeenth Centuries', *Transactions of the*

Royal Historical Society.

Foucault, M. (1979), 'What is an Author?', *Screen*, vol. 20, no. 1.

Fuller, P. (1980), *Beyond the Crisis in Art*, London: Readers and Writers Publishers Cooperative.

Giddens, A. (1979), *Central Problems in Social Theory*, London and Basingstoke: The Macmillan Press Ltd.

Girouard, M. (1979), *The Victorian Country House*, London: Book Club Associates.

Grana, C. (1967), *Modernity and its Discontents*, New York: Harper & Row.

Grana, C. (1971), *Fact and Symbol*, New York: Oxford University Press Inc.

Hadjinicolaou, N. (1978), *Art History and Class Struggle*, London: Pluto Press.

Hallé, C.E. (1909), *Notes from a Painter's Life: including the founding of two galleries*, London: John Murray.

Hamerton, P.G. (1889), *Thoughts about Art*, London: Macmillan.

Hardie, M. (1963), *Watercolour Painting in Britain*, vol. 3, London: B. T. Batsford.

Haskell, F. (1963), *Patrons and Painters*, London: Chatto & Windus.

Hutchison, S.C. (1968), *The History of the Royal Academy*, London: Chapman & Hall.

Jameson, F. (1984), 'The Cultural Logic of Capital', *New Left Review*, no. 146.

Laidlay, W.J. (1898), 'The Royal Academy: Its Uses and Abuses', *The Architectural Review*, vol. 4: 132–4.

Laidlay, W.J. (1907), *The Origins and First Two Years of the New English Art Club*, London: the author.

Lippincott, Louise (1983), *Selling Art in Georgian London*, New Haven: Yale University Press.

McKendrick, N., Brewer, J. and Plumb, J.H. (1982), *The Birth of a Consumer Society*, London: Europa Publications Ltd.

Marks, H.S. (1894), *Pen and Pencil Sketches*, 2 vols, London: Chatto & Windus.

Menpes, M. (1904), *Whistler as I Knew Him*, London: A. & C. Black.

Morgan, H.C. (1969), 'The Lost Opportunity of the Royal Academy: an Assessment of its Position in the Nineteenth Century', *Journal of the Warburg and Courtauld Institute*, vol. 32.

Pennell, E.R. and Pennell, J. (1921), *The Whistler Journal*.

Perkins, H (1972), *The Origins of Modern English Society*, London: Routledge & Kegan Paul.

Pevsner, N. (1973), *Academies of Art Past and Present*, New York: De Capo Press.

Pye, J. (1845), *Patronage of British Art*, London: Longman, Brown, Green, and Longmans.

Roberts, H. (1973), 'Art Reviewing in the Early Nineteenth Century Art Periodicals', *Victorian Periodicals Newsletter*, no. 19.

Robertson, D. (1978), *Sir Charles Eastlake and the Victorian Art World*, Princeton: Princeton University Press.

Rubinstein, D. (1981), *Men of Property*, London: Croom Helm.

Scott, John (1982), *The Upper Classes*, London and Basingstoke: The Macmillan Press Ltd.

Sennett, R. (1976), *The Fall of Public Man*, Cambridge University Press.

Shils, E. (1981), *Tradition*, London: Faber & Faber.

Skaife, T. (1854), *Exposé of the Royal Academy of Arts*, London: Piper, Stephenson & Spence.

Sloane, J.C. (1961), 'On the Resources of Non-Objective Art', *Journal of Aesthetics and Art Criticism*, vol. 19, no. 4.

Stone, L. and Stone, J.C.F. (1984), *An Open Elite? England 1540–1880*, Oxford: Oxford University Press.

Tate Gallery (1972), *Caspar David Friedrich*, London: Tate Gallery.

Thompson, E.P. (1978), *The Poverty of Theory*; London: Merlin Press.

Treble, R. (1978), *Great Victorian Pictures*, London: Arts Council of Great Britain.

Watney, S. (1983), 'The Connoisseur as Gourmet', *Formations of Pleasure*, Formations editorial collective, London: Routledge & Kegan Paul.

Webb, B. (1929), *My Apprenticeship*, London: Longmans.

White, H.C. & White, C.A. (1965), *Canvases and Careers*, New York: John Wiley & Sons.

Whitley, W.T. (1928), *Artists and their Friends in England 1700–1799*, two vols, London.

Whitley, W.T. (1928), *Art in England 1800–1820*, Cambridge: Cambridge University Press.

Whitley, W.T. (1930), *Art in England 1821–1837*, Cambridge: Cambridge University Press.

Williams, R. (1976), *Key Words*, London: Fontana/Croom Helm.

Williams, R. (1981), *Culture*, London: Fontana.

Wolff, J. (1981), *The Social Production of Art*, London: The Macmillan Press Ltd.

The politics of schism: routinisation and social control in the International Socialists/Socialist Workers' Party*

Steve Rayner

Abstract

There is a common assumption in social science, that voluntary associations founded on egalitarian principles must inevitably develop hierarchical structures with centralized control, if they are to persist through time. This paper uses grid/group analysis to suggest an approach to organizational change that is less fatalistic than the *iron law of oligarchy*.

A case study is presented which suggests that the process of routinization in egalitarian associations is far from automatic. Indeed, the members' awareness of contradiction between egalitarian principles on which the group was founded, and principles of centralized power and hierarchy in bureaucratic organizations is a problem that must be overcome by a leader who seeks to effect such a change.

Furthermore, the case study shows that social control through a centralized hierarchy cannot simply be introduced into a voluntary association. It must first pass through a phase in which institutional memory of the founding principles is eradicated through high membership turnover, and the expulsion of rival contenders for leadership. This process creates the conditions for centralized social control and the bureaucratic exercise of power.

The received wisdom of social science holds that voluntary organizations founded on egalitarian principles, can only survive by undergoing transformation into hierarchial systems. This phenomenon was clearly articulated in the sociology of religion by Max Weber (1921) as *routinization;* the gradual transformation from sect to denomination. Michels (1915), writing from a political science perspective described the same process as the iron law of oligarchy. Both can be interpreted as special cases of Tönnies' (1887) description of the general tendency of societies to shift from *gemeinschaft* to *gesellschaft* or, in Durkheim's (1893) term, from *mechanical* to *organic* solidarity.

The underlying logic of all these descriptions is that social organizations sustain themselves over time by generating increasingly complex systems of rules that become sources of inequality. It is beyond the scope of this article to argue against this general evolutionary assumption about the development of society as a whole. I shall confine myself here to the case of voluntary organizations, to argue that routinization in voluntary groups does not consist of a gradual accumulation of rules that promote internal inequality. Instead, I propose two analytically distinct steps; (1) construction of a distinctive organizational boundary, which is a necessary condition for (2) the ultimate imposition of a complex organizational hierarchy. The case I shall use to illustrate this argument is drawn from the history of the British Trotskyist movement prior to 1978. The argument itself will be framed within a formal model of the sociology of knowledge called grid/group analysis.

My justification for identifying the problem of routinization as a question for the sociology of knowledge is based on a well-known premiss shared by Weber, Durkheim, and the British structural-functionalist tradition of social anthropology. Every one of us has to achieve some sort of a match between the social constraints that govern his daily life and the ideas that he uses to explain the world that he lives in. Social life would be impossible without some principles to guide our behavior in ways that are socially sanctioned and that can be used to justify ourselves to others, as well as used to judge their actions. If any of us should find that his daily social environment and his world-view are incompatible, he may try to change either his role in the world or the social organization of which he is a part, or he may have to adjust his ideas to take account of the discrepancy. In any case, failure to achieve a convergence of social experience and explanatory ideas at some fundamental level would render any social being unable to operate effectively within his social context.

The problem of routinization is, therefore, not merely one of changing organizational arrangements. The egalitarian world outlook which leads members to band together in the first place must also be changed. The charismatic leader, or his heirs or, in some cases, his rivals wishing to develop a more hierarchical system of rules for decision making must therefore overcome an established preference for egalitarian principles of organization shared by other members of the group. We might reasonably expect this obstacle to be especially acute in those voluntary organizations which are founded in explicit opposition to the hierarchical or bureaucratic policies of the outside world, such as religious sects or anarchist and revolutionary socialist political groups. Grid/group analysis enables us to elucidate the essentially dialectical character of change at both the organizational and ideological levels.

Grid/group analysis

The organizational variables that I have chosen to illustrate the systematic connection between social organization and the ideas that legitimate it are called grid and group respectively. The definitions of each have been established elsewhere (Douglas 1978, Gross and Rayner 1985), but they can be summarized quite briefly.

The *group* variable represents the degree of social incorporation of the individual in a social unit. Where group is weak, social networks are open ended (non-transitive), while interactions with the same people tend to be infrequent and limited to various specific activities in each case. By way of contrast, where group is strong, social networks are closed (transitive), while the same people interact frequently and in a wide range of activities.

Whereas the group variable describes the range of social interactions within a social unit, the *grid* variable describes the nature of those interactions. Grid is defined as a measure of the constraining rules that bear upon members of any social grouping. Such classifications may be functions of hierarchy, kinship, race, gender, age, and so forth. Low grid indicates an egalitarian state of affairs in which no one is prevented from participating in any social role because he is the wrong sex, or is too old, or does not have the right family connections. A high-grid state of affairs is one where access to all social activities depends on one or another of these kinds of discriminations. These constraints may be imposed on people from without or within their personal social networks. Indeed, they may devote a great deal of attention to maintaining or reducing them in accordance with their own position and interests. Hence, grid constraints are measured without regard to the strength of the group dimension.

As independent variables, grid and group may be represented as a pair of orthogonal dimensions. Assessing each variable as high- or low-strength gives rise to four prototype visions of social life and characteristic world outlooks, as illustrated in Figure 1.

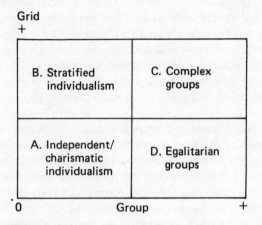

Figure 1: Grid/group typology

The absence of restrictions on social behavior arising from rules or from the prior claims of others gives rise to an independent or charismatic-individualist social environment, to be found at the extreme bottom left of the diagram.

Social institutions that make strong demands of incorporation and regulation, are located in quadrant C. Individualism and competition may not be entirely absent, but the further into C we go, the more control will be vested in formal systems until, at the extreme top-right corner, all aspects of social life are strictly controlled by hierarchical authority. That authority may be a church, a bureaucracy, or on a smaller scale, a patriarchal family head.

To the bottom right of this dichotomy between individualism and bureaucracy we find a collectivist egalitarian framework, D. In the absence of established bureaucratic procedures to resolve disputes, the reality of egalitarian groups is frequently characterized by witch-hunts and infighting between covert factions.

Finally, B is the category of stratified, often alienated, individuals. In charismatic systems there are people who, having no goods or services to exchange, get driven out of the market. In hierarchical systems there are people who are excluded from the established institutions of representation. Very often, these are people who have the fewest or the least socially valued skills in a wider social arena. They tend to be the most vulnerable in any social system.

Note that each of these four types of social structure has been generated deductively as an ideal type (Weber 1921). No real society or organization could be expected to fit one of the above descriptions in every respect. The value of such a typology is as a heuristic guide to clarify what is really similar and what is significantly different about a variety of social units that may be far apart in space and time, or to trace changes in the socio-cultural system.

The routinization of voluntary associations can, therefore, be described as the transformation of freely associating egalitarian individuals (A) into a collective bureaucratic organization at (C). However, I shall argue that this direct transformation from A to C does not occur. Rather, any attempt to transform a voluntary egalitarian association into a bureaucratic collective must first deal with the contradiction between egalitarian ideology and bureaucratic organization by means of an organizational detour through quadrant D, the witch-hunting world of strong-group egalitarians.

Although this argument is illustrated by a single case study, there are features of the grid/group model which indicate that this description of routinization is transferable to other cases and that examination of other cases reveals a similar pattern of development. My purpose, therefore, is not merely to redescribe routinization, but to answer those critics of grid/group analysis who claim that it can only describe social change; all explanation being extrinsic to the model. The account I shall give indicates that the organizational detour through low grid/high group is a product of the interaction of social and ideological pressures that are intrinsic to the definition of the grid and group coordinates. For an account of the process, we turn first to the case of the International Socialists/Socialist Workers Party (SWP) in Britain, which is drawn from my own fieldwork (Rayner 1979).

The account that I shall give is a selective history of organizational changes in the SWP during the 1960s and 1970s. Two behavioral characteristics of the organization are highlighted as the SWP passes through a low-grid/high group phase. The first is the increasing organizational intolerance of factions usually leading to wholesale expulsions of the experienced cadres who compose them. The second is the elimination of institutional memory among rank-and-file members, due to the high level of membership turnover. The crux of my argument will be that both of these characteristics enabled the original charismatic leadership, centered on Tony Cliff, to transform the SWP from a voluntary association whose egalitarian outlook required it to respect and tolerate diverse viewpoints, into a centralized Leninist bureaucracy pursuing a single legitimate interpretation of revolutionary truth.

A brief history of the Socialist Worker's Party

The history of the Socialist Worker's Party and its forerunner, the International Socialists, has been dominated by a single individual, Tony Cliff. Cliff has been a central figure in the British Trotskyist movement since 1947 when he espoused the theory that the Soviet Union under Stalin had reverted to a form of capitalism in which the surplus value was accumulated by the State. This *State Capitalist Theory* was the distinguishing ideological motif for a small group of Trotskyists that entered the Labour Party during the 1950s and 1960s.

In 1964, Cliff's group, which had grown about 200 strong, adopted the title of *International Socialists* (IS). That same year marked a change in the attitude of the IS towards the Labour Party. Previously the group had emphasized to its members, the importance of their involvement in the mass party of the British working class.

However, the group's general enthusiasm at the return of a Labour government in 1964 was to be short lived. The incomes policy, tightening of immigration controls, and support for the Vietnam war were their chief sources of dismay. The Labour Party as a membership organization went into a sharp decline and many party activists drifted out. In July 1965 the IS began a protracted process of withdrawal from the Labour Party.

The IS group rejects the Labour Party as an instrument for social change; rejects it as a milieu for mass conversion to socialist consciousness; and sees in it primarily an arena for ideological conflict, a link to a living working class audience, and a source of individual recruitment to a revolutionary programme. (Conference Resolution quoted Birchall 1975a:22)

By the beginning of 1968, IS had more or less completely broken away from the Labour Party. The change was marked by the group's newspaper, *Labour Worker,* changing its name to *Socialist Worker* in order to avoid being identified with the policies of the Labour Government. By this stage, IS was able to claim a fairly steady growth in its membership since 1964 to over 400.

Closing the boundary

1968 was a watershed for the British far-left. It was particularly notable for the emergence of student radicalism following the LSE occupation of 1967 and the focusing of popular attention on the Vietnam war. Although IS had been officially represented at the setting up of the Vietnam Solidarity Campaign (VSC), it only maintained a token presence for the first year of its operation. But by the middle of 1967, the anti-war movement in the United States had gained momentum and the emerging radical student movement in Britain was looking for a cause to adopt. At this point, IS decided to step up its involvement in the VSC. Although the bulk of the effort in getting the VSC moving had been made by another far-left grouping, the International Marxist Group (IMG), IS carried off most of the recruits which were to be made from the campaign in this period.

Encouraged by this success, IS resolved to transform itself from a propaganda group intervening in various struggles in a fragmented and localized manner into a revolutionary combat organization in the Leninist tradition. Hitherto, IS had been organized on a federalist basis whereby each branch sent a delegate to the leading body of the organization. 1968 saw the introduction of democratic centralism for the first time. It was proposed firstly that the leading body be elected nationally from a conference, and secondly, that the organization should have the explicit right to impose discipline on all of its members.

These proposals caused a considerable internal upheaval. Birchall (1975) reports that at least five factions came into existence around various positions. These ranged from libertarian opposition to centralism, to orthodox-Leninist views that the proposals did not impose a sufficiently strict discipline. The adoption of a democratic centralist constitution was agreed only after a lengthy internal debate and two stormy conferences in September and December. Birchall summarized the basis of this debate in his official history of IS.

> The heat of the debate can be partly explained by the newness of the membership – a good half had been in the group only a few months, and by the fact that many of them had come straight from the heady atmosphere of student politics. But the issues at stake were more fundamental. When the main job had been struggle in the fragments, the need had been to encourage initiative; conditions for the tenants struggle varied so greatly between say, Newcastle, Sheffield, and London, that unified directives would have been of little help to anyone. It was in fact vital to stress that comrades should not wait for directives. (Birchall 1975b:24)

Although the move was carried, there were several resignations of experienced members who found the stricter discipline unacceptable. The loss of the libertarian elements of the IS tradition can be traced to this transformation. However, despite these losses, IS doubled its total membership in 1968 to just over 1,000.

In 1971, the International Socialists was still more open to diverse viewpoints than its successor, the Socialist Workers' Party. It consisted of orthodox-Trotskyist, libertarian, and left-wing communist factions, in addition to its State Capitalist core. Duncan Hallas, a leading ideologue of the IS, claimed at the time that the International Socialists did not see itself as being the sole revolutionary party, but as an organization contributing to the development of the revolutionary left in Britain.

However, this approach was not to last much longer. The year 1972–3 saw IS intensifying its efforts in the competition to form the nucleus of a revolutionary vanguard party which was to lead the working class to power. To do this, IS made a decisive effort to develop its orientation towards industry. Whereas its main growth previously had been through Tony Cliff's lecture tours of the universities, now it set out with *Socialist Worker* to promote rank-and-file organizations and to develop factory bulletins and rank-and-file papers.

The emphasis during 1972–3 was on the creation of a traditional Leninist party structure based on workplace branches. These were principally built by student worker-priests taking up industrial employment with a view to organizing the working class. However, the factory branches which were built in this way collapsed dramatically, precisely because of the emphasis on recruitment. Workers would join in the heat of industrial struggles but, once inside, they found that the International Socialists had no strategy for work in the established trade union movement, which it rejected as being controlled by reformist bureaucrats. In an organization whose membership, drawn from traditionally trade-unionized occupations, was outnumbered two to one by those drawn from sectors which did not have a background of trade unionism, it is not surprising to find an emphasis on by-passing the trade unions and on building an alternative rank-and-file structure. It is also scarcely surprising that, in a period of Labour Party opposition, when the unions were under severe pressure from a Conservative government, workers were less than willing to desert a united trade-union movement for piecemeal rank and fileism.

The factory branches never reached fifty in number. Those that had been built soon collapsed, largely due to the failure to develop a trade-union strategy or successfully substitute the rank-and-file movement for the unions. Additional to the high turnover of individual members, structural stresses in IS began to emerge with the secession in 1971 of Workers Fight, a tiny organization that had merged with the IS only three years earlier.

The suppression of factions begins

In 1973, the International Socialists suffered a 50 per cent turnover in membership, including many of its original members. The most significant losses were those connected with the Revolutionary Opposition, dubbed the *Right Faction* by the leaders of the International Socialists. This group was expelled after publishing, internally, a lengthy critique of International Socialist Policy entitled 'What We Stand For: A Revolutionary Opposition in I.S.'. David Yaffe, one of the principal architects of the Revolutionary Opposition, attacked both of the mainstays of Tony Cliff's theoretical position, namely the Permanent Arms Economy Theory and the State Capitalist Theory. Yaffe and his colleagues had maintained an intense barrage of discussion of aspects of Marxist economics in the *Internal Bulletin* of the International

Socialists. In fact, they were eventually forced to take up a whispering campaign because they were told that they were taking up too much room in the bulletins.

It was from this time that factions, which had been previously permitted to operate quite freely in IS, became increasingly frowned upon by the leadership. By 1976, factions were only permitted during the month of discussion immediately prior to national conferences. This was part of a general process of reducing the extent to which policies and strategies were openly negotiated within IS. The outcome was the entrenchment of the Cliff leadership.

By 1974, Cliff's view of the role of IS had already shifted away from the 1971 position that IS was not itself the embryo of the revolutionary party (conference document). The balance of support on the executive shifted towards Cliff at the expense of the other tendencies which had previously given IS its informal, federalist, character and the attractive openness it had displayed between 1968–71. The executive itself was increasingly being filled with politically inexperienced students with a tendency to accept Cliff's ideas without criticism. Negotiation of policy was greatly reduced and discussion, even at the Executive level, was mainly confined to the problems of implementing Cliff's decisions.

In the face of the various internal crises of 1974 IS marched into a period of intensive activity in connection with the Portuguese Revolution. Whether it was intended to or not, this activism served as a smokescreen which diverted the membership's attention away from its own troubles. Membership fell dramatically from around 3,000 to less than 2,000. The factory branches were decimated. For example, three such branches collapsed in Hull between October and December. At the National Conference in 1974, less than half of the outgoing National Committee was reelected; an unusually high level of turnover for any far-left group.

Although there are no figures available, it is well known that the expulsion rate soared at this time. Cliff himself had a fairly narrow range of political experience, having only worked as a lecturer in a Labour College and as a part-time gardener before taking up full time responsibilities for IS. He was not able to argue convincingly against his more articulate rivals in the organization and increasingly resorted to administrative strategies to maintain his leadership. Established figures in IS, such as Jim Higgins, were attacked as has-beens who were unable to attract young militants to the organization. Roger Protz, who as editor had done much to establish *Socialist Worker* as a widely read left-wing weekly, was politically isolated by Cliff and removed from his post. This was carried out by a series of manoeuvres thinly disguised as a general shake-up to give the paper more working-class appeal. Paul Foot was appointed to this task, and at this point, sales plummeted to twelve thousand from a target circulation (admittedly never fulfilled) of thirty thousand copies a week.

Other critics emerged in 1974, some of whom were more fortunate than Protz in the strategy which Cliff pursued towards them. Duncan Hallas and Ken Applebee were among the thirteen signatories of a critical article entitled 'Socialist Worker: Perspectives and Organization', which appeared in an *Internal Bulletin* in April 1974. Of these signatories, only Hallas and Applebee remained in the organization by 1976. It would seem that Cliff decided to retain these two critics, rather than isolate them with a view to expulsion. Cliff appears to have assessed the expenditure of resources in the removal of Hallas and Applebee as being greater than the cost of accommodating them. Both were given responsible positions within the leadership, Hallas as editor of the group's theoretical journal *International Socialism*.

The campaign was carried on by the remaining eleven signatories against what they saw as the increasingly erratic Cliff leadership which was accused of wild voluntarist campaigns in both the area of rank and file work and *Socialist Worker*. Initially, the response of the leadership to these criticisms appeared to be a tolerant one. *Socialist Worker* of the 18th May 1974 described the situation as one in which, '. . . these differences arise from different assessments and are containable in the IS tradition'. However, changes in the leadership and organizational structure of the International Socialists led the critics, known as the International Socialist Opposition, to develop an extended critique of all major aspects of the organization's practice, which they rooted in Cliff's utopian political assessments. It was these same changes in the internal regime of the International Socialists, including the systematic removal of Opposition members from leading positions, that meant that the Opposition could' no longer be accommodated within the International Socialist tradition and was forced to part company with the parent organization to form the Worker's League.

The concentration of power

The most significant change in the structure of the IS in the period leading up to the expulsion of the IS Opposition was the introduction of a new constitution for the leading bodies of the group. Since the introduction of democratic centralism in 1968, the IS had been led by a National Committee of forty members, elected from conference, and an Executive of six, selected from its own ranks by the National Committee. At the 1975 IS conference, Cliff, without prior discussion, introduced proposals for a small Central Committee to replace both the National Committee and the Executive. This concentration of the national leadership was further increased by the stipulation that voting for the Central Committee should be for whole slates only, not for individuals. Of course, Cliff's slate won easily and thus precluded any minority representation on the national leadership.

The Birmingham branch, which was about sixty strong, refused from then on to abide by conference decisions. The new Central Committee sent in a Control Commission (a disciplinary committee) which expelled about half of the branch. Twickenham branch was also decimated of its leading cadres for supporting the Birmingham position. Among these was a veteran Trotskyist from the Balham Group of the 1930s, Harry Wicks. Roger Protz, who had edited *Socialist Worker*, and Jim Higgins, were among other leading IS members who were expelled during this purge. Ironically, Higgins had led the control commission which had expelled the Revolutionary Opposition the previous year. IS also lost significant groups of engineers and teachers to the new Workers' League.

In response to the issues raised by the split with the Workers' League, the Central Committee of IS set up a new body called the Party Council, consisting of delegates from branches, representative of specialist sectors, and the various front organizations of IS. However, this body had only a consultative function. It was not convened often or regularly while, over the next two years, the Central Committee became increasingly distant from the rest of the organization.

Whilst the IS Opposition was being purged, Cliff was pursuing a policy of expulsion on yet another front. The numerically tiny Left Faction, which had existed for about two years without making any significant impression on the bulk of the membership, was summarily expelled without right of appeal in October 1975 to form Workers' Power. Many IS members remained unaware of the issues on which the Left Faction was expelled. No effort was made to explain the basis of the split to anyone in the organization below Branch Committee level. But the expulsion of the Left Faction fuelled allegations by other internal opposition groups, such as IS Opposition, of increasing centralization and high-handed bureaucratic action by an undemocratic leadership.

Political isolationism

This period also marked a distinct growth in opposition to other organizations. The International Socialists attempted to disrupt the activity of the Liaison Committee for the Defence of Trades Unions and increasingly defined themselves, in organizational terms, by their opposition to the initiatives of the Labour Party, the TUC, and the Communist Party. In 1977, Cliff was the only British Trotskyist of note to refuse to join the platform at the rally at Friends House, in protest against Workers' Revolutionary Party Leader Gerry Healy's accusation that American Trotskyists collaborated with Stalin's GPU in the assassination of Trotsky. In the same year, he rejected an invitation of electoral cooperation with the International Marxist Group in fighting various by-elections.

The main focus for the oppositional politics of the International Socialists was the Rank-and-File movement, which held its first national conference in March 1974. Unlike the Liaison Committee for the Defence of Trade Unions, which was developed by trade unionists to resist the challenge of Labour's 1968 trade union legislation *In Place of Strife*, the Rank-and-File movement was not founded in response to an external threat to the organized Labour Movement. Rank-and-File was set up to oppose the traditional organizations of the Labour Movement by setting up alternative structures to what IS described as 'the bureaucracy'.

A Leninist party?

By 1976, Cliff clearly felt that he had consolidated his leadership, and he set IS firmly on a course of opposition to other left groups and to the established structures of the Labour Movement. *Socialist Worker* was accordingly instructed to raise the question of whether IS was ready to transform itself publicly into the

Revolutionary Party. It became quite clear that the leadership had already decided on this course of action and were facing the task of pulling the membership behind the move. After a period of relative uncertainty, the change was carried through and the name Socialist Workers' Party (SWP) was adopted.

However, the establishment of the SWP did not immediately herald the period of internal stability that Cliff had hoped for. Serious dissent within the party soon became apparent. Its roots lay in the expulsion of the IS Opposition in 1975, when a number of sympathisers had elected to stay in IS to fight for their position rather than join the Workers' League. Among these were Martin Shaw and Richard Kuper, who continued to press for the restoration of the pre-1975 system of national leadership.

Duncan Hallas and Chris Harman were two members of the SWP Central Committee who felt sufficiently pressed by these demands to propose extending the Central Committee from six to nine members and possibly dropping the slate system. At conference, the only branch to come out wholly in favor of Shaw's position was his own, Hull. Hallas' and Harman's proposals were accepted but were not seen as adequate concessions by Shaw's supporters. Shaw and Kuper, along with some forty others, left the SWP and formed the International Socialists Alliance.

Among those who left the SWP at this point was Mike Kidron, Cliff's son-in-law. Kidron's departure not only meant the loss to the SWP of one of its principal theoreticians but, more seriously, the loss of Kidron's publishing house, Pluto Press.

The industrial strategy of the Socialist Workers' Party was in a state of disarray by the spring of 1977. Some experienced ex-members have said that they believed that the party wanted to get into the shop stewards' movement in spite of the fact that Cliff had condemned the shop stewards some years earlier. Certainly, the obstacles to such a move were considerable since the Rank-and-File movement had been built on the basis of opposition to union bureaucracy and to the Labour and Communist Parties which dominated it. In the end, a movement based on fast-recruitment, achieved on a purely oppositional basis and lacking a programme, was bound to disintegrate. The industrial strategy of the Socialist Workers' Party stagnated whilst the organization concentrated its efforts on physical confrontation with the National Front (NF) at every opportunity.

The Socialist Workers' Party's adoption of the strategy of physical confrontation with the NF was explicitly opposed to the policies of the Labour Party, the Communist Party, and the trade unions. As such, it was a hardening of the SWP's opposition to other groups on the left, especially since, at this stage, cooperation with other groups of the far left, such as the IMG, also was minimal. The Labour, Communist, and trade unions' position was one of building up the widest possible opposition to the National Front on the basis of the threat that it posed to community relations. This course was condemned in a SWP pamphlet on the basis that socialism provided the only alternative to racism and facism.

The effect of its militant strategy towards the National Front was to provide a focus of activity for SWP members and supporters at a time when the mileage in the SWP's industrial strategy was running out. Intense activism was a means to direct members' attention away from recognising fundamentally diverse interpretations of what was taken to be a common body of knowledge. The major threat to the SWP from its rapid expansion throughout 1976–7 was that the hastily admitted, inexperienced, new members, who swelled its ranks during the anti-unemployment campaign, would find themselves with time on their hands to step back from intense activism and recognize the lack of unanimity within the SWP.

Such a rapid expansion had taken place that adequate induction and education of new members had been impossible. Many of the party's middle cadre, to whom this task should have fallen, had been expelled in the purges of 1973–6 because they posed their own threat to the Cliff leadership's plans to transform IS from an egalitarian association into a bureaucratic political institution in which power was centralized. However, despite all of the leadership's efforts, intense anti-fascist activism failed to stem the tide of resignations, just as the Portuguese activism had failed to prevent the recession in the fortunes of IS in 1974.

Another notable feature of the SWP's position in 1977 was the party's refusal to come to any sort of electoral agreement with the IMG, which had suggested joint candidates, or at least an agreement not to oppose each other, at Stetchford and the other by-elections of that year. The political basis of this rebuttal appeared to be very flimsy and certainly annoyed a number of SWP cadres who favoured cooperation to that extent. However, the leadership was clearly not prepared to risk losing substantial numbers of SWP supporters and members to the IMG by exposing them to close cooperation with the better trained membership of the IMG.

Finally, 1978 saw the further consolidation of Cliff's personal grip on the organization. Paul Foot resigned from the editorship of *Socialist Worker* over differences with the Central Committee on editorial policy and Cliff took over editing the paper. Thus, Cliff successfully altered the character of his organization over ten years, from an alliance of several mutually tolerant, but tiny, factions to a fully centralized party without recognized factions.

A Grid/group summary

Before the adoption of a democratic-centralist constitution in 1968, IS was a loose-knit federation of local voluntary groups, each containing a wide range of far-left viewpoints. Integration was therefore very weak, and hierarchy was virtually non-existent. Leadership was flexible and offices ill-defined, without established incumbents. IS members were primarily accountable to other members of their local groups. There was much of the duplication of function typical of simple egalitarianism. Negotiation of policy was widespread, involving everyone in the organization, since there were no selective principles on which to exclude any section of the membership from debate on any issue.

IS, in 1968, was more or less an alliance of diverse views. Members of IS freely belonged to a variety of different types of organizations and were also involved in established Labour-movement structures. Up until 1968, IS members had even been active members of the Labour Party. Because of the unstructured character of the organization, formal activities were relatively few and IS activity often relied on informal contact between members. All the indications point to a weak-grid/weak-group condition, relative to the highly routinized bureaucracy that was in place a decade later. However, the shift from low grid/low group to high grid/high group did not occur through simultaneous strengthening of both sorts of organizational controls.

The introduction of democratic centralism in 1968 did mark the beginning of a period of increasingly formal organization. An elementary hierarchy was introduced, with a two-tier national leadership and a two-tier branch leadership. District organization linking the branches to the national leadership was proposed but does not seem to have operated very successfully. The adjudication of disputes and negotiation of policy tended to be appropriated by branch committees and the national leadership.

These factors are indicative of a moderate increase in the strength of grid constraints operating on IS members. However, the immediate consequences of democratic centralism for institutional integration, as measured by the group dimension, were much more dramatic. The flexible federation of local voluntary associations, each responsible for its own style of recruitment and conduct, was rapidly replaced by an integrated entity, with uniform membership requirements, and an increasingly homogeneous style of branch organization. There was an increase in the range and frequency of formal activities. Informal contacts with fellow group members also tended to increase as branches became large enough to provide a fairly comprehensive social life for members, and involvement in IS took precedence over their membership of other types of organization, particularly the Labour Party and the trades unions.

Withdrawal from the Labour Party was the beginning of increasing hostility to established labour-movement structures leading eventually to the establishment of the Rank-and-File movement as an alternative to the existing trades-unions structure. Although factions were not yet outlawed in IS, the abandoning of the old federalist structure, and the separation of the organization from close contact with other movements already represented a significant shift to strong group.

The crux of my argument is that this shift to weak grid/strong group was a necessary precondition for significant routinization to occur. Cliff's initial attempt to shift from voluntary association to

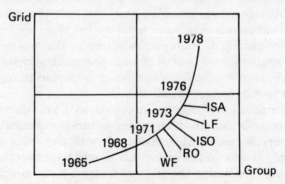

Figure 2: *Organizational change in IS/SWP 1965–78*

Leninist party was the introduction of democratic centralism in 1968. As we have seen, this attempt simultaneously to strengthen grid and group constraints met with strong resistance. The opponents of this move were not so much opposed to increasing solidarity within the movement, but to the formalization of bureaucratic control and loss of control over policy negotiation and decision making by the membership.

The transformation from loose-knit voluntary association to high group could be legitimated through the fact that IS members, as seekers after revolutionary change, saw themselves as standing apart from the larger society. Solidarity in the face of a common enemy is a credible value to charismatic individualists. On the other hand, adoption of the hierarchical style, characteristic of the world that threatens them, stands in direct contradiction to their past experiences and hopes for the future. The straightforward diagonal shift from A to C was, therefore, not a viable path for the IS to take in 1968. Even the moderate increase in grid that accompanied the move to high group was sufficient to cause a considerable proportion of the membership to give up affiliation with IS, while exit costs were still low.

The horizontal path, from A to D, established in IS the conditions for the development of high-grid organization. Rival individuals or factions, competing for leadership in low-grid organizations cannot resort to normative mechanisms for resolving disputes, such as appeals to seniority in a hierarchy or to established rules and precedents. A distinctive characteristic of low-grid ideologies is the notion that every individual's opinion carries the same weight.

However, disputants in low-grid organizations at high group are able to make use of a sanction that is not available to those at low group. At high group, a would-be leader is able to argue that his view should prevail, not because his opponent is junior or lacks access to specialized knowledge, but because his opponent is actually an outsider. The development of a clear group boundary therefore facilitates the emergence of a dominant leadership through judicious manipulation of the sanction of expulsion.

The suppression of factions was obviously a desirable step for Cliff in pursuance of his declared aim of building a militant party with a strongly centralized command structure under Leninist discipline. It also served him well in the aim, which others recognized, of securing his own power in the party. Blocking the formation of recognised factions reduced the opportunities for potential rivals to achieve intermediate leadership status legitimately and to consolidate opposition viewpoints within the party. Also, suppressing legal factions could not prevent the formation of covert factions but the uncovering of a covert faction could be used by the leadership as an excuse to legitimate the expulsion of potential rivals.

This process was clearly visible in IS during the period 1973–6 when no less than five rival factions were expelled by Cliff and his supporters. In all of these disputes, opponents accused Cliff of seeking to develop a bureaucratic or oligarchical leadership in IS. Cliff responded by accusing the challengers of deviating from the IS tradition and the binding values of the group. While experienced rivals, with a high investment in the organization, were dealt with in this fashion, the high level of rank-and-file turnover throughout the period pre-empted the maintenance of an egalitarian collective memory within IS. For the most part, rank-and-file members of IS were so new during this period of rapid recruitment and high turnover, that they were unaware generally of what the IS tradition had been. By 1976 open factionalism, a hallmark of early IS organization, had been forcibly suppressed by the leadership except for the brief period of pre-conference discussion. The new, high-grid constitutional arrangements, proposed by Cliff in 1975, were substantially in place.

Cliff had always wanted to expand his organization to the point where he could really present himself as a viable alternative to the Communist Party. However, the removal of rival leaders necessitated a shift to high group in order to remove their factional power bases. This obstructed mass recruitment and contributed to the very high turnover of members. Once the opposition factions had been expelled, and organized resistance to Cliff became very much more difficult, Cliff did not need to continue the shift to strong group which was acting against his other aim of expanding membership. Divested of the ballast formed by factions exploiting low-grid/low-group ideological themes, the SWP balloon was able to rise straight up-grid, out of the unstable quadrant D, into its relatively stable 1978 position (Figure 2). Here Cliff was able to rely on his entrenched position as leader and on his ability to impose strong-grid constraints over his members to control dissent. Therefore, the possibilities for more stable recruitment opened up.

Our examination of the SWP confirms the hypothesis of

grid/group theory, that quadrant D is organizationally unstable. We have suggested that there is a contradiction in the social relations of democratic-centralist organizations between the desire of an established leadership to reduce factionalism, in the interests of providing strong leadership for a disciplined revolutionary organization, and the desire of rival leaders to maintain factionalism, as a power base from which to challenge the leadership in the name of democracy.

The extent to which a leader will be able to introduce increasing grid constraints over his members, without causing a split, is likely to depend on the strength of the group boundary. Where the group is relatively weak even the introduction of modestly strong grid measures may produce splits and resignations. This was the pattern of opposition reaction in IS to the introduction of democratic centralism in 1968. However, as we move towards stronger group, we may expect that members will be more reluctant to place themselves outside of the boundaries. The violation of weak grid norms will have to be more extreme before members will pay the high exit costs of leaving, or risk expulsion by forming covert factions.

Summary and conclusions

The account that I have given of routinization in the Socialist Workers' Party during the period 1968–78 differs from the Weber/Michels model in three important respects.

First, it portrays routinization as a conscious strategy, instigated by leaders wishing to formalize a voluntary association into a complex organization. Although Michels does describe the manipulation by incumbents of the office of delegate to consolidate their personal position, the *iron law of oligarchy* implicitly assumes that the process is the inevitable product of irresistible social forces larger than the individual. Weber's account is even more fatalistic.

Second, the process of routinization in the SWP was not the gradual process described by Michels and Weber. There was no evolution of a customary right to the office of delegate in IS/SWP, if only because the rate of membership turnover was so rapid that most members scarcely had time to become accustomed to anything. The total transformation from voluntary association to complex organization took only one decade, whereas Weber describes routinization as taking place over a generation.

Third, the transformation of IS/SWP did not consist of the simple development of organizational inequalities. Early attempts to introduce complex organizational controls and hierarchical leadership were resisted by opponents. Only by developing a strong group boundary, and appropriating control over it through witch-hunts and expulsions, and high membership turnover was Cliff able to consolidate his pre-eminent position, and institute a fully bureaucratic system.

The foregoing account also has theoretical implications for grid/group analysis. I have suggested that a direct organizational shift from bottom left to top right does not occur because of the visible incompatibility of bureaucratic and egalitarian world views, whereas a voluntary shift from low- to high-group egalitarianism is credible, and provides the conditions for subsequent development of high-grid organization. Taken in conjunction with my account of Tangu millenarian cycles (Rayner 1982) and my reformulation of Highland Burma gumlao/gumsa cycles (Gross and Rayner 1985), we are beginning to build, through empirical research, a basis for understanding organizational and ideological change within the grid/group model. Eventually, we can hope to develop a comprehensive understanding of how the interaction of social organization and world view renders some strategies for social change viable, while ensuring the failure of others.

Note

I am grateful to the members and ex-members of the IS/SWP who assisted me in data collection and to Phil Burnham of UCL, John Reed of Oak Ridge National Laboratory, and Tom Hood of the University of Tennessee who commented on various drafts.

References

Birchall, Ian, 1975a 'History of IS, part one,' *IS JOURNAL* 76:16–24.
Birchall, Ian, 1975b. 'History of IS, part two, *IS JOURNAL* 77:22–28.
Douglas, Mary, 1978. *Cultural Bias*. Occasional Paper 35, Royal Anthropological Institute, London.
Durkheim, Emile, 1893. *De La Division du Travail Social,* Alcan, Paris, trans. 1933, *Division of Labor in Society,* Free Press, New York.

Gross, Jonathan L. and Rayner, Steve, 1985. *Measuring Culture: A Paradign for the Analysis of Social Organization*. Columbia University Press, New York.

Michels, Roberto, 1915. *Political Parties: A Sociological Study of the Oligarchical Tendencies of Modern Democracy*. Hearst, New York.

Rayner, Steve, 1979. *The Classification and Dynamics of Sectarian Forms of Organization: Grid/Group Perspectives on the Far Left in Britain*. Ph.D., University of London.

Rayner, Steve, 1982. 'The Perception of Time and Space in Egalitarian Sects: A Millenarian Cosmology' in Mary Douglas (ed.) *Essays in the Sociology of Perception*. Routledge & Kegan Paul, London.

Tönnies, Ferdinand, 1887. *Gemeinschaft und Gesellschaft*, Fues, Leipzig, trans. 1957 *Community and Society*, Michigan State University Press, East Lansing.

Weber, Max, 1921. *Wirtschaft und Gesellschaft I*, J. C. B. Mohr, Tubingen, trans. 1967. *The Theory of Social and Economic Organization*, Macmillan, New York.

The social preconditions of radical scepticism[1]

Mary Douglas

Abstract

Starting with Pascal's arguments against scepticism, this essay seeks to locate within the social structure the niche in which radical scepticism tends to flourish. The Brahminical sceptical tradition is compared with western idealist movements in the nineteenth and twentieth centuries and with sceptical trends of today. A social position that combines considerable privilege with lack of influence in an arbitrarily powerful political system gives rise to moral contradictions and insoluble problems. In such a position a denial of the reality of the world indicates a level of thought in which intellectual coherence may be possible. The converse situation, where claiming authority and holding power seem feasible, is more compatible with affirmation of reality than with its negation.

Although many religious minds are attracted by Pascal's argument for believing in the existence of God – it has been derided by logicians. So it seems good to draw attention to a modern philosopher who defends it on purely logical grounds. This is Ian Hacking, expert in the theory of probability (Hacking 1975). According to Hacking the principles of decision theory which Pascal used 300 years ago have only recently been formulated, but even so, Pascal's logic is still impeccable. Betting on the probability of God's existence, wagering the constraints of religion against the libertine pleasures open to an unbeliever, betting on the incommensurability of a chance of heaven and a chance of damnation – Pascal stands centuries ahead on game theory and the technical analysis of rational choice – the founding ancestor of modern decision theory.

Pascal (1951, Fragment 190–381) recognized that the metaphysical proofs of God were based on logical implication so remote from ordinary reasoning that they have little persuasive power against scepticism. He was specially concerned to argue a case for belief that would not rely on the authority of church doctors, nor upon the witness of the faithful, since these were already discredited by the sceptic. So he invented his wager. Modern decision theory requires an exhaustive list of the possible hypotheses of the way the world is, an inventory of possible decisions plus the different benefits from making a decision in all the possible various states of the world: from this the analyst can determine the decision most likely to pay off best. But Pascal ruled out observations of experimental data, since he would not consider reports of miracles either: this is the case of decision-making in face of uncertainty when no experiments are possible. To solve the problem he correctly used three separate arguments, called in the jargon, 'dominance', 'expectation', and 'dominating expectation'. Dominance applies when one course of action would be better, no matter what the world is like: there is more utility in preferring course A-1 than any of the other actions: then course A-1 is said to dominate. To bet that God does not exist, and to live as if that is what the world is like, will bring damnation if the bet turns out wrong. Since salvation is infinitely better than damnation, the dominance rule directs the bet in God's favor or rather in favor of living a life that is reckoned to win salvation – an important difference. Similarly for 'expectation' and 'dominating expectations', all three arguments indicate the decision to live by the rules of religion. All three arguments are valid in the sense that the conclusions follow from the premises. It is the premises that are hard to defend.

This essay, that starts with Pascal's wager, has two objectives, both rather different from Pascal's. One is to persuade some contemporary religious thinkers to be less disdainful of sociological principles and even to include them in their theological constructions of the world. The second is to use a sociological argument to locate the sources of scepticism. For these purposes, we do not need a survey of all the possible kinds of scepticism. It will not be necessary to distinguish the healthy scepticism of everyday life nor the methodological doubt of epistemology, nor the scepticisms that do not threaten discourse, but rather make it possible. The scepticism at issue is the same overall questioning of reality that Pascal himself attacked under the name of 'pyrrhònisme'. He used his decision-theory technique to establish a reasoned basis for distinguishing reality from illusion. It was a foundational problem in philosophy which he sought to solve by establishing first, the nature of man, second, the certain prospect of death and third, a testing of all the different available paths for establishing a realist view against an acceptance of uncertainty. He included as hypotheses about possible states of the world the teachings of Judaism, Islam, Montaigne, the 'dogmatists' and 'academicians'. Sorting them through, he decided that Christianity best meets the facts he finds established about the nature of man (a monster mixed of vileness and glory) and about the certainty of death. It was beside the point for Diderot to have remarked that the method of the wager could be used just as well to justify Islam. Pascal had carefully gathered up all the versions of the world and partitioned it exhaustively into two options: either there is no God, or there is a God whose characteristics are correctly reported by the Catholic Church. Hacking remarks that the strength of his logic is no help to his decisions if the partitioning of the universe is not well done. Is his list of possible hypotheses about the alternative states of the world exhaustive? Supposing God was a Protestant? Suppose He was not impressed by holy water and sacraments (or even suppose He disapproved of betting altogether?)

The argument below will focus not on God but on an anterior aspect of Pascal's partitioning: the issue of either believing in reality (especially in the reality of death) or of living in uncertainty about everything in life. He says: you are here, you are engaged in the game, you have to wager. To be indifferent, to try to withdraw from the game, is in itself a wager. Either conviction is possible or an all encompassing doubt wins the game. His real enemies are not the Protestants, Jews or Muslims, nor even the Jesuits and academicians against whom he inveighs, but the pronouncements of radical sceptics. In this choice of problem, he poses an option which is more contemporary than the choice between denominational religious forms. He thought that those especially charged in his time with expounding the claims of reason would never succeed without a modern argument. This essay assumes that scholars of today specialized in religion and philosophy will never even clarify their aims without a modern argument. Religious thinkers are not the only ones who shudder at the mention of the sociological factors. Here it will be argued that their defence against historic waves of general scepticism loses its best arm by ignoring the sociological dimension.

Many students of religion display a bias against the idea that an individual human being receives and sustains his religious beliefs in a social medium. But can they seriously discount the possibility that God, having made man a social being, allows His face to be seen only through a distorted lens, through the medium of the society which men themselves create? To say Yes, belief and society go together, to concede this, would endorse a further element in Pascal's argument. For he did not think that belief comes by a decision to believe. At issue in his wager is the idea that belief comes by living in the company of believers. He did not discount social influences. So there is a further implication for theology: could it be that the virtuous activity of avoiding damnation could entail the activity of making the society which best images God? It might also suggest that theology could not get far along its special path without studying that social medium through which God is known. And finally, on another tack, it is often remarked that an effect of the special distorting medium of our own contemporary society is to show each person related to God as an isolated individual. Theologians could well be under social constraints in this day and age to ignore the social support of belief and to emphasize the individual. If that seems plausible, then, paradoxically, those who most vehemently deny sociological determinism are by that very fact demonstrating their own intellectual dependence on shared predjudices of their society.

Religious thinkers in our times agree in taking the difference between Eastern and Western traditions as the most distinctive variation in approaches to the divine. Pascal is highly relevant on this score. For the most striking difference between the two hemispheres is the strength of the sceptical tradition in the East and its weakness in the West. Different writers on religion have selected different elements to present the contrast of East and West, yet none has hitherto focused on this fundamental point. With the publication of *Dreams, Illusions and Other Realities*, (O'Flaherty:1984) the focus is placed where it needs to be if discourse in the history of religion is not to remain in a separate sacred enclosure, fenced off from other major concerns of our time. In this new book, Wendy O'Flaherty takes her own work on the interpretation of Hindu mythology to a new depth by starting from the questions formulated by Ernest Gombrich:

Do all cultures make the same radical distinction between 'appearances' and 'reality' which ours have inherited from Plato? Are their hierarchies the same? In other words, do they necessarily accept the demand that contradictions must be ironed out and that all perceptions that clash with beliefs must force us either to change our views of the 'objective world' or declare the perception to have been a subjective experience – an illusion? (Gombrich 1973)

She sees the history of dealing with this question in the West as a long and serious combat between Platonic idealism and Humean empiricism in which our legal system keeps coming in on the side of Hume. Here it will be argued that 'What think ye of dreams?' is the contemporary way of facing Pascal's two-pronged choice. Pascal's argument took the division between dreaming and waking as the touchstone (Pascal 1951:Fragment 131–246). To the reader in the Western tradition this always seems a little far-fetched: in sleep, we think that we are awake; since we dream a lot, and since in dreaming, one dream often nests in another, is it not plausible that the other half of life in which we think we are awake is itself only a dream nested in the other dreams? Then death will be a wakening. All the flow of time and the flow of life and the sensation of various bodies, these different thoughts which disturb us, perhaps they are all illusions like the flow of time in our dreams. Who knows whether this other half of our lives in which we think we are awake is another sleep a bit different from the first? These are the very questions which the Indian literature on dreaming poses dramatically and worryingly. That tradition presents to us the logical development which Pascal wished to refute.

In Hindu and Buddhist thought, the doctrine of illusion is the single, clearest, distinguishing mark setting apart the Eastern and Western traditions. Western philosophers have been arguing with radical scepticism from the beginning of the philosophical record. But here it is a suppressed vein of thought, while in the East it is a dominant one.

Often the sceptical question is presented to us as if it only concerns the reality of particular experiences, something about stubbing toes on hard objects and feeling it hurt. Such a presentation is but a prelude to a facile dismissal. More fairly, the question is not about particular realities or certainties; it is Pascal's question of how to have confidence in speaking about reality in general. It is a technical question about how to establish a position without depending on another position that equally needs defence and that defence depending on another and so on, opening up infinite regress.

Of course, if you want discourse to proceed, it is easy to agree to avoid the whole issue of foundations. Some truce between the sceptic and his opponent can always be arranged if they so desire. They can easily agree on a conventional appeal to authority or to self-evidence. But it is a patched up truce liable to break down. The Western philosopher's favourite recourse tends to be the announcement that it has to be possible: to deny the possibility of discourse is to fall into absurdity. Or else the matter is settled by convicting the sceptic of inconsistency. The sceptic is repeating Parmenides' ancient paradox: if he says that all utterances are empty, then his own utterance is empty too. Hilary Putnam, who takes these questions seriously, seems to feel that it is a strong argument to declare that total relativism's inconsistency is a truism (Putnam 1981:124). He quotes for two kinds of inconsistency: Quine and Davidson argue that a consistent relativist has excluded the possibility of treating others as speakers or thinkers at all, while Plato and Wittgenstein argue that a consistent relativist is not even entitled to treat himself as a speaker or thinker. Reading these philosophers, it is clear that the power of total relativism and of other radical forms of scepticism should be easy to defuse. The logical arguments against allowing a conversation to be interrupted in their name are strong.

However, if the sceptic does not particularly want there to be a discourse, or at least does not want to assert any thesis of his own, his sceptical position is unassailable. As Dr. Matilal remarks, quoting the Buddhist sceptic, Nagarjuna: radical scepticism is feasible, but not stateable: if it is stated, it falls into contradiction.[2] But in the Eastern tradition, there is nothing wrong with being silent. Buddhism applauds silence. This sceptical philosophy is compatible with religious doctrines of non-commitment or non-attachment. Scepticism itself cannot be a doctrine; it can be a practice which is valued explicitly in the Eastern tradition because it leads to religious insight. It makes way for a mystical experience of the grounds of truth.

In the West, we have Hume's philosophical scepticism, but as Wendy O'Flaherty says, it is usually worked on behalf of empirical reality. Whatever else may be said of Hume, it cannot be claimed that he laid the cornerstone for a great mystical tradition. Something has been at work in the Western religious experience and its philosophical history that directs our sceptical resources into different channels.

We can try to construct some sort of overall scheme for

comparing religions of the world. Some scale that relates the degree of scepticism to the desire to maintain a community of discourse would be a start. First, at one end of the scale we would place unquestioned belief: here we would expect to find many so-called primitive religions, and also many parishes and dioceses of so-called advanced civilizations. The basic idea is that questioning and doubt can be held in check only by a strong institutional structure. Here, by definition then, religion would be directly engaged with the social order, legitimating the social machinery, making community commitments manifest.[3]

In the middle of this scale, we would place those religions whose teachings are both contested and defended in a pluralist society. The challenge to explain and define forces axiomatization. Loose, doctrinal threads will be stitched back, concepts stretched and new verbal formulae sought to meet the needs of dialogue. In this middle part of the scale, the religion stands in sophisticated engagement with the social world. In its historic controversies, Christianity gives abundant instances of how the pressure to create one unified church authority is related to the pressure to axiomatize the elements of belief, allowing for private doubt but requiring that the community of discourse be protected by a political effort at consensus.

The last point in the scale would be represented by full scale scepticism. By this reckoning, the Eastern religions would be way ahead of Christianity. Sustained scepticism is a feasible stance for those who do not expect to command or unify society, but stand apart from it. Belief/scepticism patterns have much to do with the claims of power and revolt against its claims.

The rest of the argument leads us to examine the social conditions which foster general radical scepticism. Then we should take account of sceptical movements in the west at this present time. Then, finally, we can raise questions for religious philosophy. Peter Berger (1980) maintains that Jerusalem (made to represent Western Religion) should now turn towards Benares (representing Eastern Religion). Louis Dumont (1966) holds that western political thought suffers by having let go of the concept of hierarchy which is still understood in the East. But neither recognizes that the critically distinctive element of Eastern philosophy, its scepticism, has arrived here in the West already and is thriving.

Espousing a fully sceptical philosophy leads to non-attachment, and *vice versa*, non-attachment permits a sceptical philosophy. In recognizing this we have a principle for tracing the wavering movements in Christianity away from or towards scepticism. In theology the crucial relation is that held to obtain between divine and human life. If the teaching is that they are very remote from each other, the divine an altogether unreachable, unknowable, element, impossibly distant from and superior to humanity, then we have the beginning of a religious discourse that can move to a second doctrine, that the human experience is necessarily so inferior that it can hardly be credited with reality compared with the divine; then, the latest stages of the religious discourse can progressively downgrade the human sphere so that nothing that happens in it is of any significance except in so far as it enables the human being to escape into the superior element, at whatever cost. This religious discourse can proceed either apart from or at the expense of the political community to which it can lend no support.

Our scepticism scale for comparing religions draws on a relation presumed to hold between the believer and the source of agreed authority. In the first (and the lowest) class, that of unquestioning belief, there are no cracks in the consensual system; in the second class, that of challenged and defended belief, emerging threats to community authority are seen as such and battened down. In the third and last class, belief just stands apart from authority.

Let us glance now at the subversive energies that lie dormant in religious doctrines on the nature of reality. Anyone new to this line of reasoning may question whether the protagonists in religious controversies fully recognize that authority is at stake. There is a tradition in the Humanities that assumes that ontological doubts are purely intellectual. To answer this tradition, ask whether a debater who proposes even a small doubt about the line separating reality from illusion can know that he has his hand on a powerful weapon. The answer is Yes, everyone knows and knows at once. Just imagine yourself in the unlikely situation of being confronted by a student who is never rebellious or even rude, but who seems to lack commitment to his studies. All he says to counter your rebukes is that sorrows and joys are ephemeral; grades and reports likewise; all material things are passing or illusory. Then nothing you can say matters. As an experienced pedagogue, you can see a mile off that if you concede, you have lost your grip on your class. No need for the gentle student to

75

accuse the teacher of being materialist, or to be impolite in any way; it is disruptive enough to authority to insist on the supremacy of spiritual values.

This is the context in which to appreciate the Christological debates of the second century. Witness, for example, the contest between Irenaeus of Lyons against the Gnostics: Irenaeus clearly knew that loss of concreteness and materiality meant loss of authority. On every issue, the Gnostics would spiritualize, philosophize; they also knew that a shift away from the direct personal relation between God and his people that is the distinctive feature of biblical Judaism would be a strategic shift in evading control. Laeuchli, in *The Language of Faith* (1962), says that the concept of God the Father is used 400 times in the New Testament. In Gnostic discourse the term is expanded to include Mother as well as Father; thus it loses some rather definite cognitive contours. When Fatherhood/Motherhood becomes part of the scheme of cosmic layers in which the universe is evolving, the discourse is also moved up into higher levels of abstraction. Again, in the New Testament the term 'righteousness' is equivalent to Justice. The Gnostics give it a different sense in which Justice means equality and equality means universality: thus justice becomes separated from day to day ethics and non-ethical justice is absorbed into the abstract theorizing about natural cycles of the universe. And again, in the Old Testament God addresses Israel as a nation, as a political unit, as a land. But the Gnostics would not accept the Old Testament verse (Psalms 24:1) 'The earth is the Lord's and the fullness thereof.' For the Gnostic, the earth was definitely not the Lord's, quite the contrary. The whole idea made no sense to one who thought of salvation as mental and mystical redemption. Irenaeus argued against their over-philosophizing and over-cerebralizing. He was defending a more directly, concrete and personally immediate religion. Laeuchli shows him to be fighting for each word, not so much for the word but for its particular placement in the structure that was even then perceived as the essentially Christian doctrine.

The early and continuing Christological crises are never finally settled. What think ye of Christ? Man or God? Is it obscenely blasphemous to suppose the two natures, divine and human, spiritual and material, could be combined – or is it an inoffensive, central, necessary doctrine?

Historians who trace the parting of the ways between Eastern and Western thought write as if both traditions once shared a common primitive viewpoint and at a critical moment diverged. The scepticism scale which I am here inviting you to use suggests that the major issues of authority and resistance are always capable of being translated into a choice between spiritualizing and concretizing philosophies. The question then is not to search for the historical origin but for the best analysis of the political conditions which enable one vision to win over its opposite.

In a fine essay on the genesis of the distinctive Western attitudes, Louis Dumont (1983:46–7) goes back to the very early Church, noting the views of the Fathers on the State, on slavery and private property. He finds in the early Church an ambivalent attitude to secular life: to the faithful soul embarked on life's pilgrimage the world is both an obstacle to and a necessary condition of salvation. The life of the world was neither denied nor rejected, just relativized by comparison with the beatific vision of God in paradise. The hierarchical scheme allowed great latitude in principles of government. The spot on which Dumont wants to put his finger, the defining point for the beginnings of our Western tradition, is the point at which the relation between persons and persons yields pride of place to the relation between persons and things. In the early view the things can only be means of or hindrances to salvation; they hardly counted in the hierarchy compared with relations between persons, sets of beings made in the image of God. In our own days the crucial relationships have become economic, (that is the relation between persons and things) and the hierarchy of values has disappeared under a homogenizing common denominator – material wealth. This trend is an instance of the many philosophies which dichotomize the universe between spiritual and material: sometimes a balance is held, sometimes the spiritual comes out on top, sometimes the material wins.

At the beginning of the 4th century, the emperor Constantine converted to Christianity. Then Christian thinkers (I am still following Dumont) were faced with a formidable problem. They could no longer devalue the state and the world as they had done heretofore. The state made a step towards the Church, and the Church had to take some responsibility for the secular world. Then followed frictions, disputes about doctrine, the pressure to axiomatize, resolved by denouncing heresy or by efforts to reconcile the different traditions of Alexandria and Antioch. There appears a dominant social and political concern to unify. Dumont writes:

It is remarkable that most of these debates were focused on the difficulty of conceiving and correctly formulating the union of God and man in Jesus Christ. Nonetheless, in retrospect it is this which appears to be the heart, the secret of Christianity, seen in the whole history of its development, that is to say, in abstract terms, the affirming of a real connection between this world and the other, between life within the world and life beyond it, the *Incarnation of Value* (italics his, translation mine. (Dumont 1983:51)

In its distinctive unfolding, Louis Dumont sees two crucial moments in the turning of the Western tradition away from hierarchy. The first was the fourth century conversion of the Roman Emperor and the consequent establishment of the Church. This in itself did not cause the hierarchical doctrine which balanced priestly and kingly power to be abandoned, but caused it to be very carefully enunciated. But at the second point, in the mid-century, the Pope conferred on the Frankish king the role of protector and ally of the Roman Church: almost a treaty between princes; and then in 800 A.D., Leo III crowned Charlemagne emperor in St. Peter's, Rome. The Popes now arrogated to themselves a supreme political function; they made territorial claims on their own behalf; in a later stage they could be conceived of as delegating temporal power to the emperor. By taking over this material world in the name of the spiritual one, by so nakedly throwing in its lot with political power, the Church led Western thought to abandon hierarchical principles. Paradoxically, it started the West on the slippery slope of subordinating the spiritual to the material which Dumont elaborately traces out, culminating in the rise in the 18th and 19th centuries of economic theory, our own special contribution to the cultural history of the world.

Something about the commitment to ordering and organizing other people is incompatible with nihilism, relativism, romantic idealism and radical scepticism. Cultural commitment in itself explains nothing, it is that which is to be explained. Weberian sociologists are often content to explain religious variation by reference to the spirit of the culture. But this tautology does not help to explain the great divergence between the Eastern and the Western traditions. If we are to follow up the explicit connection between the Western experience of empire and the Christian Incarnational theology (Gauchet 1984:155–75), we should take account of the sheer physical difficulty of laying the Indian subcontinent under unified control. There can be physical conditions so hostile to sustained political order that dominion is virtually impossible however strong the commitment may be. The Moguls had a great period of Empire; then, between their reign and the British Empire, there was a history of numerous local princedoms; of ephemeral, arbitrary power; a history of local dynasties under attack and overthrown. We should also recall the sanskritizing success of the Brahmins (Srinivas 1956), their universal spiritual hegemony and their self-denying exclusion from exercise of power. After a hundred years of Marxist criticism of ideology, the beliefs and values of Western intellectuals are rather well documented (Shils 1972). Their tendency to cerebralize and spiritualize the glaring social abuses of the day, though tempting a comparison with Eastern philosophy, is generally given separate treatment from the Brahmin: the differences seem overwhelming because one is the product of the Capitalist and the other of the Caste system. If we compare the position in which the Brahmins express their commitment to hierarchy, we see them in helpless contemplation of arbitrary power, wedged between rulers and exploited masses. These are the conditions of the intellectuals of Western Capitalism against whom Joseph Schumpeter inveighs (Schumpeter 1942). Their discontent and unrealism sprang, he argues, from their being trapped without esteem or dignified employment between the ruling class and the populace whose cause they espoused in furthering their own quest for higher status. Harsher than Schumpeter's measured condemnation, George Orwell (1978a) reviles the English 'highbrow with his domed forehead and stalklike neck', and the 'irresponsible carping of people who have never been and never expect to be in a position of power', and the 'emotional shallowness of people who live in a world of ideas and have little contact with reality', and above all – 'their severance from the common culture of the country' – their lack of concern for injustice. His diagnosis also depends on the relative shift in opportunities for employment: while the Empire was expanding there were rewards for ambitious men. In the stagnation of empire when the educated found themselves unesteemed, they denied political realities, espoused contradictory and impossible projects and cherished ultramontane loyalties.

Compare these fragmentary images of the post World War I intelligentsia in Europe with Isaiah Berlin's great essay on the young Russian radicals of the 1830–1840's (Berlin 1978). This is too early a date for Capitalism. The framework is the sheer weakness and arbitrary cruelty of the political system. The Russian intelligentsia were members of a dedicated order, almost a secular priesthood. On the one hand, they had glimpsed a new social order in the West, on the other, the government of the nation became progressively more difficult. As the gulf between people and rulers widened, the repression by the ruling elite became more harsh. Between the oppressors and the oppressed, a small, cultivated French-speaking class became painfully aware of the gap between Russia and the West, and of the difference between justice and injustice and of their own stake in the regime which too hasty reform might easily overturn, 'Some were reduced to cynicism, some to noble eloquence and futile despair.' Berlin identifies three social categories under Czar Nicholas 1st: a dead, oppressive government hindering change, the vast mass of the population, wretched, weak and ignorant peasants, and this small, educated class, the intelligentsia. Their ideas came to them from German Romanticism.

> For anyone who was young and idealistic in Russia in 1830 and 1840, or simply human enough to be depressed by the social conditions of this country, it was comforting to be told that the appalling evils of Russian life – the ignorance and poverty of the serfs, the illiteracy and hypocrisy of the clergy, the corruption, inefficiency, brutality, arbitrariness of the governing class, the pettiness, the sycophancy, and the inhumanity of the merchants – that the entire barbarous system, according to the sages of the West, was a mere bubble on the surface of life. It was ultimately unimportant, the inevitable attribute of the world of appearances which seen from a superior vantage point, did not disturb the deeper harmony.

A dominant element in the German romantic movement was to transpose Spinoza's science into aesthetic terms, to conceive of life as an artistic creation of some cosmic deity – to convert it from a scientific to a mystical or transcendental view of life and history.

What do these varied scenarios imply about the conditions for sceptical philosophy? Radical scepticism may flourish where an elite, educated and privileged, is faced with unacceptable arbitrary power, and is helpless to challenge it. Any equilibrium between spiritual and temporal authority is probably a precarious ideal, precarious in the East where it topples over to a fully idealized philosophy and precarious in the West where it topples to a materialist individualized philosophy. On this approach, the toppling could be reversed temporarily in either direction, according to the scope for effective responsibility perceived by the educated elite.

At this point, looking round at ourselves, we find the whole Western scene is changed. Instead of a repressed minority, the idealists – sympathetically drawn by Berlin, excoriated by Schumpeter, derided by Orwell, are now in the ascendant. When a pragmatic ruling class governed the inarticulate masses, the mainstream philosophers denounced radical scepticism wherever it reared its head: absurd, inconsistent, impossible, incoherent, unfeasible, nihilistic and so on. Anthropologists have always been attracted to cultural relativism and I do not doubt that they have relished the iconoclastic threat (Hatch 1983). Their doubts were never really threatening to the established order. The cutting edge of relativism today, as Hilary Putnam puts it (1981), derives explicitly from Marx, Freud and Nietzsche. They taught us that 'Below what we are pleased to regard as our most profound spiritual and moral insight lies a seething cauldron of power drives, economic interests, and selfish fantasies.' All ideology is now dubbed as culture-relative, with a set of unconscious, guiding assumptions whose determinants are non-rational. In vain does Putnam protest: 'If all argument were mere rationalization, it would make no sense either to argue for or to hold any views. (Putnam 1981:161) He is accusing the relativists of the most fundamental paradox of all. Naming Kuhn, Feyerabend and Foucault as the leaders, Putnam frankly identifies the politically subversive intent:

> While Kuhn has increasingly moderated his view, both Feyerabend and Michel Foucault have tended to push it to extremes. There is something political in their minds: both Feyerabend and Michel Foucault link our present institutionalized criteria of rationality with capitalism, exploitation, and even with sexual repression. Clearly there are many divergent reasons why people are attracted to extreme relativism today, the idea that all existing institutions are bad being one of them. (Putnam 1981:126)

Without going to the extremists in the philosophy of science, we cannot avoid hearing a parallel tale in every branch of social knowledge. Economics experiences a profound methodological upheaval. Tests of scientific method are applied to economic theory and it fails; its once vaunted predictions are mocked; its assumptions severely exposed to philosophic doubt, its proofs relegated to mere rhetoric (McCloskey 1983). Historiography now holds a more important place than straight history. Political philosophy finds its theory of representation built on Arrow's inescapable paradox. Jurisprudence is ferociously engaged in a debate on the legitimacy of law (Presser 1983). Literary theory would transform all human experience to the status of texts – an extreme idealist position (Rorty 1982a:139). The philosophers of science are at the centre of the storm. Science is based on a collection of provisional statements. The logicians themselves have abandoned their claims to be able to found rational discourse in reason, and also the claim to identify analytic self-evident truths. On all sides radical scepticism is advancing. Scholars in religious studies would be recluses indeed not to have heard that a crisis of epistemology is here. What think ye of dreams? What do scholars in religion feel about secular scepticism? They ought to feel liberated. It is as if they have been imprisoned since the 16th century behind a wall built to keep out the dragon of scientific objectivity. But now science and religion are no longer polarized by two distinctive kinds of reasoning. Not only the religious believers need to make a leap of faith. Not only religion lacks rational foundations – but every intellectual enterprise whatsoever is exposed to the merciless, sceptical inquiry: How do you know? By what authority? And the answers lead back in infinite regress or run in self-referencing circles. The dragon has expired in its own poisonous exhalations. But there is no victory. Radical scepticism could yet defeat us all.

Should we rejoice at being liberated by the triumphal on-sweep of radical scepticism? Does not more sophistication seem preferable to less? Is it not a position of advantage to throw doubt on earlier scholars' simplemindedness? Do they not seem like schoolboys, scrambling for grades in a well-defined world of textbook heroes and comic baddies? 'Never glad confident morning again!' Clifford Geertz sighs, half regretfully, comparing his own doubts with the earlier generation of British anthropologists who worked, after all, in a framework of Empire (Geertz 1983).

On the one hand, Western incarnational theology, with its will to consecrate institutions and make them work, tips easily towards materialist values. On the other hand, the Eastern doctrine of illusion, despairing of good institutions, easily tips towards privileged withdrawal. Choose the more sophisticated path if you will. As you do so, we shall hear you invoking metaphors of ritual cleanness. You will separate yourselves from dirty politics, and look down on those crude officers of public administration, whose minds such complicated doubts would never cross. They have a vested interest in legitimacy and so in the possibility of rational discourse. It is only the excluded elite who seriously entertain radical doubt and allow it to subvert the enterprise of communication.

In what sense do we form an excluded elite? If discourse be possible, that is the first question to ask. Have we chosen to withdraw from the murky paths of politics and power? Or do inherent processes in the machinery of government exclude us, as they excluded the Russian intelligentsia and the European intellectuals? If we are excluded against our will, then who are the tyrannical rulers squeezing us between their minions and the toiling masses they oppress? At the national level the parallel does not hold up well. But new communications technology has expanded the boundaries of effective influence from nation state to hemisphere. From the north facing southward, we cannot miss the inarticulate, miserably poor millions of oppressed. From north to south the analogy is startling. Yes – we are as keenly attached to our privileged status as any Brahmins; aware of collective guilt and indulging in idealist rhetoric as much as the Russian intelligentsia and just as despairing about the injustices committed in our name. I am not sure if we are excluded involuntarily, though I can see the imponderable machineries which we individually cannot influence. We are wedged between inhuman rulers and suffering masses. I am also convinced that if we all choose the path to subjective idealism there will be no sustained intellectual support or 'group-wise' intelligent effort to heal the widening divisions.[4]

There is another choice. Philosophers of religion could take philosophy seriously. At this point, highly accredited inquirers into the nature of reasoning converge, in a new kind of response to radical scepticism. There is no way for protecting the claims for rational foundations of discourse. The ground rules (that is the conditions for knowledge) cannot be tested and proved in the same way as discourse itself is tested. The step-by-step construction of a logical argument, correctly performed, leads to valid conclusions. But though valid, the conclusions may not be accepted as true. (Remember how Pascal was criticized for the way in which he categorized the universe.) The question of foundations is about acceptable categories, not about valid logic. So what does acceptability depend upon?

One by one the great logicians of our day are reluctantly coming out with the same kind of answer. The ultimate and only authority for the way the universe is divided up has to be the community. For Wittgenstein it is the community making rules for its life in common. For Quine it is the speech community which settles issues of sameness and identity by assigning items of the world to words and words to classes (Kripke 1982). Putnam admits appeal to cultural acceptability '. . . our world is a human world, and what is conscious and not conscious, what has sensations and what doesn't, what is qualitatively similar to what and what is dissimilar, are all dependent ultimately on our human judgments of likeness and difference (Putnam 1981:102). Nelson Goodman says of acceptability that since it 'involves inductive validity, which involves right categorization, which involves entrenchment, habit must be recognized as an integral ingredient of truth' (Goodman: 1984). Each of these philosophers is laying emphasis on the community processes for shaping the building blocks for its own logical discourse. First there begins a community engagement in a form of social intercourse: its usages entrench certain categories or ways of sorting; the entrenchment in community life gives rise to acceptable categorization upon which logical arguments are founded. Community is not separable from logic: the mistake was to suppose logic had an independent existence, held up by its own bootstraps (Barnes 1982). The foundations of rational discourse are found in community commitment to stability and coherence.

The argument seems to point in terrifying directions. We know that historical communities have founded their logic upon an utterly reprehensible categorization of the world. Is this a reason for not daring to look at the process by which acceptable categories are shaped and then entrenched? One can forgive the logicians for stopping, having come thus far. But the scholars in religion should surely see the advantages to their work of following it through. Their own professional interests should encourage them in a program of researching into how the faces of God are formed in the social process of sorting out the world. In that process there is always some fiduciary element, underwriting the prior assent which discourse needs. It is not only assent to arguments. Anyway arguments can be and are publicly contested by logic. Assent to the kinds of building blocks that logic can use emerges from hidden social processes that anthropologists uncover and which are of prime relevance to the study of religion.

Logician's reflections on the grounds of reasoning are not so remote and specialized that philosophers of religion can credibly stand aside. In a new context, Pascal's argument holds still. If they stay within their protective fortress, still imagining the fight between science and religion is being waged outside, they will likely be overwhelmed by the great waves of scepticism and they will not even recognize the new argument about religion that is pressing to be formulated.

If Pascal felt that the metaphysical proofs of the existence of God were too complicated, he would feel the same about Cartesian attempts to prove the foundations of rational thought. How would he constitute the terms of a modern wager? I am not enough skilled in decision theory to marshal the arguments for a bet on reality versus illusion, or on the likelihood of a sharp difference between waking and dreaming. To my naive eye the probable value of deciding to live by a simple faith in reality seems high. Finally, Pascal's bet was not about deciding to believe, as is commonly thought, but about deciding to live as if one believed, to live in the community of other believers. Either way he considered the decision would be validated to the extent that belief or disbelief would follow upon the choice of human company. The foregoing argument requires the community in question to be classified, not according to attitudes to reality, but according to attitudes to power and authority.

To end at this point would turn this argument into a sermon. However, the object is not exhortation to live a particular kind of good life in a particular kind of company. Here the intention is not counselling but argument. If it is true, as here maintained, that radical scepticism is an attitude that emerges in response to a distinctive form of social commitment, then theologians interested in converting the sceptics could do better than they do. They should examine the ways in which attitudes to power and authority are linked by the social fabric to attitudes to reality. Some social commitments are straightforward and satisfying; others are oblique and contradictory. There may be scope for preaching to the theologians insofar as they shirk their pastoral responsibilities by disregarding these links. In the context of this volume it should be said that philosophers of science who denounce relativism are in the same position. Denunciation carries no weight: far better to take up the cudgels of sociological comparison and work out the limits and strengths of the opponents' view. The intellectual position of the relativists can be shown to be contingent on their sense of futility or immorality of exercising power and authority, and this contingency rests in turn on their place in a social structure.

Notes

1 I thank Wendy O'Flaherty for the invitation to give the first version of this essay to the American Academy of Religion at its meeting in Dallas, December 1983, and Michel Cartry and Luc de Heusch for the invitation to give the second version to the CNRS Laboratoire, La Pensee Africaine, March, 1984. I am particularly grateful to Germaine Dieterlen and to Jeffrey Stout for hardhitting criticism. A version of this paper has appeared in *L'Homme*.
2 Matilal (1977; 1968a; 1968b) demonstrates that the Indian philosophers who founded a school of logic on the principle of negation were as rigorously rational as the analytic schools of the West and that their philosophy, by challenging other schools, forced them to organize their thought systematically. The Indian 'mystical philosophers' were serious professionals whose writing was intended to be available for rational discussion, and whose logic is inherently the same as Western logic.
3 There are many situations in which neither the words 'believe' nor 'disbelieve' apply. See Pouillon (1979).
4 Schumpeter's word for the kind of social know-how he felt was so often lacking in the European intellectual.

References

Barnes, S.B. (1982), 'Reference', unpublished paper for the Edinburgh Science Studies Unit.
Berger, Peter (1980), *The Heretical Imperative: Contemporary Possibilities of Religious Affirmation*, Doubleday.
Berlin, Isaiah (1978), *Russian Thinkers*, edited by Henry Hardy and Aileen Kelly, originally in *Encounter*, 1955.
Dumont, Louis (1966), *Homo Hierarchicus*, Paris, Gallimard.
Dumont, Louis (1983), *Essais Sur l'Individualisme, Une Perspective Anthropologique sur l'Ideologie Moderne*, Paris, Seuil.
Gauchet, Marcel (1984), 'Fin de la Religion?', *Le Debat*, 28, 155–75.
Geertz, Clifford (1983), 'Slide Show; Evans-Pritchard's African Transparencies', *Raritan*, Fall, 62–80.
Gombrich, E. (1973) 'Illusion and Art', p. 193–243 in Gombrich and Gregory (1973).

Gombrich, E. and Gregory. R.L. (eds) (1973) *Illusion in Nature and Art,* London, Duckworth.

Goodman, Nelson (1983), 'Notes on the Well-Made World', *Erkenntnis,* 19, 97–107, and forthcoming republication in Goodman (1984).

Goodman, Nelson (1984), *Of Mind and Other Matters,* University of Harvard Press.

Hacking, Ian (1975), *The Emergence of Probability,* Boston, Cambridge University Press.

Hatch, Elvin (1983), *Culture and Morality, the Relativity of Values in Anthropology,* New York, Columbia University Press.

Izard, M. and Smith, P. (eds) (1979), *La Fonction Symbolique,* Paris, Gallimard.

Kripke, Saul (1982), *Wittgenstein on Rules and Private Language,* New York, Blackwell.

Laeuchli, S. (1962), *The Language of Faith: Introduction to the Semantic Dilemma of the Early Church,* N.Y., Abingdon Press.

Matilal, Bimal Krishna (1968a), *Navya-Nyaya Philosophy,* Mass., Harvard University Press.

Matilal, Bimal Krishna (1968b), 'The Navya-Nyaya Doctrine of Negation' in Matilal (1968a).

Matilal, Bimal Krishna (1968c), 'The Semantics and Ontology of Negative Statements', in Matilal (1968a).

Matilal, Bimal Krishna (1977), 'The Logical Illumination of Indian Mysticism', Inaugural Lecture delivered before the University of Oxford, Oxford, Clarendon Press.

McCloskey, Donald N. (1983), 'The Rhetoric of Economics', *The Journal of Economic Literature,* 21, 481–517.

O'Flaherty, Wendy Doniger (1984), *Dreams, Illusions and Other Realities,* Chicago, Chicago University Press.

Orwell, George (1978a), 'Your England', chapter from Orwell (1978b).

Orwell, George (1978b), *Inside the Whale,* edited by Colin Bell and Sol Encel, New York, Pergamon.

Pascal, Blaise (1951), *Pensées sur la Religion et sur quelques Autres Sujects,* edited by L. Lafuma, fragment 190–381.

Pouillon, Jean (1979), 'Remarques sur le verbe "croire" in Izard and Smith (1979).

Presser, Stephen (1983), Rorschach Lecture.

Putnam, Hilary (1981), *Reason, Truth and History,* Boston, Cambridge University Press.

Rorty, Richard (1982a), 'Idealism and Textualism', Chapter 8 in Rorty (1982b).

Rorty, Richard (1982b), *Consequences of Pragmatism.*

Schumpter, Joseph (1942), *Capitalism, Socialism and Democracy,* New York, Harper Bros.

Shils, Edward (1972), *The Intellectuals and the Powers and Other Essays,* Chicago.

Srinivas, M.N. (1956), 'A Note on Sanskritization and Westernization', *The Far Eastern Quarterly,* 15, 4, 481–96.

The values of quantification*

Jean Lave

Abstract

Standardized forms of knowledge, such as systems of measurement and money, and the formal arithmetic taught in school, may be thought of as attempts to dominate the definitions of the situations of their use and forms of knowledge in practice. Ethnographic research on middle class American adults shopping in supermarkets, managing family finances, and trying to lose weight in a dieting organisation suggest, rather, that calculation and measurement procedures are generated in situationally-specific terms which both reflect and help to produce the specific character of activities in daily life. At the same time, the values embodied in the standarised forms of quantitative knowledge discussed here, especially values of rational objective utility, appear to be resources employed expressively in everyday practice. A politics of knowledge is thus embodied in mundane transformations of knowledge and value through activity constituted in relation with its daily settings.

1 Introduction

There is a considerable tradition in anthropology that treats

* An earlier version of this paper was presented at a meeting on 'Visualisation and Cognition' organised by Bruno Latour at the Ecole Nationale Supérieure des Mines, Paris in December 1983. A French translation of the paper is to appear in a special volume of *Culture-Technique* edited by Bruno Latour. My thanks to him and to Michael Murtaugh, Olivia de la Rocha and Katherine Faust who are responsible for the field research on which the discussion is based. I wish to thank colleagues who fought with and against various versions of this paper, improving it the while: Mary Brenner, John Comaroff, Olivia de la Rocha, Sam Gilmore, Michael Kearney, John Law, Michael Murtaugh and Carole Nagengast.

scientific activity as a specialized mode of thought (Levy-Bruhl 1910; Durkheim 1912; Malinowski 1925; Horton 1973, to name but a few). It is also clear that definitions of 'cognition' have consistently been cast in normative scientific terms (cf. Barnes 1973). Dualistic distinctions between prescientific and scientific cultures, minds, methods and societies have created simplistic, obfuscating divides across the social sciences (Latour 1983b). Psychologists who are quick to dismiss the idea of 'primitive modes of thought', for instance, are quite willing to shift to an argument that scientific thinking is nevertheless quite distinct from 'everyday modes of thought'. It was in an attempt to reconsider this division that I began research on arithmetic practice among Vai and Gola tailors in Liberia and among citizens of California in the United States as they shop for groceries in the supermarket, try to lose weight by joining a commercial dieting organization, cook meals in their kitchens, manage family finances, participate in experiments and take math tests.

Any dichotomous theory simultaneously specifies what unites as well as what separates its two poles. A 'great divide' might be thought of as a specification of the level, or point of articulation between that which is general and shared, and that which is specific and differentiated. The unspoken unity underlying divisions between 'prescientific' and 'scientific' cultures is the unquestioned equation of a culture with uniformity in certain kinds of knowledge and the means by which knowledge is produced, and/or transmitted. Thus, 'great divide' theories in anthropology (as elsewhere) have both reflected and defined politically and socially significant distinctions separating societies that are knowledgeable and powerful from those that are not, but couched in apparently value-neutral dichotomies between 'civilized' and 'primitive' cultures, 'scientific' and 'everyday' spheres of activity and/or modes of thought.

Perhaps this state of affairs reflects acknowledgment in the past of relations of a certain kind between knowledge and power. A macro-political view of the meaning and locus of 'power' would lodge it at the level of state, nation, society, or (the primitive analogue of the nation) and 'culture'. Kinds of knowledge, modes of thought, have then been assimilated to the same template as those of power, locating uniformity of action, knowledge and belief within cultures, and at the same time marking the critical differences as those between cultures. In functionalist theory the mechanisms of assimilation have typically been those of cultural transmission (with verisimilitude – that is uniformly for all, across generations, within the society) and the educational institution. The latter has been assumed to have a unified style (e.g., formal, informal, nonformal), characteristic of a whole culture. These uniform units cluster into two categories of societies: those with formal education (read 'schooling') and those without (read 'no schools').

Great divide theories have been criticized repeatedly in the past (e.g. Goody 1977; Latour 1983b). Theories of practice provide the currently predominant alternative to this view. Practice theory treats knowledge and power as indivisible, but gives primacy to the interest-driven actor (DiMaggio 1979; Ortner 1984), actors being knowledgeable and powerful in different degrees, manners and variably in different arenas of action. The term 'interest' unifies connotations of knowledge and power, reflecting quite accurately the theoretical position of its users. And heterogeneity of modes of knowing, and power, is built into this position. But their location in individual practice makes it difficult to avoid a new form of utilitarian individualism, so long as practice is viewed as the action of individuals engaging value-loaded power in action and knowledgeable action in their everyday routines. As one possible alternative, practice may be thought of as a property or product of interaction between social system and individual action. I am trying to move in this direction, assuming integral relations between knowledge and power, but also trying to explore the theoretical advantages and disadvantages of locating them in complex relations between individual practice and sociocultural order (Comaroff 1982: in preparation).

The context for the working out of this argument has been a group of empirical studies on arithmetic practice in everyday situations. The research raises questions about relations between social institutions (schools, supermarkets), theories of cognition, everyday practice, and beliefs about practice. It may be helpful in avoiding the pitfalls of great divide theories and utilitarian views, to identify alternative points of articulation between culture and the politics of knowledge and its production, as a basis for respecifying critical points of unity and divergence and different units of analysis.

At the beginning of the project some of the dangers of great divide theories were clear: two, specifically methodological, implications seemed to follow from, and typify research in, this genre of research. The first was the systematic *differential* investigation of opposed categories such that one is treated as residual, defined only as the negative side of the focal category and investigated not at all. Such is the fate of 'everyday thinking' (e.g. Levy-Bruhl 1910; cf. Barnes 1973). There are studies of general, abstract, logical 'scientific' cognitive tasks, but few studies of everyday practice. Therefore, one place to begin to change the specification of relations between 'scientific' and 'everyday' thought is with careful observational studies of everyday activity. The second typifying characteristic, more focally centered in research on cognition, has been the practice of excising it from its customary contexts in order to carry out controlled investigation in laboratories, then treating experimental task 'performances' in the laboratory as if they had no social context. To begin to reformulate the (ostensibly politically neutral) 'cognitive' nature of scientific or any other practice requires investigations of activity in context.

These concerns have strongly shaped the analysis, which focuses on arithmetic activity in multiple contexts by the same individuals. In the sections to follow evidence is presented for a non-cognitive, non-culturally uniform, view of situationally specific arithmetic activity in everyday contexts. This is followed by discussion of the kind of articulation that seems to characterize relations between standard arithmetic forms intended to dominate everyday practice and that practice itself.

2 Signs of situational specificity

I have come to the view that reformulating relations between everyday practice and the politics of knowledge rests on reconceptualizing relations between persons acting and the physical/social contexts in which they act in dialectical terms that stress their integral, mutually constitutive, relation. But if this conceptualization is to stand, then at the very least it should be possible to produce evidence of the situational specificity of activity. My research has focused, therefore, on discontinuities in performance of arithmetic activity by the same persons in different settings, and on analysis of the processes of arithmetic used in those settings.

An earlier example of this research may serve as an illustration of the method. Among tailors – craftsmen in Liberia – I carried out ethnographic research on craft apprenticeship as a form of education, then learning-transfer experiments based on uses of arithmetic in tailoring work and school arithmetic (Lave: in preparation). Tailors with various combinations of tailoring experience and schooling took part in the experiments. The results did not support a conventional functionalist view of schooling as the purveyor of abstract, general arithmetic skills, nor further, the presumably unique role of schooling, as opposed to other forms of education, in teaching universally transferable general arithmetic. There was roughly equal transfer from schooling and tailoring experience to tasks similar to those learned in each setting, but very little transfer from either one (1977). More importantly, procedures used in the experimental setting – paper and pencil place-holding algorithms, elaborate, effortful paper and pencil tallying and button-counting routines – were not observed in the tailor shops. A further round of observational research on everyday arithmetic practice in the shops provided a basis for analysis of the tailors' arithmetic activities in work settings. And, indeed, these arithmetic procedures were quite different from those employed by the same individuals in the experiments (Reed and Lave 1979).

In the Adult Math Project in California, test problems were created after observational work in supermarkets, with the same pattern of results. A pencil and paper arithmetic test included problems formally equivalent to ones observed in the market. For example, a comparison of two boxes of laundry soap to see which would be the better buy is formally equivalent to comparing two ratios. Algorithms taught in school were used without question in the test situation; no pencil and paper, but instead quite different kinds of problem solving processes were observed in the super-market.

But there was a simpler, more startling difference between test and supermarket arithmetic. In price arithmetic calculations in the supermarket, shoppers, though they fumbled and often made errors early in a calculational sequence, essentially never made an error in the final outcome. In 90 per cent of the arithmetic episodes the shopper correctly solved the problem and identified the best buy. In formally comparable problems in the math testing situation the same people averaged 57 per cent correct.

Other researchers are beginning to report similar findings. Cognitive psychologists in Recife, Brazil have approached children selling produce in open air markets. The researchers acted as difficult customers so as to pose a number of arithmetic problems for the children. These researchers then created a special arithmetic test for each child with all and only problems the child had confronted in the market. The children's arithmetic was correct 99 per cent of the time in the market; and 65 per cent of the time on the math test. All the children were having difficulty with arithmetic in school. (Carraher and Schliemann 1982; Carraher, Carraher and Schliemann 1982; 1983). Scribner's research among workers in a commercial dairy in the U.S. provides yet another similar set of findings (1984; Scribner and Fahrmeier 1982).

In somewhat different circumstances a high school teacher has described the same performance differences among his students, all of whom had a history of failure in mainstream classrooms:

> I dropped in on the Tierra Firma Bowling Alley. . . .One day I ran into the dumbest kid in the dumb class. . . .He was getting ready to go to work, he told me. Fooling around until five, when he started. What did he do? I keep score, he told me. For the leagues. He kept score for two teams at once. He made fifteen bucks for a couple of hours. He thought it was a great job, making fifteen bucks for something he liked to do anyway, perhaps would have done for nothing, just to be able to do it.
>
> He was keeping score. Two teams, four people on each, eight bowling scores at once. Adding quickly, not making any mistakes (for no one was going to put up with errors), following the rather complicated process of scoring in the game of bowling. . .
>
> I figured I had this particular dumb kid now. Back in eighth period I lectured him on how smart he was to be a league scorer in bowling. Naturally I then handed out bowling-score problems. . .The brilliant league scorer couldn't decide whether two strikes and a third frame of eight amounted to eighteen or twenty-eight or whether it was one hundred eight and one half. (Herndon 1971:93–5).

Nor could girls who bought shoes or boys with paper routes, both of whom made correct change routinely, solve comparable problems invented by Herndon in the classroom.

There are good reasons not to jump to the conclusion that extraordinary success in everyday settings was somehow the result of the 'simpler demands of everyday life'. For the arithmetic demands of the bowling alley were certainly more complex than Herndon's word problems in the classroom; in our research the test problems were formally equivalent to those we observed shoppers formulating and solving in the supermarket; and for the market vendors in Recife *only* the problems a child had attempted to solve in the market were included in the formal test at school.

There is another common argument about relations between everyday and school activities that is brought into question by these findings. Official competence/performance distinctions hardly make sense when people do better in settings other than school and tests and when school math algorithms are not often used in settings other than school and formal examinations. Testing at the end of the school career is treated as the last, best measure of general arithmetic competence, and it is assumed that ability to solve arithmetic problems recedes as alumni move further away in time and space from schooling. The AMP data fulfil this expectation as far as *school* algorithmic arithmetic is concerned; there is a strong negative correlation between age and test performance. But performances in the supermarket, measured in various ways, are not related either statistically or in terms of problem solving procedures, to age nor to success at the algorithmic formulae taught in school. It is difficult to support the argument for general, school-acquired competence under these circumstances. The signs point to situationally-specific, variably-successful arithmetic activities as a better description of both school and everyday practice. The near-perfect arithmetic in everyday settings provides evidence of the qualitatively different organization of arithmetic in different settings.

3 The character of situational specificity

It is proposed here that situational specificity of arithmetic practice comes about because there are integral relations between activities like grocery shopping and settings like the supermarket. Let me first suggest what this doesn't mean – and also why it might make sense. Examples may then help to make plainer a dialectical conception of the relation between activity and setting. This conception depends on the development of a differentiated concept of the context of activity, leading to a discussion of arena, setting and context.

'Situational specificity' probably is not usefully thought of in the conventional, abstract sense that people are required to respond to the flow of continually newly experienced conditions, according to the convention that reality is flux, no two moments identical. A relationship between activity and setting arises more immediately because familiar activities tend to take place in settings that are in many respects fashioned, culturally, to be a part of the activity – the surfaces, objects, furnishings, spaces, paths, two dimensional inscriptions, the work and intentions of other people in the same location, and other paraphernalia of some particular activity, such as grocery shopping. Even if the supermarket organization is antagonistic to the basic goals and interests of shoppers, there is agreement, established in ways that transcend any particular shopper or store management, about what objects, what procedures, what inscribed information, how customarily arranged, are available for use in the activity of shopping. The store has won many of the agonistic struggles for the cultural formulation of supermarket arenas – most information considered vital to shoppers is in very small print; prices are given as prime numbers, making calculation difficult; a whole series of strategies in placing and pricing products are notoriously favorable to management in the war between store and shoppers. On their part, shoppers have indirectly contributed to the existence of unit pricing, generic brands, special sales offers, and nutritional information on packages. They have also produced as a general cultural phenomenon, perhaps neutral in this particular arena, categories of groceries that are used in placing things on shelves and in looking for them; and family consumption patterns that in rough ways constrain the customary volumes, weights and units in which things are sold. Not to use these structured characteristics of the world in which activity takes place would be a poor 'cognitive' strategy, it seems to me.

From this point of view, the notion that algorithms, making no use of characteristics of the setting, that is, 'pure cognitive' strategies, should be the arithmetic strategy of choice make no sense. But this is not an argument that arithmetic strategies in school and supermarket differ because in the market one uses information stored in the environment while in school tests not. If such a difference were sufficient to account for specificity, it would locate its origins in a changing environment, or in a person's (normative) permissible relations with it. This explanation for situational specificity argues that cognition is an epiphenomenon of the environment. In contrast, an integral relation between activity and setting means that neither could exist in the form in which it is realized except in relation with the other. Neither an explanation that accounts for situational specificity in purely cognitive terms (i.e., as a variable realization of basic stable competence) nor a purely environmental explanation of variation across situations seems appropriate when grocery shopping and supermarket settings are taken to be cultural, and culturally coordinated productions. When viewed as political in character the 'value-free' connotations of 'cognition' and 'environment' are also brought into question (see below). So far I have appealed to general ideas about the organization of grocery shopping activities and supermarkets in relation with one another. Examples from the supermarket data may help to make such a view more plausible.

Conventional analyses of arithmetic activity characterize it as a linear process, beginning with information handed to the problem solver disguised in the form of a problem to be solved. Take the problem $\frac{2}{3} \times \frac{3}{4} = ?$. The problem solver is to figure out what arithmetic operation is called for in the problem. Then calculations should take place (2×3; 3×4; $6/12$), and if everything has gone well the answer, unknown at the beginning, should now appear. Contrast this with a formulation of arithmetic problem solving wherein the realized activity is mutually constituted with the setting in which it takes place. In the kitchen, for example, it appears that the process of solving the same arithmetic problem involves integral relations of hand, eye, setting and calculation, and might be described as an activity-generating arithmetic experience. In Adult Math Project research (cf. de la Rocha in preparation) we observed dieting cooks at work in their kitchens, and sometimes posed problems for them to solve. When one dieter prepared a lunch that included cottage cheese, the researcher asked:

> Suppose your allotment of cottage cheese for lunch is three-quarters of the two-thirds cup the Weight Watchers program allows? How much would you put on your plate? The problem solver began the task muttering that he had had calculus in college. . .(a typical chagrined acknowledgment of differences between school math and everyday practice). After a long pause he announced that he had 'got it'. From that moment on he appeared certain he was correct, even before carrying out the procedure. (So much for the linear character of problem solving, where the answer is supposed to come last.) He filled a measuring cup two-thirds full of cottage cheese, dumped it out on a cutting board, patted it into a circle, marked a cross on it, scooped away one quadrant, and served the rest.

'Take three-quarters of two-thirds of a cup of cottage cheese' is the problem statement. But it is also the solution to the problem and the procedure for solving it. The environment was used as a calculating device insofar as the solution was simply the problem statement, enacted. At no time did the Weight Watcher check his procedure against a paper and pencil algorithm, which would have produced $\frac{2}{3} \times \frac{3}{4} = \frac{1}{2}$ cup. Instead, checking occurred through the coincidence of problem, procedure and enactment. In the face of this and many similar examples, we have abandoned the goal of assigning arithmetic problems to unique locations – in the head or on the shelf – or labeling one element in a problem-solving process as a 'calculation procedure' another as a 'checking procedure'. It may even be difficult to distinguish a problem from its solution.

It might be argued that though people make use of the environment in solving problems, and scramble relations between solutions, problems and procedures, problem solving is basically cognitive and body and setting are only channels for expressing the results. But this and other examples recommend the view that activity is mutually constituted with the setting in which it takes place in a vitally integrated way. This proposition is not easy to confirm through observation partly because it is so difficult to find counterexamples. Here is one, however, that may help to make the integral character of person acting-in-setting clear.

A shopper and the observer were walking toward the frozen food case in the supermarket. The shopper wanted to buy a package of frozen enchiladas. Until the shopper arrived in front of the frozen prepared foods display it was as if she were not just a physical but a cognitive distance from the enchiladas. In contrast, she and the enchiladas, in each other's presence, brought into being an entirely different quality to the activity:

Shopper: (speaking hesitantly, walking towards the display, eyes searching the shelves to find the enchiladas): Now these enchiladas, they're around 55 cents. They were the last time I bought them, but now every time I come . . . a higher price.
Observer: Is there a particular kind of enchilada you like?
Shopper: Well, they come in a, I don't know. I don't remember who puts them out. They move things around too, I don't know.
Observer: What is the kind you're looking for?
Shopper: Well, I don't know what brand it is. They're just

enchiladas. They're put out by, I don't know. (Discovers
the frozen Mexican dinners.) Here they are! (Speaking
vigorously and firmly). They were 65 the last time I
bought them. Now they're 69. Isn't that awful?

Before arriving at the display she could not generate much
information about the enchiladas. But when she faced the display
she constructed, or reconstructed *in setting,* the brand, the former
price of the enchiladas and her first coherent statement about them
– all at once. Not all of this knowledge could be accounted for in
terms of receiving or processing information written on enchilada
packages. In fact it seems likely that she had not located the
particular brand she intended to buy, at that moment, but only
placed herself in relation with the place in the display she had been
searching for; thus the idea that she and the setting together
constructed her knowledge about enchiladas. The contrast between
her manner before and after constituting 'enchilada-news' in-
setting illustrates a difference not easy to pin down in the course of
ongoing activity, because activity and setting must be caught in
transit (in this case before the informant finds the enchiladas) to
see the contrast with what I take to be the mutual constitution of
activity and setting when she finds them.

However, to argue for the mutually constitutive character of
whole-person activity in setting, creates a new problem, or rather,
makes salient contradictory aspects of everyday usage of the term
'context'. On the one hand, this term connotes an identifiable
durable framework of activity, with properties that transcend the
experience of individuals, exist prior to them, and are entirely
beyond their control. On the other hand, context is experienced
differently by different individuals. Both are valid aspects of
experience. Our solution has been to differentiate them into the
'arena' of activity and its 'setting'.

The supermarket, for instance, is in some respects a public and
durable entity: a physically, economically, politically, and socially
organized space-in-time. In this aspect it may be called an 'arena'
within which activity takes place. The supermarket as arena is not
negotiable directly by the individual. It is outside of, yet
encompasses the individual, providing a higher-order institutional
framework within which setting is constituted. At the same time,
for individual shoppers, the supermarket is a repeatedly experienced,

personally ordered and edited version of the arena. In this aspect it may be termed a 'setting' for activity. Some aisles in the supermarket are part of the arena but not the setting for a given shopper. Setting is not merely a shopper's personal 'mental map' of the supermarket, but a relation between arena and shopper. If the arrangement of the store is changed, the setting changes as well. It might be thought of not as a static phenomenon, like a map, but rather as an historically rich, unfolding process.

The separation of concepts of arena and setting makes it possible to conceive of person-acting-in-setting without denying the existence of macrosocial structures and their immediate realizations in the form of, say, supermarkets, or denying what I take to be primarily tautologically constructed cultural relations between the political economy of supermarkets and activity within them.

It has been proposed here that person-acting-in-setting, differently in different settings and arenas, is a useful unit of analysis; the relations among the parts of this whole are dialectical ones. One of its virtues is that it stands in conflict with concepts of uniform knowledge or ways of knowing in 'unitary cultures'. Taken seriously, it deflates the usefulness of 'great divide' comparisons. This concept, person-acting-in-setting, at the same time locates significant differentiation at the level of individual practice in culturally structured situations (rather than at the level of general, decontextualized modes of thinking and knowing, kinds of cognition, or cognitive stages). Classification of sociopolitical structures into mutually exclusive categories takes place not between types of societies, but at the level at which people organize their activities, are organized by their activities, and by the arenas in relation with which setting as well as activity is generated.

To this point I have sought to establish that there is substantial situational specificity of cognitive activity, that scepticism is warranted concerning the value-free character of activity, cognitive or otherwise. It has been argued that on-the-ground realizations of political economy, such as supermarkets, are neither immediately addressable, nor realized in directly interactional terms, by individual actors. At the same time arenas and actors are intimately, dialectically connected through setting, in activity. These are preconditions for discussing the politics of everyday practice.

4 Ideology of practice and belief

Both the argument for the specificity of arithmetic in different settings and the analytic distinction between arena and setting underline the complexity of relations between what have often been treated as value-free, universalistic systems of knowledge and their practical enactment. Latour (1983a) has suggested that standardization of money, of bureaucratic record keeping and of systems of measurement may be analyzed in the same terms as the employment of inscription technology in the agonistic struggles among scientists to dominate each other through the imposition of their version of facticity. In this section, and the next, school algorithmic arithmetic, a universalistic system of knowledge, is considered as an example of potential dominance through standardization. But it appears that the major effect of schooling may well be to purvey an ideology of everyday practice, rather than methods for solving math problems.

Since the initiation of math curricula in schools in England about 1750 when the curriculum was borrowed from everyday practice (Cohen 1982), schools have tried to replace the everyday arithmetic procedures of commerce, craft and the domestic scene with arithmetic of pedagogical, institutional design. Other conceivable approaches such as reviewing, supporting or enhancing everyday arithmetic practices have been rejected since about 1820, more strongly since the turn of the century. This gradual process was intended to transform everyday practice into the field of application of school-taught arithmetic algorithms. The success of this trend is arguable, on the basis of our findings. To clarify this point requires a distinction between an ideology of arithmetic practice and everyday arithmetic practice, itself. Each operates on the other, but they cannot be reduced to the same thing. Perhaps in discussing this distinction the analysis can contribute to the solution of the puzzle posed by Latour (1983a) of why higher mathematics and print inspire faith. The data on arithmetic practice seem relevant, for arithmetic in the supermarket is a subject that commands belief and despair in the average grocery shopper.

The place-holding algorithmic arithmetic taught in schools depends on spatial display and hence on visualization; it is intertwined with print, and almost always given two dimensional spatial representation, in ways that do not occur in the supermarket. The question is, if arithmetic activity is constituted in setting, in situation-specific ways, what happens to universalistic standards such as algorithmic math? If general algorithms are transformed into local procedures, what kinds of transformations occur, and how?

Schooling could be described as attemping to dominate the practice of everyday arithmetic through the inculcation of universalistic standards of calculation, that is, through the teaching of place-holding algorithmic arithmetic. At the same time it teaches school children about money, another universal form of standardization. The monetary system is taught only in the same context as math, in arithmetic classes. The association of this specialized system of quantity with general arithmetic emphasizes, if only by implication, the rational, objective nature of all kinds of calculation, whether numerical or monetary. But a comparison of problem solving process data in school-like tests and supermarket shows that the procedures used to solve arithmetic problems in the supermarket do not conform to those taught in school (and that most school taught procedures are partially forgotten soon after the completion of schooling).

In a school-like situation people use algorithmic place-holding techniques, with borrowing, carrying and paper and pencil routines for long division, multiplication and division of fractions, and manipulation of decimals. By contrast, in the supermarket, the same people use varied techniques for solving any given type of problem, rather than an algorithm; they invent, (or borrow) units with which to calculate, i.e. 'six packs' of beer, a week's-worth of apples; people change, decompose and recompose problems and use the environment as a calculating device. They do what I call 'gap-closing' arithmetic (after Bartlett's pioneering work 1958). That is, in order to have an arithmetic problem, the shopper has to see both a problem and the partial form of a solution at the same time. The process of solving problems appears to be dialectical, rather than linear, as the problem and the information with which to solve it change each other, iteratively, until a coherent pattern of relations is constructed. Problem 'resolution' may be a more apt label in the supermarket than problem 'solving'.

However, procedures are not the only goals of school curricula and school does not fail completely to affect its alumni. Let us look more carefully at the practice of arithmetic in the supermarket to see why. Grocery shopping activity is seen as 'routine' by the shoppers we studied (Murtaugh 1985). Local supermarkets in

California stock an average of 7,000 items among which shoppers may choose. Shoppers see the supermarket as the only possible place to obtain 'necessities'. And a major part of life is to be carved out by these choices.

For example, a shopper who was preparing to go to the market might ask a series of questions, thus: I am going to a dinner party. Should I take pears in apricot sauce and vermouth, or just buy a package of cookies? If I decide to prepare the pears, can I find ripe ones in the supermarket?

What about breakfast cereal? Some types have more vitamins than others. The kids must not have too much sugar. I must keep insisting on the healthier brand.

It appears to shoppers that there is an abundance of choices in the supermarket; choices that matter in the creation of style, texture and substance in life outside the supermarket. Many of the products chosen are viewed as 'basic' necessities. Certainly shopping itself is seen as a necessary and urgent chore, and shoppers believe it is possible to be a good or a poor shopper. Those who dash through the store saving time apologize for their profligate ways. Those who do not have full time jobs put effort into the chore. They believe they have not only a right but a duty to agonize over their choices, and that shopping can be done in an ideally frugal way. They take it to be potentially an objective test of their rational and utilitarian acumen. But to an outside observer, watching this process of choosing groceries and the value people invest in the process, what is salient is the culturally constructed, almost mythological, character of this subjective view. Shoppers' premises about the necessity, purpose and style of shopping reflect a belief that the particular political economy of consumerism they experience in their daily lives is inevitable, the only imaginable possibility.

In particular it is instructive to consider the role of price arithmetic in the process of choosing groceries. Analysis of ethnographic data shows that grocery shopping activity unfolds in relatively discrete segments, as the shopper stops in front of one display and chooses an item to put in the cart, then moves on to another display. Within a particular shopping segment size and brand are taken into account, in that order, in making decisions, while price and quantity are considered at the end of decision processes (Murtaugh 1985). Most of any such decision process is a matter of qualitative decision-making, concerning what ingredients are needed for particular menus, to fit family food preferences, nutrition, kitchen storage capacity, and so on.

In fact, in analysis of some 800 grocery item selections, the typical incident of price arithmetic calculation occurred in the following circumstances. If a decision process based on qualitative characteristics of a product became stalled when the shopper had but two, or at most three remaining alternatives to choose among, price arithmetic was used to arrive at a unique selection. It was called into play, then, only when a pair of alternatives looked approximately equally good, and a choice on qualitative grounds appeared arbitrary. Arithmetic activity in these cases was both an expression of, and a medium for, dealing with stalled decision processes. It was, among other things, a move outside the qualitative characteristics of a product to its characterization in terms of a standard of value, money. In the supermarket, calculation may be the most immediate means at hand for asserting the rationality of grocery choices when qualitative criteria of choice have been exhausted. Indeed, a good case can be made that shoppers' ideological commitment to rational decision-making is evidenced by their justificatory calculations and explanations, for the alternative is to declare that choices as constrained as those for which price arithmetic are invoked are arbitrary and hence not worth the effort required to explain them.

It might be argued that a difficult choice made in quantitative terms is not arbitrary, since it fulfils rational utilitarian values directed at saving money. But shoppers' desires to save money are more powerfully accomplished by choosing a supermarket where prices are generally lower than other supermarkets, and by general choices of food quality – it is possible to subsist on steak and champagne or bread and beer, but not for the same price. By the time the activity is reduced to choosing one among several acceptable cans of tomatoes, the contribution of price arithmetic to overall frugality must be quite small. (And for what it's worth, there is no statistical relationship between family income and the frequency of price calculations in the supermarket.)

If there is no good, functional, utilitarian explanation of price arithmetic, and the choices it addresses are arbitrary, what does price arithmetic mean to those who use it? To begin with it may be helpful to consider what it is people do *not* know about their arithmetic activities in the supermarket. We searched grocery shopping transcripts for evidence that people were aware of the arbitrary character of price arithmetic calculations and found only one:

> One shopper, referring to a television commercial in which an animated package of margarine gets in an argument at the dinner table, selects this brand and comments ironically:
> *Shopper:* I'll get the one that talks back.
> *Observer:* Why?
> *Shopper:* Others would have been more trouble.

Further, and a second clue to the role of price arithmetic in the supermarket, the shoppers had not the slightest idea that they were extraordinarily efficacious at arithmetic problem solving in that setting. Instead they apologized for not doing 'real math', or not knowing any math. My thesis is that the ideology that insists on the nonideological, objective, 'natural' character of arithmetic and money, (partly by disguising the latter as a form of arithmetic in school), gives arithmetic in the supermarket, still intertwined with money, a special primarily ideological role in the production of rational utilitarian accounts of choice.

One shopper, for example, who found herself buying a bag of noodles in the presence of the observer, first explained the qualitative reasons for the purchase. She was accustomed to using noodles in two specially prepared dishes, for which one bag was just the right amount; and her kitchen had limited storage space. Both considerations led her to purchase small quantities. But she also felt embarrassed at being observed not to purchase the best buy, the most frugal alternative available. She defensively identified a better buy:

> It's four pounds, and what did I buy? Two? Oh, there is a big savings. Hmm, I might think about that next time, figure out where I can keep it. I actually try to look for better prices. I used, I guess I used to, and I was so much in the habit of it that some of the products I'm buying now are leftovers from when I was cutting costs. And I usually look. If they have something on sale, you know, a larger package of macaroni or spaghetti or something, I'll buy it.

In this example price arithmetic preempted other values, superseding qualitative criteria of choice, and thereby expressing a commitment to utilitarian rationality. The shopper's past decisions to reject large-size packages on the basis of cooking requirements and kitchen storage capacity were not seen as sufficient justification for her habitual purchase, when challenged by the presence of an observer. In the transcribed conversation she made a claim that she valued price very highly as a criterion of choice, emphasizing that her current financial state did not require stern economic restraint (as in the past when she was 'cutting costs'). In the presence of the observer she produced a half-commitment to future 'rational' action; but it seemed unlikely to occur once the observer was absent, relieving her of an implicit demand for a rational account of her choices. For such an account contradicted the other (not un-utilitarian) criteria she customarily employed.

A highly valued belief in rational empiricism and utilitarian calculation permeates American society as a whole, and is not limited to lessons taught in school. I insist, however, that it is in part transported from school into the supermarket because AMP participants (and others under observation in everyday settings, e.g. Kempton 1982) apologize for what they see as the inadequacy of their everyday arithmetic practice. It is only in the context of the hegemonic intentions of schooling that such pervasive beliefs about everyday practice could plausibly arise.

There are two closely related, but distinct meanings to the idea of an ideology of practice. The present section has focused on widely held beliefs about the values that math activity embodies (indeed, is uniquely designed to embody in this culture) concerning the rational utilitarian objective quality of arithmetic calculation. The other meaning of 'an ideology of practice' refers to prescriptions for practical action that are embedded in standardized systems of knowledge in relation to realized practice in everyday situations. In the next section I shall consider how various systems are used; whether reproduced as intended, or transformed or abandoned in everyday situations.

5 Ideology of practice and action

It appears that the ideology of rational empiricism has a sufficiently powerful impact that people devalue their own arithmetic practice and greatly underestimate its efficacy; it leads them to introduce quantitative rationalization into qualitative decision processes at moments when they might just as well flip coins. This raises questions about the degree and kind of penetration of standardized unitization into the organization of everyday activity, for there is no evidence that the standardized place-holding algorithms taught in school are used in everyday settings such as the supermarket. The discussion may be broadened at this point to include the monetary system and systems of measurement as well as school algorithms. We have been investigating money management practices and the uses of measurement devices in the grocery shoppers' households, asking what happens when the standardized unitization of these systems meets the organization of everyday activities. If standardized unitization either imposes its form on, or is inserted into, segments of ongoing activity, it would constitute evidence for the dominating character of these systems in everyday practice. This does not seem to be the case, however.

Thus, in interviews with shoppers about family money management, they described the ways in which money came into the family, was held in various 'stashes' and then spent. It is noteworthy that while almost all families used the strategy of depositing paychecks into a collective family account, partly in order to shed the individualistic identity of these funds as a person's wage, they also re-elaborated the ways in which they held funds in forms that reflected and sustained major family activities and interests. That is, even in the face of values that promoted the collective character of the family, money was 'stashed' in a variety of small and purposefully incommensurate bank accounts, wallets, socks and teapots, to create differences between kinds of expenditures. Family relationships were reflected in the ways in which money was thus decomposed. The spouses in first-marriage families created several joint stashes, distinguished by the purposes of anticipated expenditures; second-marriage families separated accounts, even duplicating them for a single type of expenditure, especially for different children in the family. Our data confirm the work of others (e.g. Mary Douglas 1967) that a universal standard of value and medium of exchange is not seen as an economic advantage. People create incommensurate bank accounts to control the liquidity of their funds. There remains a question of why they create a particular configuration of stashes. After all, they could choose to keep a single family fund of money and to do elaborate bookkeeping. Instead, when a matter of money becomes salient people act with it, stash and move it in a manner shaped by on-going activity. Our analysis suggests that enormous effort goes into creating paths and flows of money which both produce and reflect the specific character of different value-expressing activities of daily life.

The same description fits measurement activities among AMP participants. Gay and Cole (1967) describe measuring devices among the Kpelle of Liberia as specialized for specific jobs in contrast with the universal, standardized, interchangeable units of measure to be found in Western societies. Our data suggest that the measurement systems that Gay and Cole observed among the Kpelle appropriately describe measurement practices (as opposed to an ideology of universalistic systems of measurement) in this society as well. As with money, people create multiple, rich connections between measuring things and the organization and meaning of the activity in which it is germane. It should not be surprising, then, to find special purpose 'stashes' (to borrow a metaphor) of numerical information lying about the household. Such is indeed the case. A survey of a local ten-cent store produced a list of more than 80 separate measuring and calculating devices intended for home use. Inventories of the homes of AMP participants demonstrated an impressive number of such special-purpose measuring devices, used in the course of specialized activities. Cooking a roast and making candy utilized different thermometers, as did learning the air temperature outside the house, the engine temperature of a car and checking a child's body temperature for fever. All were designed with emphasis on the substantive particularities of their intended uses.

Standardization has the effect of attempting to impose a definition of situations of use, as schooling tries to impose general algorithmic math on variously organized ongoing activities. Yet if implicit requirements are successfully imposed, so that money, measuring and especially arithmetic problem solving methods are used in their standard forms, then they must become central, structuring foci of activity. Under such circumstances one might expect thermometers to come only in sets divided at critical units on the scale of temperature such as freezing and boiling points. Money might be stashed, as in a cash drawer, according to its internal units of organization, the twenty dollar bills in one account, the coins in others. But in fact, in the activities of which they form a part, in the settings in which they are generally found, their use is rarely an end in itself. Thus, the particular unitization of money in a given family shapes spheres of exchange so that they are commensurate with activities, social relations, values and occasions on which decisions must be made or issues resolved. But the units of money so formed are not commensurate with each other. In effect their discontinuities create fields for action. Activity-infused stashes and measurement devices have action-producing capacities because they are activity-organized arithmetic rather than arithmetically organized activity. Incidentally, and too briefly (see Lave: in press), this transformation of standardized phenomena within everyday practice is at the heart of the efficacy of arithmetic in supermarket, bowling alley and Brazilian open air markets.

There is a parallel between the implicit stipulation of salience and scope of calculational activity embedded in standardized money and measurement systems and general place-holding algorithms learned in school and the organization of cognitive tasks in experimental settings. Psychologists set up situations in the laboratory such that the display of cognitive 'skills' is the main activity. But arithmetic and other activities typical of experimental tasks almost always play accommodating, minor roles in everyday activity. Such things as classification, remembering and calculating, might be expected to display remarkable plasticity and variability across activities-in-settings most especially as they easily take on different degrees of centrality in different situations.

6 Conclusions

If arithmetic practice is situationally specific, for which the evidence looks increasingly strong; if in the supermarket everyone appears to attach similar 'rational, objective' significance to arithmetic procedures they absorbed in school and are intended to exercise in the supermarket arena; and if these meanings are brought into play in the situation-specific handling of problems very generally; and if researchers and shoppers alike have mistaken the pervasive ideology of arithmetic practice for an adequate description of everyday practice; then, I would argue, to account for the shoppers' arithmetic activity, requires a theory of relations among practice-in-setting, ideologies of practice and institutional arenas.

Such an approach to theorizing about cognition, one that takes practice into account, differs from conventional theory in at least two ways. One shift is a move away from value-free interpretations of particular forms of cognitive activity such as arithmetic. The other is a move to locate all activity, cognitive or otherwise, in its settings. In this view, cognitive activity is value-laden and integrally related with the (value-laden) settings in which it takes place. This non-neutral, value-generating characteristic of activity derives from the fact that minds are integral parts of the body – call them persons – and they are always uniquely located in time and space. Where persons are automatically defines where they are not: in this sense all action creates value. In less abstract ways, money, measuring, and especially the supermarket examples demonstrate that transformations of standardized forms of money and math that occur in everyday situations both give value to certain social relations and activities and settings, and take on value through action in setting.

All of these events could be described in terms of some unit of knowledge/power. But if arithmetic varies from situation to situation, and further, is not to be located in cognition or in culturally organized arenas alone, surely the same principle is relevant in analyses of interests (or other terms representing a synthesis of knowledge and power). Further, if part of any value-creating activity is to maintain the categories of activity of which it is the product (money stashes offer an example), then its characterization as value-infused becomes appropriate on reflexive grounds that go beyond the simpler notion of value-creating action.

Bloor suggests that a truly different, sociologically constructed, mathematics would 'look like error or inadequacy. . . An alternative mathematics might also be embedded in a whole context of purposes and meanings which were utterly alien to our mathematics.' (1976:95–6). Perhaps everyday arithmetic, which researchers and shoppers only *believe* to be error-full and inadequate, is not a candidate for a 'different' mathematics. But just as everyday practice is analytically distinct from ideologies of practice, perhaps formal mathematics deserves a comparable review. It was, after all, a Platonic invention that gave Western mathematics its status as universal and ideal and thereby established the conditions for its hegemonic legitimacy. Everyday math which is simultaneously in the head and on the shelf and is acted out and shaped by ongoing activity, breaches the dominating integrity assumed to be the main characteristic of higher mathematics. The mixed business of arithmetic activity in everyday circumstances contains some of the same elements and operations as higher powered mathematical knowledge, but in practice its involvement in producing and being produced in ongoing activity *does* violate the attributed locus of math as a separate and abstract verity.

That is, built into the platonic ideal is a politics of mathematics, one that is elaborated in the academic and technological world in which we live. As an *ideology* of practice it goes unchallenged in any sphere of life, one ironic way in which boundaries between 'scientific' and 'everyday' thought do not exist. However, its domination only partially penetrates everyday practice (and indeed scientific practice, but that is another argument). Instead, everyday arithmetic might be thought of as, on the one hand, the active quantification of myriad values. And on the other hand, and in contradiction, this practice sustains dominant cultural values concerning the platonic, rational meaning of quantification in ongoing everyday practice in all settings.

This helps to account for the pervasive adherence to great divides between scientific cultures and prescientific cultures or for that matter, everyday thought. But in moving toward a view that value-creating activity-in-setting provides an articulation point between individual experience and room-sized realizations of sociocultural order (culturally-structured arenas), practice in all settings may be accorded a general unity across cultures and spheres of activity; at the same time it suggests great diversity in the location of what might be called knowledge and the values that impel its uses; and divisions between ideologies of practice and practice itself.

References

Barnes, B. 1973. 'The comparison of belief-systems: Anomaly versus falsehood.' In *Modes of Thought*, eds R. Horton and R. Finnegan. London: Faber & Faber.

Bartlett, F.C. 1958. *Thinking: An Experimental and Social Study*. New York: Basic Books.

Bloor, D. 1976. *Knowledge and Social Imagery*. London: Routledge & Kegan Paul.

Carraher, T. and Schliemann, A. 1982. 'Computation routines prescribed by schools: Help or hindrance?' Paper presented at NATO Conference on the Acquisition of Symbolic Skills. Keele, England.

Carraher, T., Carraher, D. and Schliemann, A. 1982. 'Na vida dez, na escola zero: Os contextos culturais de aprendizagem da matematica.' *Caderna de Pesquisa*. 42:79–86. Sao Paulo. Brazil.

Carraher, T., Carraher, D. and Schliemann, A. 1983. 'Mathematics in the streets and in schools'. Unpublished manuscript. Recife, Brazil: Universidade Federal de Pernambuco.

Cohen, P.C. 1982. *A Calculating People: The Spread of Numeracy in Early America*. Chicago: University of Chicago Press.

Comaroff, J.L. 1982. 'Dialectical systems, history and anthropology: Units of study and questions of theory.' *The Journal of South African Studies* 8(2):143–72.

Comaroff, J.L. In preparation. *Capitalism and Culture in an African Chiefdom: A Study in Anthropological Dialectics.*

de la Rocha, O. in preparation. 'The use of arithmetic in the context of dieting: A study of practical problem solving.' Ph.D. dissertation. University of California, Irvine.

DiMaggio, P. 1979. 'Review essay on Pierre Bourdieu.' *American Journal of Sociology* 84(6):1460–74.

Douglas, M. 1967. 'Primitive rationing.' In *Themes in Economic Anthroplogy.* ed. R. Firth. A.S.A. Monographs 6:119–47. London: Tavistock.

Durkheim, E. 1912. *The Elementary Forms of the Religious Life.* (tr. 1915). London: George Allen & Unwin.

Gay, J. and Cole, M. 1967. *The New Mathematics and an Old Culture.* New York: Holt. Rinehart & Winston.

Goody, J. 1977. *The Domestication of the Savage Mind.* Cambridge: Cambridge University Press.

Herndon, J. 1971. *How to Survive in your Native Land.* New York: Simon & Schuster.

Horton, R. and Finegan, R. (eds) 1973. *Modes of Thought: Essays on Thinking in Western and non-Western Societies.* London: Faber & Faber.

Kempton, W. 1982. 'The folk quantification of energy.' *Energy – The international journal.*

Latour, B. 1983a. 'Visualization and cognition: An introduction to the debates.'

Latour, B. 1983b. 'Comment redistribuer le grand partage?' *Revue de synthese:*III S. No. 110.

Lave, J. 1977 'Cognitive consequences of traditional apprenticeship training in West Africa.' *Anthropology and Education Quarterly.* Vol. 8:177–80.

Lave, J. in press. *Culture, Cognition and Practice.* New York: Cambridge University Press.

Lave, J. In preparation. *Tailored learning: Education and Everyday Practice among Craftsmen in West Africa.*

Levy-Bruhl, L. 1910. *How Natives Think.* (Reprinted, London: Routledge & Kegan Paul, 1966.)

Malinowski, B. 1925. 'Magic, science and religion.' In Joseph Needham (ed.), *Science, Religion and Reality.* Macmillan Company.

Murtaugh, M. 1985. 'A hierarchical decision model of American grocery shopping.' Ph.D. dissertation, University of California, Irvine.

Ortner, S.B. 1984. 'Theory in Anthropology since the Sixties. Comparative Studies in Society and History.' 25(1):126–66.

Reed, H.J. and Lave, J. 1979. 'Arithmetic as a tool for investigating relations between culture and cognition.' *American Ethnologist,* 6(3):58–82.

Scribner, S. (ed.). 1984. 'Cognitive studies of work.' *The quarterly newsletter of the laboratory of comparative human cognition.* 6(1 and 2) (special issue).

Scribner, S. and Fahrmeier, E. 1982. 'Practical and theoretical arithmetic: Some preliminary findings.' Industrial Literacy Project, working paper No. 3. CUNY.

'Interests' in political analysis

Barry Hindess

Abstract

This paper argues that interests have consequences in so far as they
provide actors with reasons for action, and that actors may find reasons
for action in interests they ascribe to themselves and in interests they
ascribe to others. This argument undermines many of the ways in
which concepts of interests have traditionally been used in social and
political analysis. Section I is an introductory discussion of the uses of
concepts of interests in political analysis. Section II discusses the place
of interests in the explanation of action and Section III discusses
connections between interests and actors' social location. A brief
conclusion summarises the main arguments of the two central sections.

1 Introduction

'Interests' is one of the most widely used and most disputed
concepts in political discussion. To say that a policy, practice, or
state of affairs is in the interests of an individual or group is to
suggest that the individual or group would somehow benefit from
it. That much, at least, is generally agreed. Interests in that sense
may be regarded as providing explanations of action. Many
commentators would agree with Connolly's assertion. 'Every
explanatory theory of politics includes somewhere in its structure
assumptions about persons and their real interests' (Connolly,
1983, p.73). Interests are used to provide justifications for actions
said to be performed on behalf of others, for example, by
politicians or social workers. Because they are thought to provide

explanations they may also be employed in the course of attempts to estimate how others are likely to act.

Socialist political analysis in Britain, for example, is often conducted in terms of the actions of classes and of certain social categories (women, blacks, youth) and the scope for conflicts or alliances between them. What is at stake here is the idea that membership of a class or category defines an interest that exists independently of the practices of political parties and other organisations, and irrespective of whether the individuals concerned recognise it as their interest (Hindess, 1983). The interests of a class or social category are supposed to be a function of its position in relation to other classes and categories. Interests identified in this way can perform a number of functions in socialist political discussion. First, they may be used in explanation. For example, it is often argued that the Labour Party gains working class support in so far as it appeals to the interests of the working class, and loses support in so far as it betrays those interests or reduces that appeal (e.g. Cripps et al., 1981, chapter 8; Panitch, 1976). Second, they may be used to justify or evaluate some aspects of the policy of a party, union or government. Policies may be supported or opposed in the name of the interests of the working class, pensioners, and other interest groups. Third, they may appear as features of the situation to be taken into account in assessing the potential support that may be won for some particular policy or programme.

Marxism provides perhaps the best known source of theoretical foundations for such a concept of interests. Marxism regards class interests as in some sense given in the structure of class relations, and proceeds to the analysis of political institutions and organisations as their more or less adequate embodiments or representations. I have argued that that approach has unacceptable political consequences (Cutler et al., 1977, 1978; Hindess, 1983). Indeed there is an important sense in which it makes political analysis redundant: if politics is reducible to the representation of interests given by some underlying social reality, then the representations themselves – the practices of parties, unions, state agencies, and the like – are clearly of secondary importance. Rather than consider the social distribution of interests as given to politics from elsewhere we should consider instead the conditions in which political concerns and interests are formed and the ways in which their invocation may play a role in political life. For the moment notice that if interests are regarded as given by a social reality that is supposed to underlie and explain political activity, then they are 'objective' in two senses. First, they do not depend on any subjective awareness on the part of those whose interests they are supposed to be. Second, they have an objective reality that socialist parties have to recognise as a precondition of effective political practice.

I have discussed this notion of 'objective' interests and its consequences elsewhere. What should be noted here is that there is more to the notion of objective interests than the assumption that the content of those interests be given to politics from elsewhere. In the concluding chapter of his general discussion of the forms of collective action Tilly (1978) clearly recognises that there may be a problem with treating collective interests as given. For example: 'Mobilization, collective action, and acquisition or loss of power, frequently alter a groups' interests' (p.228). Here a dynamic character is assigned to the distribution of collective interests, but Tilly continues to treat the division of the population into the groups or categories to which those interests are assigned as given in an extra-political structure of social relations (cf. the Introduction to Berger, 1981). The interests of a group or category are determined by its position in that structure, with the result that the contents of interests may change with the relative positions of the contending groups. Only if the basic structure of class relations is an extra-political given in this sense can politics be regarded as ultimately reducible to struggles between them. That presumption of a given distribution of the population into interest groups or categories may have a limited plausibility in the short term. At any particular moment many political interests and concerns must be regarded as effectively given – but only in the sense that they cannot be changed readily or in the short term by any of the forces currently engaged in political activity. But to say that many interests have to be accepted as given for the purposes of immediate practical politics is not to say that they have to be accepted as theoretically given in political analysis or that they should be regarded as unchangeable in the longer term. The argument here is not that politics alone, still less political activity in the immediate term, is the source of all effective political interests and concerns. Rather it is that the activities of governments, parties and other movements have consequences that are too important to be ignored – not only for the forms of collective action and organisation that may be adopted, but also for the formation and distribution of political interests within the population.

But the explanatory use of interests is by no means restricted to the marxist tradition. For example, Weber treats values and 'material' interests as giving distinct and generally opposed reasons for action. Or again, the pluralist tradition in American political science analysed political life in terms of the interactions of more or less organised interest groups, on the assumption 'that people participate in those areas they care about the most' (Polsby, 1959, p.235). The interests at stake in political life are therefore the ones that people organise around and campaign for. Critics of that tradition do not dispute the explanatory use of interests. Instead they argue that certain interests may be prevented from providing an effective basis for political action – either because they are excluded from the sites in which decisions are taken or because the agents whose interests they are fail to recognise them (Lukes, 1976; cf. Hindess, 1976, 1982).

These examples are restricted to questions of political analysis but what they illustrate are general features of the uses of concepts of interests in social enquiry. First, interests are supposed to be relatively stable properties of actors and their specification normally involves some reference to the possibility of intentional action. They define some of the objectives that actors set themselves, or would set themselves if only they were in a position to do so. Interests belong to that broad class of entities that have been supposed, by social scientists and others, to provide actors with ends, and therefore with reasons for action. Other members of that class include values, preferences, wants, fears, dislikes, desires, needs, habits, and impulses.

How do interests relate to and differ from these other items that may provide actors with reasons for action? Hirschman (1977) has shown that there have been considerable changes in the way interests are conceptualised in relation to other possible sources of motivation. In the modern period interests are generally thought to differ from values in a relatively clear way: to promote actors' interests is supposed to be beneficial to them, while to promote their values need not benefit them at all. Many would follow Weber in suggesting that an actor's values are, or may be, freely chosen, but no-one would suggest that interests are a matter of choice in the same sense. Or again, interests differ from impulses in being relatively stable. But what of needs, wants, and all the rest? The question is frequently addressed, and there is little sign of agreement on the answer (e.g. Barry, 1965; Connolly, 1983; Reeve and Ware, 1984).

Second, interests appear to provide an explanatory link between action and social structure. On the one hand they provide actors with reasons for action and on the other they are derived from features of social structure. Actors have interests by virtue of the social conditions in which they find themselves, as members of a particular class, sex, age group, or community, as victims of monopoly power or multinational companies, etc. The problem here, of course, is that different features of the conditions in which actors find themselves may be used to specify different, and sometimes conflicting, sets of interests (Berger, 1981). The identification of such cross-pressures and their effects has been an important theme in several traditions of political analysis, for example, in discussions of the affluent worker thesis, status inconsistency, contradictory class locations (Abrams et al., 1960; Crosland, 1960; Goldthorpe et al., 1968; Campbell et al., 1960; Lipset, 1968; Wright, 1978).

Finally, the link between action and social structure raises the question of real interests. If interests are things that actors possess as a function of their membership of a class or social category then the possibility must be considered that actors may not always recognise their own interests. For example, children, the elderly and the insane may be regarded as having at best a limited capacity to recognise what their interests are, thereby providing rationales for the interventions of relatives and professional agencies. In political analysis the possibility of the misrecognition of interests has been elaborated in many different ways, for example, in marxist notions of false consciousness, in Lukes' three-dimensional view of power, and in Gramscian notions of hegemony and rule by consent. I have discussed some of the problems with these positions elsewhere (Hindess, 1982). What should be noted here is that this notion of interests takes us beyond the recognition that what an actor's interests are may be specified in different ways by the actor concerned and by various other actors – or by the same actor in different circumstances. It goes further to suggest that some of those interests are more real than others. The notion that actors have real interests then poses the problem of just how those interests are to be distinguished from the rest. For liberal political thought, with its concern for liberty of the individual, this problem is more than merely academic: it poses the further problem of the conditions in which actors may reasonably be judged incapable of recognising their own interests, so that others may be justified in acting' on their behalf. The debate on these problems is interminable. (See Reeve and Ware, 1984, and the references therein.)

I argue that many of these questions, and the debates around them, stem from a failure to recognise the specific place of interests and related concepts in the explanation of action. First, the formulation (and therefore the existence) of interests is always dependent on definite discursive and other conditions. Secondly, the specification of interests is always open to dispute: interests are not given properties of individuals or groups. In particular, they should not be regarded as structurally determined. Thirdly, problems of the correct definition of interests in social analysis are frequently misconceived; but there are important questions to be asked about the conditions in which actors will acknowledge one set of interests rather than another, or in which the appeal to certain interests can be effective. Finally, I argue that the use of interests as a form of explanation of action is not necessarily wrong, but it is seriously incomplete.

II Interests and actions

Reasons and decisions

An actor is a locus of decision and action, where the action is in part a consequence of the actor's decisions (Hindess, 1985). Human individuals are actors in this sense, and so are state agencies, capitalist enterprises, political parties, and various other bodies. Analysis of what actors do, their actions, the struggles they engage in and the relations between them, therefore includes analysis of their decisions. The notion of interests that are real but not recognised by the actors whose interests they are has little to offer by way of explanation of *their* actions – although others may sometimes claim to act in their name. On the other hand, there is little point in insisting on the *reality* of certain interests if they are recognised by those whose interests they are said to be. Interests may provide reasons for action if they are recognised by the actors concerned. It makes no difference to the effectiveness of those interests in providing reasons that they might, on some account of

117

real interests, be mistaken. What the appeal to interests that are real but not recognised usually suggests is that what has to be explained is not so much the decisions that actors take, and the reasons for them, but rather an absence: a non-existent state of affairs (in which actors do pursue their real interests) is posed as a measure of the present and the problem is to explain away its non-existence. The problem is why certain objectives, the real interests, are not pursued, rather than the investigation of those that are.

Contrary to Connolly's claim, quoted above, explanatory accounts of politics need make no assumptions about actors' real interests. If the concept of interests is to play any part in the analysis of action it can only be because interests are thought to relate to the decisions of particular actors, and therefore to their actions. Actors formulate decisions and act on some of them. The concept of interests refers to some of the reasons that may come in to the process of formulating a decision, to act or to do nothing, to support some policy or party, to oppose it or to abstain, and so on. Actors' decisions may relate to their own interests or to the interests of others, and they may relate to reasons of other kinds, to values, sudden impulses, or whatever. What matters here, of course, is not that the word 'interests' should appear in the formulation of reasons for a decision. Interests can also be said to provide reasons for a decision if the reasons that are formulated relate to the benefit or well-being of some actor or actors. The interests of employees in a factory may be said to be involved in a decision to resist its closure, even if the word 'interests' is not used in their deliberations.

Interests that provide no actor with reasons for action can have no social consequences. They are effective in so far as they provide reasons for actors' decisions. Two aspects of this conception of the connection between interests and action are important here. First, interests are effective, in the sense of having social consequences, as conceptions: they must be formulated if they are to be perceived, and if they are not formulated directly then they must be reflected in reasons that are formulated. This point may seem trivial, but we shall see that it has important consequences for the ways in which interests may be said to have political repercussions. The problem with discussing interests in terms of the visual imagery of perception is that it can divert attention from what is required for reasons to be formulated. If interests are things that may or may not be perceived, then what has to be explained is actors' perceptions: under what conditions will they see, or fail to see, . . . It is a problem of the subjectivity of actors and the effects of social conditions on their subjectivity. To say that interests are formulated is to insist on a further set of questions concerning the conceptual or discursive conditions necessary for certain reasons to be formulated at all. It is only if the appropriate reasons can be formulated that particular interests can be effective elements of social life.

Second, interests not only provide reasons that enter in to some process of assessment, but they are also, at least in principle, products of assessment themselves. On some accounts of action there may be reasons for action that do not themselves depend on assessment. Two, possibly three, of Weber's four types of action involve reasons of this kind. There are certainly problems about the characterisation of such reasons, but they need not concern us here. To say that a policy or state of affairs is in the interests of an actor is to say that the actor would benefit from its implementation. It follows that what the actor's interests are in any given case is always potentially open to dispute. Interests are reasons that may themselves require further justification: they depend on assessment or the possibility of assessment. To locate interests within the realm of reasons that are themselves open to assessment is to say that the range of possible interests depends on the forms of assessment available to the relevant actors. Interests depend on the forms of calculation and means of posing objectives and of locating themselves and others in relation to those objectives that are available to actors.

Interests and forms of assessment

Interests depend on forms of assessment: if they are to provide potential reasons for action it must be possible to present them as the outcome to some process of assessment ('this strike is in the interests of the miners because. . .'). What is involved here is the construction of an account of the actors' situation and of how they might be affected by particular changes or actions. In many situations a variety of distinct and competing ways of assessing the interests of specific actors or groups of actors will be available. Assessments may be produced using cost-benefit analysis, horoscopes, geomancy, or what seems to us some more rational process. The point is simply that they are the result of some definite process employing particular conceptual means of specifying the actor's situation and possible changes within it. Interests are the product of assessment. They do not appear arbitrarily, out of nowhere, they are not structurally determined and they cannot be regarded as fixed or given properties of actors. I return below to the issue of structural determination. Interests are always open to dispute, and the interests of particular actors may be differently identified by the actors concerned and other agencies, or by the same actors at different times. Does this matter? Does the assignment of conflicting sets of interests to the same actors pose problems for the use of interests in social analysis?

Consider the question of what interests are or may be effective in particular sites of action, social relations or struggles. The first point to notice is that this question has nothing to do with questions of the accuracy or 'validity' of the attribution of interests. The attribution of interests is effective, in the sense of having social consequences, not because it is valid, but rather because of the part it plays in the reaching of decisions by some actor or actors. In the 1984 miners' strike, for example, distinct and conflicting conceptions of the interests of the miners have been effective. The miners' interests have been at issue in the decisions of miners who support the strike and in the decisions of miners who oppose it. Which position is correct is itself a matter of dispute, and the conduct of that dispute has consequences in the changing pattern of support for the opposed positions – but it is not the 'validity' of one attribution of interests rather than another that determines what support it has.

To say that interests are subject to assessment is to say, secondly, that their specification is open to dispute. There may, for example, be disagreement as to the consequences of the pursuit of a particular assessment of an interest. Political conclusions derived from some assessment of what the interests of the working class (or the miners or owner-occupiers) are, are always in danger of being undermined by alternative assessments. Again, to say that interests are effective in so far as they provide reasons for action is to say that those reasons are articulated by particular agencies, by individuals or by organisations such as governments, trades unions or political parties. The interests involved in the reasons they articulate may be their own or ones they attribute to others. Trades unions may, for example, calculate their own interests and those of their members, and they may also calculate the interests of various other constituencies, the labour movement, the working class, the unemployed, etc. Other agencies may also claim to identify the interests of those constituencies and to act in pursuit of them. There is no reason to suppose that the interests of the unions or their members as calculated by these various agencies will coincide, still less that they will necessarily correspond to assessments of their interests by union members themselves. Indeed, there have been well known cases where the politics of a union are contrary to those of a majority of their members.

The interests that have social consequences are not always those acknowledged by the actors to whom they are attributed, and it is not the validity of the attribution that secures their effectiveness. To investigate the political repercussions of interests it is necessary to begin with the assessments of interests (their own and others) by various agencies (unions, parties, factions, individuals) and with the decisions they make on the basis of those (and other) assessments. There is no reason to suppose that the interests assigned by various agencies to particular actors, to the unions, the working class owner-occupiers, or whatever, will coincide. Nor, of course, should we assume that actors' own assessments of their interests have any effective priority in determining the decisions of those who claim to represent them. Political parties and other organisations make their own assessments of the interests of those they may claim to represent, they do not merely aggregate their interests. They do more than merely aggregate by working to create or specify the content of the interests they represent. They may also do much less, in so far as they fail to represent the concerns acknowledged by their members or supporters. In these respects, the interests represented by political parties cannot be seen simply as the more or less adequate reflection of the distribution of interests within the electorate (Hindess, 1983).

To say that interests depend on forms of assessment is to say thirdly that their attribution is not arbitrary or a matter of entirely free choice. Interests are effective only in so far as they play a part in the formulation of actors' decisions. Actors make decisions and try to act on them, but that does not mean that there are no limits to what they are able to decide or that they can always do what they have decided to do. The decisions they formulate and the reasons that enter into those decisions depend on the discursive means available to them, and actors have very little choice over what those means are. Actors may work to change how they think, but they cannot adopt new discursive forms at will. Consider again the example of the 1984 miners' strike. The claims of those miners who support the strike and the claims of those who oppose it involve assessments of miners' interests that are far from arbitrary. Both sets of interests are products of definite modes of assessment of what the miners' interests are that are well-established in mining communities in Britain. Both sets of interests can provide reasons for decisions within the decision-making procedures of the miners' union. Other conceptions of the miners' interests are certainly possible, but to be effective they would have to provide possible reasons within the current means of reaching decisions and of assessing what their interests are. For example, the claim that the miners' interests consist in the sacrifice of one goat for every ten members of a pithead branch would have no purchase within current forms of assessment and decision-making.

Actors are clearly limited in the extent to which they can choose the forms of assessment employed by or available to them. But that is not to say that those forms of assessment are uniquely determined by their social location. Rational choice theories of political or economic behaviour tend to assume that actors' forms of thought are uniquely determined by their rationality and social location: political leaders and ordinary voters may calculate in different ways as a function of their different positions, but they are both essentially rational. I have discussed these positions elsewhere. What should be noted here is that if actors' forms of thought are given by their social location, or if rationality is a property of the actor *qua* actor, then there is no difficulty about what interests they will identify or what conclusions they will draw from them. The problem here is that in many contexts the forms of assessment available to actors allow the formulation of a variety of distinct and conflicting reasons, objectives and decisions. This possibility provides considerable scope for dispute and also for the persuasion, propaganda, and other forms of political work intended to change people's assessments of their interests and how they might be served. What interests or reasons for action are acknowledged in any given case depends not only on the forms of assessment available to the actors, but also on other conditions, including the work of individuals, political parties, unions, and other agencies, in support of some assessment of interests and against others.

Validity

Finally, to distinguish questions of what interests are effective from questions of their validity is not to say that questions of validity therefore have no place. There are obvious cases where it is reasonable to question the correctness of an attribution of interests. However, this is not a matter of correspondence to some objectively determined real interests. The point rather is that the attribution of interests implies the claim that those whose interests they are said to be will benefit in some way from their successful pursuit. The validity of such claims is of obvious importance to political actors (including many social scientists). They are open to question in at least two respects: there is, first, the question of whether the supposed benefits are really benefits at all, and, secondly, the question of whether they are likely to be realised by pursuit of the interests specified. In some cases there may be clear and unambiguous answers to such questions. There would not be much dispute, for example, about the claim that the interests of the British people are served in the maintenance of elementary public health measures. But in general the attribution of interests is not so clear-cut, and an important part of political debate consists in disputes over the attribution of interests and how they might best be pursued. Such disputes can have significant effects on the balance of political forces around the issues in dispute – and sometimes more generally when the disputed issues are part of a wider ideological polarisation.

III Interests and social relations

Perhaps the most common approach to the explanation of interests is to locate them in terms of some concept of social structure. Actors have interests as a consequence of their position as members of a group or class in relation to members of other groups or classes. Most forms of marxism analyse the distribution of interests in terms of a structure of class relations, which in turn is largely a function of definite relations of production. Sociological critics of marxism, such as Dahrendorf and Parkin, see the structure of class relations rather differently, but continue to account for interests in class terms. Others analyse the distribution of interests in terms of group rather than class membership. These positions share a view of interests as reflecting actors' location within a structure of social relations. The concept of interests then appears to provide an explanatory link between structural location and actors' behaviour.

What are the consequences for this 'structural' analysis of interests, of insisting that actors do indeed make decisions and act on them? I have argued elsewhere that the concept of actor outlined above cannot be reconciled with any concept of society as a functioning whole governed by some unifying principle (central values, mode of production, or whatever) and producing necessary effects on actors as a consequence of their position in its structure (Hindess, 1985). This section develops that general argument with specific reference to the concept of interests. I argue first that interests do not function as a mere transmission between actors' social location and their behaviour, and then move on to consider other ways in which actors' social location may have a bearing on their assessments of interests.

There are several reasons why the notion of interests as given by or reflecting social structural location is unsatisfactory. Consider first the notion of real interests, interests that are supposed to have an objective reality but are not necessarily recognised by those whose interests they are thought to be. If they are not recognised then they cannot provide those actors with reasons for action. Interests that are real but unrecognised provide reasons for action only in the case of other actors, who may claim to recognise the interests without necessarily sharing them. Real interests in this case are ascribed to those for whom they do not provide reasons for action. Concepts of interests that are real but not recognised by those they are ascribed to may well have social effects – for example, in the actions of political parties and sects, the decisions of parents, teachers or social workers – but they provide no explanatory link between the social location of actors and their actions.

Such cases apart, we are concerned with interests in so far as they relate to the decisions of particular actors, and therefore to their actions. How far can interests that actors recognise as their own be explained as reflecting their social location? We have seen that if interests are to provide reasons for action it must be possible to present them as the outcome of some process of assessment. There are two kinds of problem here for the view of interests as reflecting social location. First, I have argued above that the forms of assessment available to actors are not uniquely determined by their social location. It follows that the interests actors recognise and act upon cannot be uniquely determined by social location either. There is a partial recognition of this point in those analyses that seek to identify 'cross-pressures' on actors as a function of distinct aspects of their social location – for example, in Olin Wright's notion of contradictory class locations (Wright, 1978). What is at issue here is the idea that interests are determined by membership of particular social categories, and that the complexity of social life is such that these categories are not mutually exclusive. Unfortunately, such cross-pressures approaches merely complicate a position that is fundamentally flawed, namely, the view that actors' forms of thought are determined by their social location.

Second, leaving aside the issue of competing forms of assessment, actors' assessments of interests (their own and others') are not determined simply by the form of assessment they employ. First, the forms of assessment may leave considerable scope for interpretation. This is clear enough in the case of actors using geomancy or a manual such as I Ching. But indeterminacy and therefore scope for interpretation can also be found, for example, in non-trivial uses of cost-benefit analysis and in the forms of political calculation employed by even the most sophisticated groupings on the left. Second, in considering actors' reasons for action we are not generally concerned with the deliberations of perfectly rational actors. Unlike the idealised puppets of rational choice theory, actors' deliberations are rarely completely pro-grammed by the form of assessment employed in any given case (Hindess, 1984). Their conclusions are reached through complex internal processes which may vary from one actor to another and within the same actor over time.

These points undermine the idea of interests as an explanatory link between actors' social location and their actions. But to dispute that link is not to say that there are no connections between the interests that actors recognise and act upon and their location in sets of social relations. It is merely to say that those interests should not be seen as given by or reflecting actors' locations. Indeed, if actors act on the basis of their decisions, and if those decisions involve complex internal processes, then we should not expect the connections between actors' social location and the interests they acknowledge to conform to any one general model (Hindess, 1985). Nevertheless several possible kinds of connection can certainly be indicated. Some of these are to do with the availability of discourses providing means of assessment, and others are to do with means of action and its impact.

I have argued that interests depend on forms of assessment and that they must be formulated (or reflected in reasons that are formulated) if they are to be effective in the sense of having social consequences. The possibility of formulating particular interests and reasons for action depends on the availability of appropriate discourses to the actors in question. Foucault's discussion of medical discourses shows some of the ways in which the availability of specific discourses may be restricted to the occupants of particular positions within medical institutions (Foucault, 1973) and his later work has suggested a variety of connections between discourses and power relations (Foucault, 1971, 1980). The availability of the professional discourse does not of course guarantee that 'professional' interests will be formulated, let alone acted upon, in every case. The point rather is that the possibility of formulating certain 'professional' interests is effectively restricted to those able to deploy the appropriate professional discourse. For a different, non-professional example, consider how the development of specialist managerial techniques over the last century has affected the differential availability of sophisticated means of assessing the performance of large public and private organisations. Or again, the cultural and educational diversity of all but the smallest societies is enough to ensure that means of assessing their situation are not equally available to everyone.

What these examples show is that there are several ways in which individuals may differ with regard to the forms of assessment available to them at any given time. What is available may not be used, and limitations on what is available may be changed, for example, through education or specialised training. Nevertheless, what is available to an actor at any given time is not a matter of choice. The differential availability of discourses providing means of assessment gives one set of connections between actors social location and the interests they are able to formulate.

A rather different set of connections concerns not so much the availability of discourses but rather their pertinence to particular actors. The formulation of interests involves actors in the assessment of conditions and in locating themselves and others in relation to those conditions and possible changes in them. For example, socialist discourses elaborating on the interests of the working class and other groups that might be regarded as its allies may well be available to actors who are not in any of these groups. Chartered accountants may have no difficulty in identifying the interests of the working class, women or blacks, in terms of the discourse of, say, *Militant*, without being able to locate their own interests in any clear way in terms of that same discourse. Many workers will confront similar problems in relation to the discourse of the CBI or Institute of Directors. Or again, part-time women workers may have some difficulty locating themselves in relation to trades union discourses conducted in terms of the 'family wage'. There is, of course, nothing about these problems that is inescapable. The general point is that if certain actors are unable to locate themselves in relation to the conditions they confront in terms of a particular discourse then they will not employ that discourse to identify their interests. There is nothing to stop socialist parties, say, from modifying their analyses to try to take account of such problems – as most socialist groups in Britain have tried to do in the case of women.

Two final sets of connections between actors' social location and the interests they recognise and act upon concern the means of action available to them and the differential impact of social conditions and changes in those conditions. If interests provide actors with reasons for action, then the interests they formulate will depend on the possibilities for action that are (thought to be) open to them. What those possibilities are will depend not only on the forms of assessment employed by actors but also on the means of action available to them. All employees in a manufacturing enterprise may be affected by its strategies towards investment, product and marketing development – and in that sense they all have an 'interest' in what those strategies are. But, with the rare exceptions of some cooperative enterprises, they are not equally well placed to act on the determination of those strategies. The interests that are formulated by senior managers on the one hand and wage-labourers on the other with regard to those strategies may well differ – both because they will be affected differentially but also because they have radically different means of acting on them. The means of action available to workers, and therefore the interests they formulate, will, of course, depend not only on their position within the organisational structure of the enterprise but also on the extent of unionisation, the strength of shop steward organisation within the enterprise, and so on.

As for the differential effects of social conditions, consider the example of the structures of the markets for various categories of housing in Britain. They have implications for the formation of political interests because conditions in those markets and changes in them have differential effects on the households and organisations that operate in them. Such patterns of differential effect provides the conditions in which parties and pressure groups attempt to identify interests and develop policies in relation to them.

Some words of warning may be in order at this point. First, to insist on differential impact here is not to say that political interests to do with housing can be read-off from the structures of housing markets and changes in them. The point rather is that the differential effects of social conditions have consequences for the pertinence of political appeals and campaigns for different sets of actors. Secondly, housing conditions should not be regarded as an extra-political given. The political significance of housing has been transformed in Britain since the war, to a large extent as a result of government policies. Neither the character of the housing stock and the structures of the housing market, nor the pattern of political concerns and interests around housing issues, are readily amenable to change in the short term through political action. But it would be absurd to regard them as given to political life by something entirely outside it – by economic growth, affluence, or whatever (Abrams et al., 1960). There is no original pre-political pattern of interests which politics could be said to represent or react to. I have used the example of government policies here in order to make the point. But it is clear that governments are by no means the only bodies whose activities can transform the conditions to which actors relate in formulating their interests.

IV Conclusion

I have argued that interests have consequences only in so far as they provide some actor or actors with reasons for action; that they must be formulated or find expression in reasons for action that are formulated; and that actors may find reasons for action in interests they ascribe to themselves and in interests they ascribe to others. The notion of interests that are real or objective (unlike other interests that actors may believe themselves to have) has no explanatory significance with regard to the actions of those whose interests they are thought to be. Interests are either acknowledged by the actors to whom they are ascribed, or they are not acknowledged by them. In the first case, the reality or objectivity of the interests has no bearing on their reasons for acting as they do. In the second case they provide no reasons for action to those whose interests they are said to be: that is, they play no part in the explanation of the action of those actors, although other actors may well claim to act in their name.

The interests that actors act upon are not given by their social location, but I have suggested several respects in which they may be connected with actors' locations in sets of social relations. These connections are to do with: differences in the availability of discourses providing means of assessment, and differences in their pertinence to different sets of actors; the differential access to means of action; and the differential impact of social conditions and changes in them. There are definite connections between actors' social locations and the interests they acknowledge and act upon, but there is no simple correspondence between the two. Actors are not mere creatures of their position in sets of social relations, of their class or gender or whatever. The forms of assessment available to them are rarely so limited as to be given uniquely by their social location. The conclusions of their deliberations depend on complex internal and discursive processes: they are not determined solely by the forms of assessment employed.

It follows that there is no possibility of interests functioning as a mere transmission between social structure on the one hand and what actors do on the other. Interests cannot provide the means whereby the structure of society produces its effects. No doubt some readers will be disturbed by such blatant undermining of the notion of social structure as an entity operating outside of and above actors, and manipulating them to produce its necessary effects. In fact there is nothing to regret in the loss of that conception of social structure. To say that there is no such thing as a social structure which produces its effects through the manipulation of the actors ensnared within it is not to say that there are no relatively pervasive and enduring social conditions. Nor is it to say that social life is reducible to the constitutive actions of human individuals: first, there are actors other than human individuals; secondly, actors do indeed make decisions and act on them, but neither their means of reaching and formulating decisions nor their means of acting on them are determined solely by the actors themselves. Their decisions and actions always depend on 'social' conditions, but those conditions will be of the most diverse kinds and there is no need to assume an essential 'structure' to which they all refer.

Interests are conceptions. If they are to have consequences it must be possible for them to be formulated or to be expressed in reasons that are formulated. The interests that are formulated by actors depend on the discourses they are in a position to employ and the forms of assessment of conditions those discourses provide. How do interests relate to, and differ from, other items (values, desires, aversions, etc.) that may provide actors with reasons for their actions? I have indicated how interests may be said to differ from impulses and from values: interests relate to a calculation of benefit but the same cannot be said in general about impulses or values. But it may be more useful finally to question the importance that is sometimes attached to the drawing of such distinctions. It is far from clear that distinctions drawn between, say, interests and values in terms of certain moral discourses will be equally pertinent to all forms of assessment employed by actors. If we are concerned with actors' reasons for action and with what makes it possible for those reasons to be formulated, then it may be more important to concentrate on the discourses available to and employed by them, and on the forms of assessment of conditions and of locating themselves and others in relation to them that those discourses provide. In this respect the use of interests as a form of explanation of action is not necessarily mistaken, but it is certainly seriously incomplete.

References

Abrams, M., Rose, R. and Hinden, R., 1960, *Must Labour Lose?*, Harmondsworth, Penguin.
Barry, B., 1965, *Political Argument,* London, Routledge & Kegan Paul.
Berger, S., 1981, *Organizing Interests in Western Europe,* Cambridge University Press.
Campbell, A., Converse, P.E., Miller, W.E. and Stokes, D., 1960, *The American Voter,* New York, Wiley.
Connolly, W.E., 1983, *The Terms of Political Discourse,* Oxford, Martin Robertson.
Cripps, F., Griffith, J., Morrell, F., Reid, J., Townsend P. and Weir, S., 1981, *Manifesto,* London, Pan.
Crosland, C.A.R., 1960, *Can Labour Win?*, Fabian Tract, 324.
Cutler, A., Hindess, B., Hirst, P.Q. and Hussain, A., 1977, 1978, *Marx's Capital and Capitalism Today,* London, Routledge & Kegan Paul.
Foucault, M., 1971, 'Orders of Discourse', *Social Science Information,* 10,2.

Foucault, M., 1973, *The Birth of the Clinic*, London, Tavistock.

Foucault, M., 1980, *Power/Knowledge*, Brighton, Harvester.

Goldthorpe, J.H., Lockwood, D., Beckhofer, F. and Platt, J., 1968, *The Affluent Worker*, Cambridge University Press.

Hindess, B., 1976, 'On Three-Dimensional Power', *Political Studies*, xxiv.

Hindess, B., 1982, 'Power, Interests and the Outcomes of Struggles', *Sociology*, 16,4.

Hindess, B., 1983, *Parliamentary Democracy and Socialist Politics*, London, Routledge & Kegan Paul.

Hindess, B., 1984, 'Rational Choice Theory and the Analysis of Political Action', *Economy and Society*, 13.

Hindess, B., 1985, 'Agents and Social Relations', M. Wardell and S. Turner (eds), *The Dissolution of Sociological Theory*, London, George Allen & Unwin.

Hirschman, A.O., 1977, *The Passions and the Interests*, Princeton University Press.

Lipset, S.M., 1963, *Political Man*, London, Heinemann.

Lukes, S., 1976, *Power: A Radical View*, London, Macmillan.

Panitch, L., 1976, *Social Democracy and Industrial Militancy*, Cambridge University Press.

Polsby, N., 1959, 'The Sociology of Community Power', *Social Forces*.

Reeve, A. and Ware, A., 1984, 'Interests in Political Theory', *British Journal of Political Science*, 13.

Wright, E.O., 1978, *Class, Crisis and the State*, London, New Left Books.

Interactive-orientation and argumentation in scientific texts

Steven Yearley

Abstract

Sociologists have frequently sought to explain people's beliefs and claims to knowledge in terms of those people's interests. Yet in every case the knowledge/interest connection is an interpretative and revisable one and, moreover, people may have many possibly-ascribable interests. Accordingly the ascription of interests in any particular case is fraught with difficulty. However, actors themselves appear regularly to engage in this kind of interpretative work. Using concepts from sociolinguistics and conversation analysis, this study illustrates through the example of one famous scientific paper how written scientific arguments can be seen to depend on this kind of work also. The study proposes that scientific arguments have a specific interactive orientation, and that technical texts can be seen to operate as a nexus of persuasion, action and belief.

Introduction

It has been a recurrent practice in the sociology of knowledge to seek to explain the origins and support for particular knowledge claims in terms of actors' social interests (Barnes 1977; Foucault 1970:196–200). In the last ten years this procedure has been systematically applied to scientific knowledge as well as to other forms of knowledge more commonly acknowledged to be socially variable (Barnes 1977:1–26; Yearley 1984:118–20; Barnes and Shapin 1979). Recent commentators have argued that this practice is unsatisfactory since it tends to imply that both social interests and knowledge claims are fixed and specifiable entities. These commentators propose, on the contrary, that interests may be very variable and that ascriptions of interests and beliefs are necessarily open and revisable (Woolgar 1981; Yearley 1982). The fundamental practice of this form of the sociology of knowledge accordingly appears to depend on a method which ossifies and reifies the posited variables. And although this objection has largely been made with respect to the sociology of scientific knowledge, similar observations occur in other fields as in Hindess' (1982) consideration of political interests. Still, it must also be accepted that the general pattern of reasoning according to which people's beliefs are ascribed to their interests is widespread in lay interaction as well as in the sociology of knowledge (Woolgar 1981:379–86; Mulkay and Gilbert 1982:171–80).

A possible resolution of this paradoxical situation – where there is apparently widespread support for a flawed procedure – is suggested in a recent study of scientific argument (Callon and Law 1982). The proposed interpretation is that people's interests are postulated or constructed in the course of appeals to those interests. In principle, it may be possible to ascribe many interests to specific persons, but arguments are set up so as to align with *possibly ascribable* interests. Arguments, it is said, are aimed at 'enrolling' people's interests. One of the situations in which such a process would be anticipated is in the course of a written scientific argument. In this case the process can be redesignated in terms of what, following the work of Iser (1974; 1978) on literary texts, may be termed the 'implicit reader'.[1]

Iser argues that texts postulate a reader with certain characteristics (beliefs, concerns and so on) and that the sensefulness and development of the text depend upon the response of this implied reader. The implied reader is clearly an abstraction from any particular actual reader, but Iser maintains that actual readers are influenced by this postulated one. Iser's schema perhaps seems a little speculative and, in any case, was worked out in relation to literary, fictional texts. It may, however, offer a general indication of how texted arguments operate and thus clarify the mechanism of knowledge presentation. In this way it would suggest how attributes like interests are brought to bear in technical, factual debates through the interaction of text and reader. To examine this possible mechanism of interaction and enrolment this paper will be concerned with the analysis of a famous and influential scientific text.

The text to be considered is one that has received a great deal of attention from historians of science; it is Hutton's first major expression of his theory of the earth. A celebrated eighteenth-century geologist, Hutton was engaged in scientific activities from his early twenties when he studied medicine in Paris and Leyden (Playfair 1805; Eyles and Eyles 1951). His wide-ranging scientific interests persisted through his involvement in chemical manufacture and farming. By 1783 when the Royal Society of Edinburgh was formed he was apparently well prepared to deliver a paper on the theory of the earth. His paper (Hutton 1788) was read over two meetings in 1785 and published three years later.[2] In 1795 a vastly extended version was published which included illustrative material and lengthy replies to his critics (Hutton 1795). In general terms the theory maintained that the earth was unknowably old and that it was constantly being reformed by the reconsolidation of eroded materials. The power activating this system was the earth's internal heat which allowed the eroded sediments to be fused together and which supplied the force needed to uplift the new rock strata, formed on the ocean floors, to the level of the continents. For this reason his theory was often referred to as 'Plutonist' and that of his opponents as 'Neptunist'. His work has attracted a great deal of scholarly attention and has been praised by historians of geology on a number of grounds including: its recognition of the importance of heat; its correct conception of the antiquity of the earth; its emphasis on erosion and the re-formation of rock strata; and its insistence on the constancy and naturalness of geological processes and change (Bailey 1967; Gerstner 1968; Davies 1969: 154–96; Porter 1977: 184–97).

While early commentators explained his achievement in terms of a sloughing off of impediments to the scientific attitude and of the adoption of the correct methodological presuppositions (Geikie 1962: 314ff), more recent historians have begun to be concerned with the integrity of his ideas and the suffusion of his geological theory with non-scientific conceptions. Religious and philosophical notions have been interpreted as constitutive of his theory (Grant 1979; O'Rourke 1978). For example, it has been proposed that his commitment to the uniformity of geological processes was more closely related to deistic views on the earth's durability and perfection than to a realisation of the 'scientific necessity' of uniformitarianism (Dean 1975). Where some historians have seen evidence in Hutton's text of his belief in inductive methods or 'the propriety of a scientist going directly to nature . . . there to study earth processes' (Bailey 1967: 32), others, like Grant (1979: 32), have claimed that:

a grasp of the meaning of the text presupposes a grasp of a
central theological problem which, although barely visible in
the text, is nevertheless constitutive of the theory.

On this interpretation, the text displays Hutton's preoccupation
with teleological reasoning. Yet others claim that the theory stems
from a rationalist, proto-Kantian philosophy of science and that,
in O'Rourke's words (1978: 11–12), 'the real argument [is merely]
masked by the teleology'.

These interpretations are clearly very different but they do show
some significant similarities. For one thing, they all claim to be
revealing the true basis of the argument embodied in the text.
Second, they each refer to a philosophical foundation for the
validation of the theory (respectively inductivism, teleologism and
rationalism) which is supposedly evidenced in the text. In no
instance, however, is the structure of Hutton's text examined for
an explanation of these diverse allusions. Instead they each
suppose that there must be some general principle of knowledge
evaluation – exposed or covert – which does figure decisively in
Hutton's work. These commentators' procedures would seem to
suggest that allusions to philosophical principles are common in
Hutton's text and this raises a question about the function of such
allusions in making it a successful text. But at the same time the
existence of at least three readings indicates that the implied
reader is not a close constraint on actual readers. Because of its
historical success and apparent textual complexity it seems
therefore that Hutton's text may be a useful medium for
investigating how readers are influenced by texted arguments.

The justification of knowledge claims in Hutton's 1788 paper

Hutton's paper was divided into four sections: 'Prospect of the
Subject to be treated of' (pages 209–24); 'An Investigation of the
Natural Operations employed in consolidating the Strata of the
Globe' (225–61); 'Investigation of the Natural Operations employed
in the Production of Land above the Surface of the Sea' (261–85);
and 'System of Decay and Renovation observed in the Earth'
(285–304). The second of these concerns the formation of rocks
while the third deals with general uplift and with volcanic action.
The 'Prospect' is of a more general nature, and the fourth section
is primarily concerned with marshalling earlier material in support

of the general perspectives announced in the 'Prospect'. In order to address the most empirical areas of Hutton's work I shall initially examine the claimed bases for knowledge assessment found in the intermediary sections – I shall commence with the second.

From Hutton's introductory comment one could easily be led to accept O'Rourke's point about the teleological basis of Hutton's presentation, if not Grant's insistence on the teleological assumptions which pervade and legitimate his thought, for Hutton (1788: 209) claims that:

> When we trace the parts of which this terrestial system is composed, and when we view the general connection of those several parts, the whole presents a machine of peculiar construction by which it is adapted to a certain end.

Yet immediately at the beginning of the second section the reader is cautioned that, in regard to understanding the consolidation of rocks:

> If we are not informed in this branch of science, we may gaze without instruction upon the most convincing proofs of what we want to obtain. If our knowledge is imperfect, we may form erroneous principles, and deceive ourselves in reasoning with regard to those works of nature, which are wisely calculated for our instructions. (Hutton 1788: 225)

In the 'Prospect', a conviction of the teleological arrangement of the world is presented as quite apparent and self-evident enough to direct our knowledge. Yet when it comes to the introduction of factual material, it is said to be correct, specific factual knowledge which *precedes* teleological insights, even though in general terms these may be known to be the desiderata. As I described above, a great deal hangs, for interpreters of Hutton's work, on the question of which considerations were primary for him: narrowly empirical, teleological or epistemological ones. Within his own text however, Hutton appears to be ambivalent about it.

It is therefore important to examine more closely the authorisations of knowledge employed in the second section. Thus, an explicit statement is given of the basis for assessing the opposing 'Neptunist' interpretation of rock formation on the sea-bottom:

The action of water upon all different substances is an operation
with which we are familiar. We have it in our power to apply
water in different degrees of heat for the solution of bodies, and
under various degrees of compression; . . . consequently, we
are to look for no occult quality in water acting upon bodies at
the bottom of the deepest ocean, more than what can be
observed in experiments which we have it in our power to try.
(Hutton 1788: 226)

In this passage there is no suggestion that knowledge derives
anywhere but from common experience, nor that there are
refractive criteria by which scientific knowledge about the natural
world should be assessed. Indeed, experimental trials which bring
knowledge within the reach of 'everyman' are proposed as the
explicit basis for assessment. Equally, when discussing the
origination of flint as it occurs in organic petrifications, Hutton
suggests that the pattern of the siliceous penetrations could only
have arisen from the injection of molten, rather than solvated,
material. He emphasises that:

There cannot be a doubt with regard to the truth of this
proposition; for as it is, we frequently find parts of the
consolidated wood, with the vascular structure remaining
perfectly in its natural shape and situation. (Hutton 1788:
234–35)

A similar espoused view on knowledge evaluation – that simple
observation is routinely capable of deciding questions in an
unproblematic manner – is commonly found elsewhere in this
section. Thus:

. . . in order to decide this point, with regard to what is the
power in nature by which mineral bodies have become solid, we
have but to find bituminous substances in the most complete
state of coal, intimately connected with some other substance,
which is more generally found consolidating the strata, and
assisting in the concentration of mineral substances. But I have
in my possession the most undoubted proof of this kind.
(Hutton 1788: 240)

According to the conception presented in these accounts of
knowledge evaluation, truth follows easily from observation and

even a grasp of nature's fundamental powers is simply linked to isolable empirical proofs.

Furthermore, Hutton sometimes invokes the claims of other scientists. For example, after arguing that bodies of (what would now be called) elemental metals could only be formed by the action of heat, Hutton appeals to their widespread occurrence as proof of the global influence of heat. Then:

> For the truth of this assertion, among a thousand other
> examples, I appeal to that famous mass of native iron,
> discovered, by Mr Pallas, in Siberia. This mass being so well
> known to all the mineralists of Europe, any comment upon its
> shape and structure will be unnecessary. (Hutton 1788: 238)

At the very least, it has been demonstrated in this section that the warranting in Hutton's text is not exclusively performed through reference to teleological or rationalist principles. Indeed, the opposite is rather more applicable: as has been found in other analyses of formal scientific presentations, the author's knowledge is portrayed as arising directly from observation. Moreover, the purported knowledge of other (presumably neither rationalist nor teleologically-disposed) authorities is adopted as a textual basis for belief without any caveats concerning the transformation of these authorities' philosophically ill-founded knowledge. Accordingly it appears that the informational sections of Hutton's text are provided with evaluational criteria based on an inductive view-point. This is not to say that there are not alternative characterisations of proper reasons for belief or of evaluative principles available in the same text. I shall briefly examine these before moving on to consider, at first abstractly and then textually, the place of these various characterisations within Hutton's scientific discourse.

In commenting on alternative bases for knowledge evaluation I shall commence with non-inductivist elements in the second section of Hutton's paper, and then turn to the 'Prospect' and its characteristic range of references. Early in the second section, he introduces the role of time as a geological agent:

> Though the continuance of time may do much in those
> operations which are extremely slow, where no change, to our
> observation, had appeared to take place; yet, *where it is not in
> the nature of things to produce the change in question*, the

unlimited course of time would not be more effectual, than the
moment by which we measure events in our observations.
(Hutton 1788: 226)

In this case, a knowledge of the 'nature of things' is opposed to
observational knowledge since, by definition, observation cannot
discriminate between immeasurably small changes and immut-
ability. How such knowledge arises is not specified on this
occasion, but it re-appears four sides later in a methodological
statement:

If, therefore, such an agent [as steamy exhalations] could be
found acting in the natural place of strata, we must pronounce it
proper to bring about [processes which we deduce must go on
there]. (Hutton 1788: 230)

Here, a prior knowledge of the natural place of strata informs the
selection of the agents which must effect the unobservable changes
which the strata are known to undergo. Principles of an undis-
closed origin permit determinate, substantive interpretations of
general empirical issues, by allowing Hutton to recognise the
'natural' condition of parts of the earth. Such an external criterion
of naturalness might be furnished by deistic teleology or by a
proto-Kantian transcendental deduction of the properties of a
knowable world. These non-inductivist evaluative appeals provide
some licence for the views of commentators like Grant and
O'Rourke; it must, however, be recalled that such appeals are far
less numerous than inductivistic ones so that any straightforward
assumption that they correspond to Hutton's real thoughts appears
suspect.

In the 'Prospect' one does not have to look far for comments
which apparently bespeak a dependence upon sources of knowledge
prior to empirical investigation. Thus:

Where so many living creatures are to ply their respective
powers, in pursuing the end for which they were intended, we
are not to look for nature in a quiescent state; matter itself must
be in motion. . . . (Hutton 1788: 209)

Here, a claim to substantive knowledge is authorised by a
teleological warrant ('the end for which they were intended'), and
the implied knowledge of teleological arrangement is located

beyond the text. It is also suggested that such general principles direct the course of the ensuing empirical investigation:

> To acquire a general or comprehensive view of this mechanism of the globe, by which it is adapted to the purpose of being a habitable world, it is necessary to distinguish three different bodies which compose the whole. (Hutton 1788: 211)

The choice of categorisation is 'necessitated' by a knowledge of the world's purpose.

The latter part of the 'Prospect' is largely concerned with establishing the basic constituents of the globe – seemingly in accordance with the above quotation from page 211. When one reads how this is achieved, however, rather different perspectives emerge. Hence:

> *that which renders the original of our land clear and evident, is the immense quantities of calcareous bodies* which had belonged to animals, and the intimate connection of these masses of animal production with the other strata of the land. (Hutton 1788: 218)

The agency which generates 'clear and evident' knowledge is part of the world's natural composition. A similar point of view persists up to the close of this section, since Hutton remarks that:

> From every view of the subject, therefore, we are directed to look into *those consolidated masses themselves, in order to find principles* from whence to judge of those operations by which they had attained their hardness or consolidated state. (Hutton 1788: 224)

Thus, in these pages, the emphasis is directed towards the knowledge-generating capacity of the world's objects themselves, and away from the application of prior principles. How should one interpret this switch of evidential bases?

In general, one can say that Hutton makes reference to different evaluative systems on different occasions and that in broad terms, allusions to particular systems are clustered. An inductivist basis is the commonest, while philosophical bases are somewhat less frequent and not entirely consistent. It does not appear tenable to select only some of the philosophical references (say, to teleology) as an index of Hutton's thought. No simple enumerative assessment of allusions can plausibly depict the degree of his commitment to various evaluative principles. A better appreciation of the significance of these allusions will derive from an analysis of the role they play in the practical medium of Hutton's text. For an indication of the practical argumentational or persuasive task accomplished by reference to general principles it will be necessary to look for the moment beyond scientific texts and textual analyses altogether.

Formulations and conversation analysis

Much of the pioneering work on the sociology of language was done in relation to informal, everyday interaction. Language use in such contexts is often directed to situations where actions and interpretations are not agreed or specified in advance. Unlike fictional texts where the reader is at least in some senses enthralled, conversational language may often be concerned with the control and influencing of the direction of interaction. Thus there is an initial functional similarity between conversational language use and the enrolment functions of scientific texts. The branch of the sociology of language most concerned with conversational interaction, conversation analysis, may therefore assist in the examination of Hutton's paper. However, many of the features of conversational interaction which have proved most susceptible to analysis (features such as sequencing, openings and closings, and speaker-selection) are explicitly and exclusively interactional. In turning this work to the study of historical scientific texts very few of the analyses can be transferred directly. But I suggest that there is an everyday model available for understanding at least one type of scientific allusion to philosophy. This model will provide a means of addressing the textual role of philosophy in Hutton's paper.

A phenomenon observed by Garfinkel and Sacks (1970), and developed by Heritage and Watson (1979), is that in the course of interaction people sometimes formulate the thing which it is that they are doing. Conversational turns in which this is done are termed formulations, thus:

> A member may treat some part of the conversation as an
> occasion to describe that conversation, to explain it, or

characterize it, or explicate, or translate, or summarize, or
furnish the gist of it, or take note of its accordance with rules, or
remark on its departure from rules. That is to say, a member
may use some part of the conversation as an occasion to
formulate the conversation . . . We shall speak of
conversationalists' practices of saying-in-so-many-words-what-
we-are-doing as *formulating*. (Garfinkel and Sacks 1970: 350–1)

While Garfinkel and Sacks are concerned with formulating as an
ethnomethod of establishing types of social action, the later
authors' interest is in the conversational properties of formulations.
Both pairs of authors consider primarily interactional material
where a need for the monitoring of the conversation can plausibly
be tied to the use of formulations. I shall argue, however, that the
capacity to identify what it is that one is doing in performing such-
and-such an action has a broader use. Before developing this
hypothesis it will be advantageous to examine what kind of role
formulations fulfil in the common run of things.

Heritage and Watson, in their extensive analysis of the
conversational role of formulations, are primarily concerned with
what they term 'formulations of gist'. They examine how hearers,
but also speakers to a lesser degree, take the opportunity to put
forward statements of what the conversation (cumulatively) is
about. They note that formulations are rarely employed in the case
of uncertain or precarious understanding; such contingencies are
customarily met with a questioning device. Rather:

we may grossly say that the primary business of formulations is
to demonstrate understanding and, presumptively, to have that
understanding attended to and, as a first preference, endorsed
. . . formulations constitute a members' method for providing
that the conversation *has been* and is *ongoingly* a
self-explicating colloquy. (Heritage and Watson 1979: 138–9)

Thus, it is their claim that formulations operate to demonstrate the
meaning of specific conversational turn(s); to explicate a participant's understanding of this meaning; and to signify the grasp of
the overall conversational event. The role of formulations in
denoting comprehension and offering a reading of that comprehension, is particularly developed by the authors. They argue that
negations of candidate readings of the meaning of conversations
invite a great deal of interactive trouble, whereas to accede to a

formulation is simultaneously to endorse the whole conversational interaction. Acceptances of formulations are therefore regarded as normatively preferred.

Heritage and Watson seek to explain this normative implication of formulations by suggesting that:

> it is possible to locate a basis for the preference for confirmation of formulations in what Pollner has termed the presupposition of a world-essentially-known-in-common. (Heritage and Watson 1979: 144)

Since the conversation rests continually on the assumption of a common experiential world for its intersubjective transparency, denials of formulations throw potentially into doubt the whole basis of the conversational undertaking. In formulating one must however display one's understanding. A characteristic feature which the authors ascribe to this display-function is the use of 'pro-terms' (viz pronouns and other substitutive locutions), whose successful employment exhibits conversant understanding through the overcoming of the potential ambiguity of deixis. In long conversational turns or protracted interchanges, formulations may be employed to indicate cumulative understanding. Such possibilities may even be institutionalised, as in judges' summings-up, where the authors contend, the potential importance of the summing-up turn is indicated by its restriction to certain persons or offices (Heritage and Watson 1979: 150). Finally, they note that formulations are customarily met with a decision as to whether to accept them or not, and it is suggested that the formulation/decision couple constitutes an adjacency pair (Heritage and Watson 1979: 159; Wootton 1975: 65–71).

With these points in mind, I shall briefly review what Heritage and Watson have to say on the construction of formulations. They characterise the content of formulations as consisting in the preservation, deletion and transformation of previously occurring material. An illustrative instance will clarify what is meant by these seemingly contradictory features:

> [a radio interview with a 'Slimmer of the Year': following a detailed story about the distress caused by the consciousness of unattractiveness resulting from overweight]. . .
> I: You really were prepared to commit suicide because you were a big fatty

S: Yes, because I – I just didn't see anything in life that I had to look forward to. . . (Heritage and Watson 1979: 132)

Here, in the interviewer's formulation of the slimmer's former state of mind, the slimmer's foregoing story is recouched in new terms whilst preserving salient constituents and deleting excess detail. As was mentioned above, adequate paraphrasing exhibits understanding; literal repetition usually denotes a query rather than successful comprehension. Whilst, as the authors make clear, within their rubric there are many ways of accomplishing a formulation, there does seem to be one recurrent approach which I consider to be of special interest. This approach, where one formulates by invoking a generality, is exampled twice in one of their excerpts:

[concerning a patient who has difficulty in taking food under certain social circumstances]. . .
Dr: So what you're saying is that you're self conscious. . .
Dr: You conform for the sake of con:formity. . . (Heritage and Watson 1979: 134)

In this case, the formulation is achieved by demonstrating, through reference to a well-known syndrome or generality, that the patient's talk is recognised and understood. Unfortunately, neither Garfinkel and Sacks nor Heritage and Watson provide any more general account of the composition of formulations. Neither do they specify the ways in which paraphrases are recognised to be adequate formulations.

In Cuff's engaging study of a radio debate about a family's personal problems, he analyses the role of experts in setting forth the upshot of the accounts given by the family members. He observes how one expert:

blends and integrates many of the previous materials in the talk to provide not only an 'overall' view of the organisation of the family, but also possibly to give an 'expert's' view or version of it. (Cuff 1980: 66)

As in the example of the doctor above, an authoritative way of participating in interaction is to furnish an expert's formulation of what has gone on. The expert does not provide just another version, but a view which locates all that has been done as culminating in that view. The authority of the formulation of gist also inheres in the fact that it is established with respect to general principles of expert knowledge, and moreover in the exhibition of this connection.

To summarise, then, formulations offer a proposed interpretation of the preceding talk for validation. Because of their interactive location they invite ready acceptance and may lead to interpretative difficulty if they are opposed since further background assumptions are thereby also challenged. However, they do not oblige agreement. They influence and constrain the direction of inter-pretation – but loosely. Their role is thus very akin to the presumed process of enrolment or reader-implication. They tend to favour one interpretation but are not fully compelling.

The conversation-likeness of scientific formulations in formal contexts

There exist at least two preliminary justifications for expecting to find formulations in scientific discourse. First, as is shown by conversational analysis, formulations occur relatively frequently, and appear often in circumstances where an agreed outcome is both sought and displayed. Since science is normally informational, formulations could reasonably be expected to occur with at least average frequency. Second, the institution of 'conclusions' to scientific papers suggest that there are occasions in such texts for the job of summing-up which, according to Heritage and Watson, is often associated with formulations. The point that I particularly wish to examine, however, is whether there are any significant links between formulations, allusions to philosophical principles and espousals of specific evaluative bases, within Hutton's geological text. My interest, therefore, will not be in scientific formulations as such, but in seeking to show that the role of philosophical allusions in his text can be understood by use of the concept of formulating.

Initially, to demonstrate that there are formulations in formal scientific texts and to study their composition, I shall consider an example of summing-up from the informational section of Hutton's paper. This passage has been chosen not for its philosophical referents but for its unobjectionable status as a summing-up. At the beginning of the third section of his article, Hutton reviews the argument's progress:

[In this section] We seek to know that operation by means of which masses of loose materials, collected at the bottom of the sea, were raised above its surface, and transformed into solid land.

We have found, that there is not in this globe (as a planet revolving in the solar system) any power or motion adapted to the purpose now in view; nor, were there such a power, could a mass of simply collected materials have continued any considerable time to resist the waves and currents natural to the sea, but must have been quickly carried away, and again deposited at the bottom of the ocean. But we have found, that there had been operations, natural to the bowels of this earth, by which those loose and unconnected materials have been cemented together, and consolidated into masses of great strength and hardness; those bodies are thus enabled to resist the force of waves and currents, and to preserve themselves, for a sufficient time, in their proper shape and place, as land above the general surface of the ocean. (Hutton 1788: 261)

To many readers, especially those convinced of Hutton's correctness, this is a good, straightforward summing-up; even to opponents, I consider, it would appear unremarkable. It is interesting to note, therefore, that this passage possesses the characteristics of a formulation as specified above. There is deletion: of factual material on particular rock types and on operations in the earth's bowels; there is transformation: 'great strength' is a new term describing rocks; and yet the order of the argument, the emphasis on the sea's agency, and the term 'cementing' are all different forms of preservation. This summing-up displays the formal features of a formulation; it says-in-so-many-words what the arguer has been doing. In some ways, this identification may seem trivial given one's commonsense familiarity with summings-up. However, I suggest that it will be interesting to ask what may be learned about scientists' summing-up (or conclusions) by considering them in the light of knowledge about the functions of other formulations.

Through extensive studies of everyday language use, both ethnomethodology and functional linguistics have developed the claim that no use of language is innocent of interactional effect. A fundamentalist view of science would hold, on the contrary, that regardless of their linguistic garb, scientific arguments are paramountly transparent and depend on nothing save simple statement in order to be properly persuasive. On this view, the need for conclusions in scientific papers at all would appear rather inexplicable. A moderate solution might be that conclusions perform a psychological function in aggregating the proceedings of a whole turn at writing, and in reminding the reader of things which must be prominently attended to. However, as was indicated above, conclusions depend on paraphrase, including deletion. They announce the upshot of a foregoing argument. Conclusions do not consist in the repetition of arguments but in stating-in-so-many-words what the arguments (successfully) have argued. Given this creative and innovative role, it is hard to see how conclusions can be understood as innocent. Rather they must be interpreted in functional terms (Kress 1976: vii–xxi and 26–31).

We now consider that all scientific arguments are potentially revocable and therefore in a sense incomplete. Accordingly summings-up can be viewed as a way of drawing out the intended implications of foregoing arguments, of limiting objections to those arguments, and of attempting to establish their correct, unobjectionable upshot. Of course, according to this perspective conclusions are potentially contestable. If one examines Hutton's remarks in the above passage, (such as the comment that 'there is not in this globe . . . any power or motion adapted to the purpose' of forming continents 'nor, were there such a power, could a mass of simply collected materials have continued any considerable time') it is clear that in an important sense these are new assertions. Hitherto, for example, specific hypothetical proposals about consolidation were called on, whereas now there are definitive and counterfactual statements. One could accept earlier statements and yet contend the summing-up. The functioning of the conclusion depends on it extending beyond earlier claims whilst appearing to issue directly from them.

Scientific conclusions are not alone in having this property; as was mentioned earlier, formulations generally invite a decision as to their acceptance. The adjacency pairing of a decision indicated the contestability, and hence the innovativeness, of formulations. I shall examine formulation/decision structures in Hutton's text more closely in the next section, but it will suffice to note here that the summing-up passage above is followed (Hutton 1788: 262) by a discussion of how certain one can be of its claims, and that an earlier formulation was resolved with an injunction to the reader to go and see (Hutton 1788: 233). Both these specific references and the general work on formulations suggest that summings-up are orientated to decisions about their propriety. This finding supports the earlier suggestion that scientific papers should be interpreted as an interpretatively persuasive or enrolling medium. In the next section the formulations in Hutton's text will be studied in more detail and their connection to philosophical allusions investigated.

The distribution and anatomy of formulations in Hutton's text

It has been suggested that Hutton's text incorporates formulations as integral elements in its overall construction. It has also been proposed that some scientific formulations involve reference to methodological or meta-scientific principles and that such formulations should be regarded as related to the broader type in which generalities are called on to formulate an individual instance. Finally, because formulations are frequently tied to decisions, one would anticipate that scientific formulations too should invite decisions, and that, given the persuasive orientation of scientific writing, grounds for returning an affirmative decision might be furnished within the text. Since my concern is not with formulations per se, but with Hutton's philosophical allusions, this study will henceforth deal only with formulations which illuminate the practice of invoking philosophical principles. In the following table I have exhaustively recorded references to philosophical bases for evaluation in the third (informational) section of his text. I have also noted all the formulations with which they are associated, although it is not my claim that these are all the formulations in this section.

From Figure 1 it can be seen that out of thirteen instances of philosophical talk, only one (PX) was not involved in a philosophical formulation (PF) or decision (PD). Within Hutton's text, formulations are recognised by the use of paraphrased, re-stated points to describe where the argument has reached, what it amounts to, or what the general upshot is. Decisions are sections of text following formulations which warrant, and enjoin an affirmative response to, the preceding formulation. Some formulations occur which are couched in terms of the empiricist account of evaluation which characterises the majority of the informational text; yet these formulations (EF's) may then be certified by reference to philosophical bases for knowledge evaluation. By philosophical I

contents \ page 200+	61	62	63	64	65	66	67	68	69	70	71	72	73	74	75	76	77	78	79	80	81	82	83	84	85
	EF	PD		EF	PD	EF		EF			PF	PF	PD	EF	PD	PX			EF		PF		EF	EF	PD
						PD		ED			ED	ED	PF										PD	PD /	PF
												EF													

TOTALS:

EF . . . PD	=	7
Other EF	=	2
PF alone	=	3
Other PF	=	2
PX	=	1
PF + PD + PX	=	13

KEY:
- EF = Empiricist formulation
- ED = Empiricist decision
- EF / ED = Empiricist formulation followed by decision on same page
- PX = Additional references to philosophy
- PF = Philosophical formulation
- PD = Philosophical decision
- PD / PD = Philosophical decision spanning consecutive pages

The remainder comprises unremarked accounts unassociated with uses of philosophical bases for evaluation

Figure 1: Inventory of allusions to philosophical principles in the third section of Hutton's paper

mean both putative methodological rules of scientific action and *a priori* sources of substantive knowledge claims, such as metaphysics and religion. Thus, my category of philosophical allusions embraces both the types of resource (rationalist proto-Kantianism and deism) which are commonly regarded as particularly influencing Hutton's thought.

The second and fourth EF . . . PD structures (264–5 and 272–3) illlustrate well the common role occupied by teleological reasoning and invocations of the philosophy of science. Rather lengthy quotations are required to demonstrate this point:

EF | The supposition, therefore, of the subsidence of the former ocean . . . is beset with more difficulty than the simple erection of the bottom of the former ocean; for, *first*. There is a place to provide the retirement of the waters of the ocean; and, *secondly*, there is required a work of equal magnitude; this is, the swallowing up of that former continent, which had procured the materials of the present land.

PD | . . . Such an operation as this would discover as little wisdom in the end elected, as in the means appropriated to that end; for, if the land be not wasted and worn away in the natural operations of the globe, why make such a convulsion in the world to renew the land? (Hutton 1788: 264–5)

EF | Here is a comparison formed of two mineral substances. . . The solidity and present state of the one of these is commonly thought to be the operation of fire; of the other, again, it is thought to be that of water. This, however, is not the case. The immediate state and condition of both these bodies is now to be considered as equally the effect of fire or heat. The reason of our forming such a different judgement with regard to these two subjects is this; we see, in the one case, the more immediate connection of the cause and the effect, while, in the other, we have only the effects from whence we are in science to investigate the cause.

PD | But, if it were necessary always to see this immediate connection, in order to acknowledge the operation of a power . . . we should lose the benefit of science, or general principles, from whence particulars may be deduced, and we

should be able to reason no better than the brute. Man is made for science; . . . but he does not always reason without error. In reasoning, therefore, . . . care must be taken how we generalize; we should be cautious not to attribute to nature, laws which may perhaps be only of our own invention.
(Hutton 1788: 272–3)

Both of these examples begin with formulations: the problem of how to explain the ocean's subsidence has been treated in detail before the assessment that the whole idea is 'beset' with difficulties; similarly, a detailed comparison of the properties and origins of lava and marble precedes the second synopsis. These formulations operate in empiricist terms: it is said to be the facts which lead to the difficulty addressed. Subsequently, the philosophical perspective of, respectively, teleology and rational man is employed to endorse the formulation. Yet, it is crucial to note that the implications of the philosophical perspective are informed by the details of the formulation. The philosophical generality is only potent when viewed through concrete, particular assertions about the subject matter which the philosophy is supposed to illumine (Mulkay and Gilbert 1981).

On five occasions, allusions to philosophical bases of evaluation occur as PF's. I shall examine these by first considering the PF which stands alone on page 273 (Hutton 1788):

The immediate question now before us is not, if the subterraneous fire, or elevating power, which we perceive sometimes as operating with such energy, be the consolidating cause of strata formed at the bottom of the sea; nor, if that power be the means of making land appear above the general surface of the water; for, though this be the end we want to arrive at ultimately, the question at present in agitation respects the laws of nature, or the generality of particular appearances.

This formulation of what the 'question now before us is' undertakes the role of directing enquiry rather than of carrying out much summing-up work. The other solitary PF's perform a similar task: the one on page 281 re-states a foregoing argument about the igneous origin of whinstones and the like in order to introduce the next step of the argument, rather than to elucidate an upshot; and the one on page 285 serves to direct the overall argument (legitimately) into the concerns of section four of the paper. That these single PF's do less substantive work than the EF . . . PD structures accords well with my earlier claim about the limited potency of purely philosophical arguments, whereas it appears to contradict the views of commentators who regard Hutton's philosophy as actively constitutive of his geological theory. That the two PF . . . ED structures do rather more substantive work, and that in both cases the assertional force is textually located more on the ED component would appear to support my reasoning. In both instances (concerning the formation of marble, and the persistence of the active role of heat in the earth) lengthy, elaborate ED's contrast with brief PF's.

Finally, it will be necessary to examine the apparent exception formed by the philosophical reference on page 276. This passage is concerned with establishing that violent volcanic eruptions are not disruptive of the world's purpose. While it is not immediately associated with any formulation, it is my contention that it should be regarded as the complement of the PD of the previous page, which had certified an earlier formulation of volcanic agency by outlining the providential consequences of such agency. Thus, the PX is not separated from the EF by anything save a PD. Accordingly, it may be regarded as the second part of the PD, since its adjacency and senseful connection with the formulation are unimpaired. It is therefore possible to claim that the presence of philosophical bases for knowledge evaluation in the third section of Hutton's text is restricted to their role in formulatory units. As such, these philosophical allusions perform directive, confirmatory, and summarising work but are responsible for no original introductions of information within the structure of the text. Indeed, its commonest location, in the decision components of EF . . . PD devices, indicates the *ex post facto* argumentative force of general, philosophical principles. It is my suggestion that this pattern is borne out in the second section of Hutton's paper, from which I quoted earlier. Readers are invited, because of the inevitable brevity of this analysis, to check this point themselves.

Formulating in Hutton's conclusion

At the level which has been analysed here – the level of textual invocations of bases for knowledge evaluation – the fourth section of Hutton's paper is nearly consistently characterised by allusions to philosophical bases for knowledge, and especially to teleology. Moreover, and of particular significance in the light of the above examination of occasions for different types of evaluative basis, these references are not restricted to formulations. There are formulations with philosophical components, as in the comment, after an empiricist section concerning the features of fossil materials, that:

> Having thus ascertained the state of a former earth, in which plants and animals had lived, as well as the production of the present earth, composed from the materials of a former world . . . by pursuing in our mind the natural operations of a former earth, we clearly see the origin of that land, by the fertility of which, we and all animated bodies of the sea, are fed. (Hutton 1788: 293)

However, there are also occasions on which philosophical grounds for evaluating knowledge are used initially, rather than in re-statements of claims. This initiatory function is performed in at least five instances (on pages 291, 294, 296, 300 and 301). Thus, one reads that:

> In order to understand the system of the heavens, it is necessary to connect together periods of measured times, and the distinguished places of revolving bodies. It is thus that system may be observed, or wisdom, in the proper adapting of powers to an intention. In like manner, we cannot understand the system of the globe, without seeing that progress of things which is brought about in time, thus measuring the natural operations of the earth with those of the heavens. (Hutton 1788: 296)

The direction of enquiry towards the disclosure of 'wisdom' is quite explicitly avowed here without the informational issue of mensuration having featured in the preceding paragraphs. Almost equally unanticipated is the later comment that:

> It is not necessary that the present land should be worn away and wasted, exactly in proportion as new land shall appear; or, conversely, that an equal proportion of new land should always be produced as the old is made to disappear. It is only required that, at all times, there should be a just proportion of land and

153

water upon the surface of the globe, for the purpose of a
habitable world.

Neither is it required in the actual system of this earth, that
every part of the land should be dissolved, in its structure, and
worn away by attrition, so as to be floated in the sea. . . . Many
. . . irregularities may appear, without the least infringement
on the general system. (Hutton 1788: 301)

In this case, whilst erosion had been previously discussed in
empiricist terms, no specific claims about the global distribution of
wasting had been made. Hence, the teleologically based reasoning
for a balanced pattern of erosion does not merely formulate prior
contentions, but contributes novel claims. The other three
examples are less distinctly concerned with novel information and
its evaluation support. They resemble formulations in that they
begin with re-statements of the immediately preceding information,
but they include fresh claims of their own with a solely philosophical
legitimation. Thus, in this fourth section of Hutton's paper,
philosophical allusions are commonly tied to formulations although
they occasionally contribute novel knowledge claims with a purely
philosophical warrant.

On the other hand, many of the empiricist sections have a
formulatory form. On pages 288–9, four consecutive paragraphs
of material with empiricist warrants commence with specifications
of what it is that 'we' are doing:

. . . we are now to take a very general view . . . We have
already considered. . .; we are now to investigate. . . We have
already observed . . . Therefore . . . we shall have learned . . .

A similar tendency can be detected throughout this section. It is
my suggestion that the differences between the textual organisation
of this section and that of the earlier (informational) section of
Hutton's paper can be ascribed to their roles. The fourth, final part
of the paper contains Hutton's conclusion and, I suggest, its
characteristics are dominated by its concluding role. Even at the
commencement of this part it is suggested that the geological
theory has been completely put forward already:

[Considerations on the orderliness and disorderliness of the
globe] find the most perfect explanation in the theory which we
have been endeavouring to establish; for they are the facts from

whence we have reasoned, in discovering the nature and
constitution of this earth. (Hutton 1788: 285)

Thus, the whole of the fourth section is presented in the form of a
formulation of the foregoing theory. The details of the theory are
restated in the empiricist portions of this fourth section, which
explains their presentation in terms of summings-up. And the
philosophical allusions all serve to elucidate (*ex post facto*) **the
legitimacy, and indeed the inevitability, of the geological theory on a
priori** grounds. Accordingly, it is possible to contend that Hutton's
references to philosophical bases for knowledge evaluation within
this particular paper all occur as components of formulations.

Conclusion/formulation

Using the example of Hutton's celebrated scientific text, it has
been possible to examine how scientific arguments effect their
influence on readers or recipients. Because of the apparent
agreement of historical commentators about the prevalence of
philosophical allusions in Hutton's text it was decided to focus on
this feature. From a study of this feature the (by now widely
accepted) view that readers are actively presupposed in the text's
construction has been confirmed. But the existence of discrepant
readings of Hutton's theory means that texts cannot be supposed
to be routinely effective in enthralling readers. This analysis has
investigated how texts can be said to be constructed to influence
readers without being held to dominate them.

The way in which this occurs is suggested by analogy to the
interactive functions of language highlighted by conversation
analysts. Conversation analysis suggests that a question, for
example, is normatively followed by an answer. While this does
not mean than an answer is automatically provided after any
question, it does indicate that the next utterance (or action) after a
question will be interpreted in the light of the question's having
been asked. Many types of response, such as a change of topic,
would therefore be seen as evasions. A conversational turn creates
an interpretative space which does not constrain what can next be
said or done but does limit the interpretations which can be placed
on subsequent utterances or actions. Similarly Hutton's text can be
said to project a readership which it then aims to persuade (or,
more precisely, a readership with certain characteristics which it

seeks to satisfy) but this procedure is not automatic. The text does, however, limit the space for the reader's interpretative work. Subsequent studies will be required to show whether this mechanism is repeated in other aspects of Hutton's text beside the philosophical allusions. These components have been selected for study simply because of their enduring appeal for historical commentators. Equally, the texts of other scientific authors must be considered and even other kinds of technical or factual text. But this study has, at least, provided further grounds for regarding arguments as interactive – both fashioning and enlisting readers' interests – and, through the analogy to control in the conversational situation, has proposed a mechanism through which the projection and enrolment of interests operates. In this way it has sought to clarify how technical texts operate as a nexus of persuasion, action and belief.

Notes

I should like to express my gratitude to John Law for his helpful comments on the first draft of this paper.
 1 For a review of the analyses of the implied reader and their connections with the work of semioticians see Culler (1981) chapters 3 and 5.
 2 Hutton (1788) is helpfully reprinted with an editor's introduction as Eyles (1970).

References

Bailey, E.B. 1967. *James Hutton – The Founder of Modern Geology*. Amsterdam: Elsevier.

Barnes, Barry 1977. *Interests and the Growth of Knowledge*. London: Routledge & Kegan Paul.

Barnes, Barry and Shapin, Steven (eds) 1979. *Natural Order*. London and Beverly Hills: Sage.

Callon, Michel and Law, John 1982. 'On Interests and their Transformation: Enrolment and Counter-Enrolment'. *Social Studies of Science* 12: 615–25.

Cuff, E.C. 1980. 'Some Issues in Studying the Problems of Versions in Everyday Situations'. University of Manchester, Department of Sociology, Occasional Paper No 3.

Culler, Jonathan 1981. *The Pursuit of Signs*. London: Routledge & Kegan Paul.

Davies, G.L. 1969. *The Earth in Decay*. London: MacDonald.

Dean, D.R. 1975. 'James Hutton on Religion and Geology: the Unpublished Preface to his *Theory of the Earth* (1788)'. *Annals of Science* 32: 187–93.

Eyles, V.A. (ed.) 1970. *James Hutton's System of the Earth*. New York: Hafner.

Eyles, V.A. and Eyles, J.M. 1951. 'Some Geological Correspondence of James Hutton'. *Annals of Science* 7: 353–62.

Foucault, Michel, 1970. *The Order of Things*. London: Tavistock.

Garfinkel, Harold and Sacks, Harvey 1970. 'On Formal Structures of Practical Actions'. In McKinney, J.C. and Tiryakian, E.A. (eds). *Theoretical Sociology*. New York: Appleton-Century-Crofts: 337–66.

Geikie, Archibald 1962. *The Founders of Geology*. New York: Dover Reprints.

Gerstner, P.A. 1968. 'James Hutton's Theory of the Earth and his Theory of Matter'. *Isis* 59: 26–31.

Grant, R. 1979, 'Hutton's Theory of the Earth', in Jordanova, L.J. and Porter, Roy (eds). *Images of the Earth*. Chalfont St Giles: British Society for the History of Science: 23–38.

Heritage, J.C. and Watson, D.R. 1979. 'Formulations as Conversational Objects'. in Psathas, George (ed.). *Everyday Language: Studies in Ethnomethology*. New York: Irvington: 123–62.

Hindess, Barry 1982. 'Power, Interests and the Outcome of Struggles'. *Sociology* 16: 498–511.

Hutton, James 1788. 'Theory of the Earth'. *Transactions of the Royal Society of Edinburgh* 1: 209–304.

Hutton, James 1795. *Theory of the Earth with Proofs and Illustrations*. 2 vols. Edinburgh: Cadell and Davies (vol. 3 1899. London: Geological Society).

Iser, Wolfgang 1974. *The Implied Reader*. London: Johns Hopkins.

Iser, Wolfgang 1978. *The Act of Reading*. London: Routledge & Kegan Paul.

Kress, Gunther (ed.) 1976. *Halliday: System and Function in Language*. London: OUP.

Mulkay, Michael and Gilbert, G.N. 1981. 'Putting Philosophy to Work: Popper's Influence on Scientific Practice'. *Philosophy of the Social Sciences* 11: 389–407.

Mulkay, Michael and Gilbert, G.N. 1982. 'Accounting for Error: How Scientists Construct their Social World when they Account for Correct and Incorrect Belief'. *Sociology* 16: 165–83.

O'Rourke, J.E. 1978. 'A Comparison of James Hutton's *Principles of Knowledge* and *Theory of the Earth*'. *Isis* 69: 4–20.

Playfair, John 1805. 'Biographical Account of the Late Dr James Hutton'. *Transactions of the Royal Society of Edinburgh* 5: 39–99.

Porter, Roy 1977. *The Making of Geology*. Cambridge: CUP.

Woolgar, Steve 1981. 'Interests and Explanation in the Social Study of Science'. *Social Studies of Science*. 11: 365–94.

Wootton, Anthony 1975. *Dilemmas of Discourse*. London: Allen & Unwin.

Yearley, Steven 1982. 'The Relationship Between Epistemological and Sociological Cognitive Interests'. *Studies in History and Philosophy of Science* 13: 353–88.

Yearley, Steven 1984. *Science and Sociological Practice*. Milton Keynes: Open University Press.

The question of ideology: Althusser, Pecheux and Foucault

Mark Cousins and Athar Hussain

Abstract

Althusser's essay on ideology revived Marxist analyses of ideology, and charted a path for their further development. Michel Pecheux's *Language, Semantics and Ideology* is undoubtedly the most imaginative attempt to develop Althusser's sketch of theory of ideology. The first part of the paper deals with Pecheux, and goes on to show that his reformulation of the category of interpellation in Althusser leads in the end to the dissolution of the category of ideology itself. This is not a failure but a symptom of the fundamental difficulties which beset the problem of ideology as it has been posed. The second section of the paper is devoted to an examination of the implications of Foucault's analyses for the discussions of ideology.

1 Introduction

Marxist theories of ideology move in profound conformity with the dominant lines of thought within sociology. Society is conceived as an object of a special type, a type strictly distinguished from other objects. One element of its special character is that it functions as a coherent entity and must be conceived in that light. An enduring and constitutive condition of this object is that it is conceived as the product of two elements – agency and structure. Taken together the action of agency and structure upon each other produce society. But to know this, to know how society is produced in this way, a special type of knowledge is appropriate – the social sciences. Such a knowledge is both a knowledge of objects and causes, what we may call theory and a capacity to place phenomena which are encountered into a relation with such a theory, so that they might be explained, interpreted, understood, 'read', analysed, in sum raised up from the mundane world in which they are met.

But of course, this elementary and simple claim cannot expect to gain much acceptance within the social sciences. For *within* sociology what is most clamorously present is not this fundamental identity but rather the sound of controversy. Theoretical differences proliferate, it seems to some that there is no core to sociology. These differences, these disputes present a surface of theoretical decisions which cannot be reconciled. In particular, how the structure of society is conceived, how human agency is conceived, how one determines the other, how they interact, all these theoretical issues produce interminable quarrels. Yet if disputes are real and not just a babble there must be a question, or series of questions, to which conflicting answers are addressed. We may think of this level of questions as the *a priori* of possible answers, of positive answers. Disputes occur only where there is a domain in which positive claims may be asserted. Now it is the *a priori* of possible answers which, we would argue, links Marxist theories of ideology and other sociological theories. Controversy can only take place within a controversy, dispute presupposes a positive problem.

The precise point at which Marxist theories of ideology are completely embedded in sociology is in the problem which may be called that of *representations*. For arguments about the relation of social structure and agency crystallize around the issue of representations. Representations are the point of juncture between social structure and human agency, which may be variously conceived as a distinction between the society and the individual, or between the social and the psychical, or between the mode of production and the subject. All such dichotomies require a space in which the action of such elements work their way into that product we call society. In this sense what Foucault has called the human sciences since their inception have been centrally concerned with the issue of representations, the realm in which the elements of structure and agency combine to form that particular object the social totality.

That is perhaps why no term in the social sciences is quite as loaded and burdened as that of 'representations'. It stands at a point where so many different problems intersect, at a point onto which so many theoretical issues are displaced. Merely consider how many different usages the term has to bear. Things may be said to represent other things, which are absent, by reflecting them or signifying them. In this sense 'representation' raises questions about how such representations occur and about how what is represented is related to the representation. Or the question may be about how individuals incorporate or respond to or even are an effect of representations. In this sense the problem of representation raises questions about what effect representations have upon humans, or about how relations of effects of meaning are established between humans and representations. Or the question may be how true representations are, how they may distort what they purport to represent. In this sense the problem of representation raises questions of the assessment of truth, error and knowledge in an epistemological sense. Or the question may be to what extent apparently disparate social phenomena are related by a relation of representation, such that one may be said to represent or express the other. In this sense the problem of representation raises questions of causality, the way in which one thing can determine another as its representation. All these different usages are strung together as problems of representations.

As if there were not enough, all these problems are introduced into the question of the status of sociology as a distinctive type of knowledge. Knowledge of representations, of their relations and their effects is not given to spontaneous forms of experience; it has to be produced and uncovered by social analyses. The problem of the investigation of representations is always at the same time an investigation of what is unconscious from the point of view of human experience, an investigation of the 'unthought' so that it might be 'thought' by sociology. This 'unthought' character of representations is what makes sociology possible as a distinct branch of knowledge. 'Representations' are what escape consciousness and are brought to light. In this sense social analyses have always been concerned with what is unconscious. The unconscious is a constitutive element of the problem of representations.

These things are problems which are shared by differing schools of thought. But in this paper we restrict ourselves to examining a particular Marxist theory of ideology. We have chosen to examine the work of Michel Pecheux both because of its exemplary rigour, and because it jams all these problems together in a particularly interesting form. His enterprise, however, ultimately fails as a necessary consequence of attempting to resolve all the different problems of representations in one theoretical scheme. We also think that the fact that these different problems appear to require a general solution is itself a consequence of attempting to analyse social relations by reference to a social totality. For this reason in the second part of the paper we sketch out Foucault's analysis which dispenses with the category of totality and eschews any reliance on the notion of ideology.

2 Althusser and Pecheux

In the work of Louis Althusser and his associates there is a central thesis concerning human consciousness, or experience. It is that the human subject is presented with objects for experience in such a way that commands complete assent; that there is a compelling evidentness about what exists, and a compulsive self-evidentness about the subject who experiences what exists for it. Of course this 'evidentness' is the very instrument which conceals from the subject the imaginary character of the relation of the subject to the objects of its experience. The subject sets off, unwittingly and every day, in a fictional direction. And it does so, not just by way of the church, the school, the office or the factory but also by way of wherever it is they manufacture philosophy. For the same rules apply here; the materials of the subject and his experience are fashioned and refashioned into models which make the evidentness of the subject ever more systematic and secure.

This is why Althusser's work takes as one problem something which is usually counted as two problems; the analysis of theoretical error and the analysis of social relations. In his hands the criticism of philosophical positions (idealism) and the attempt to construct a (materialist) conception of knowledge is the same thing as the attempt to construct a systematic theory of social relations. This is much more than the conventional Marxist insistence that certain philosophical positions 'represent' in some way particular social or political positions. What is characteristic of Althusser's arguments is that in a certain sense what theoretical error 'represents' is nothing less than the spontaneous and general form of human experience. Idealism, or empiricism as it is called in *Reading Capital,* is the elaboration at a theoretical level of what is evident to humans. And what is evident to humans, is imaginary in respect to knowledge, and may be called Ideology; hence Althusser's insistence that ideology is always already there.

This dramatic proposition determines a theory of Ideology,

161

whose outlines Althusser sketched (Althusser 1971). In it two elements are bound together. Firstly he is concerned to identify the elementary form of experience. He accepts that experience shall be that of a subject, but argues that the subject far from being without conditions is an effect. Human experience is an effect, as Althusser puts it, of being interpellated as a subject. Human experience is always given in a subject-form. Not only given but *kept* in a subject-form. For the crucial side-effect of interpellation is that the process whereby the subject has been constructed is completely concealed from it. And in the place of this construction is installed an imaginary relation. The subject's spontaneous experience is that he has always been such, that he is himself the space from which he speaks and acts. He sees what he sees and he knows what he knows. Human subjects misrecognise the conditions of their own construction, and thus in the elementary forms of their experience are caught up in relations which are imaginary. These relations are not illusions, nor are they hallucinations. Indeed they are a necessary condition of the working of any social relations. But nevertheless viewed from the side of scientific knowledge they must be classed as misrecognition.

In this way epistemological concerns are intertwined with the analysis of social relations. The two meet in the theory of Ideology, and they have definite implications not only for ideological struggle but for philosophical and theoretical work. The struggle against 'idealism' is made all the more difficult because 'idealism' is the immediate form of experience given to subjects. That I think and therefore that I am; that I perceive things which exist and come to know them; in short the evident experience of experience, all this in Althusser's argument not only constitutes the grounds of idealism/empiricism but is its strongest ally – quotidian life. Idealism/empiricism has, does, and will receive its daily confirmation and validation of experience because that daily experience of subjects is constructed in the same imaginary relation which idealist philosophy spins. In this, materialism has the task of an inverted Penelope. The shroud which it spends all day unpicking is mysteriously rewoven by the following morning. Idealism always engulfs the work of materialism. It therefore becomes a strategic necessity to work out the connection between idealism/empiricism and the experience of subjects.

If Althusser's chapter 'From Capital to Marx's Philosophy' in *Reading Capital* is read alongside the paper on Ideology, it is clear how the epistemological theses upon ideological knowledge relate to the analysis of subjects' experience. And it is in relation to this problem that the work of Michel Pecheux may be considered. Althusser's paper identified interpellation as the mechanism by which individuals become subjects, but it provides only a cursory indication of that mechanism. Michel Pecheux in *Language, Semantics and Ideology* (Pecheux 1982) attempts to rectify and advance the conception of interpellation, especially in relation to the problem of meaning. His text stands as a dashing, acute and inventive attempt to sustain and develop the Althusserian position. The extent to which it cannot, is itself a tribute to the text, to its unflinching recognition of what must be argued if that position is not to fall. Pecheux is concerned to elucidate the relation of interpellation and especially the means by which the subject takes itself as self-evident, by which its status as an effect, a construction, is concealed and annulled. He does this by developing the use of psychoanalytic concepts which had been hinted at in Althusser. He deals directly with the relation of ideology and the unconscious. But this part of his contribution is made by a lengthy detour; an examination of the history of philosophy's attempt to grasp certain ambiguities in meaning. This history, he claims, still dominates contemporary linguistics. In this strategy Pecheux follows Althusser's own: that the structure of ideological relations can best be conceptualised after working through philosophical theses. The 'errors' and impasses of the latter, when worked over and through, themselves contain the secret of the former. The structure of idealism condenses and epitomizes the mechanisms of ideology.

However, we leave aside Pecheux's discussion of the problem of meaning and concentrate on his elaboration of the mechanism of interpellation. It will be remembered that for Althusser ideology 'hails' individuals as subjects. Not only does it hail them in the sense of catching their attention but it succeeds so completely that subjects spontaneously misrecognize the conditions of their productions as subjects, their 'vocations', and they accept what ideology produces in them with a blithe assertion of its evidentness, that this is indeed how it is. At the heart of this misrecognition is the spontaneous impression that existence is really quite simple, as simple in fact as the logicians' examples drawn from history, astronomy and geography. Everything is like the knowledge of battles, stars and rivers. It is obvious that words name things, it is obvious that you and I are subjects. But for Althusser any investigation of the mechanisms of ideology must start by seeing that this obviousness is in fact one of the effects, perhaps *the* effect of ideology. Interpellation is the mechanism not simply of constituting subjects but of installing in them a profound sense of the obviousness of their position. Subjects are not frogs always waiting to be kissed back into being princes.

How does interpellation work? Althusser relies upon two traditional Marxist examples to stage it for us as a little theoretical theatre: the police and God. A policeman shouts 'Hey, you there'; someone turns round. He believes that it is he who is hailed, that the 'you there' referred to him. Or again, religion addresses individuals as God speaking through it to You. Pascal's Christ says 'It is for you that I have shed this drop of my blood.' The subject may respond to this voice; in assenting to the voice of God it recognizes that God has called out to it. It is the subject who has been called. Now given the first example of the policeman, interpellation might seem to involve the subject who is interpellated, the subject who interpellates and the action of interpellation. But God? So it must be *ideology* which interpellates. God is that which the subject recognizes as hailing him. So the relation of interpellation is what Althusser calls an imaginary relation, an imaginary relation of God(S) to the subject(s). Yet this is more than just being accosted by an imaginary being, and believing it to have recognized one, and then to recognize it. We recognize, in this case, that we are subjects through the Subject; we are thus subjects to the Subject. We are made in His image after all. So much so that in his turn, his Son was sent as a human subject to enact the drama and promise which is given to human subjects – that they may return and re-enter the Lord's bosom. To elucidate this theatre with greater precision, Althusser abandons the voice, and stages the drama in terms of the looking glass.

His task is to elucidate what he means by 'the duplicating of the Subject into subjects and of the Subject itself into a subject-Subject'. (Althusser 1971 pp. 180–1), which he takes to be a theoretical account of the relation of God and believers. The relation is what he calls *speculary:* in the glass (and not at all darkly) they see the Subject to which they are subjected. But this speculary relation is *double*; they also see the subject which is interpellated. It must be themselves, that is it must be us, of whom I am one. Finally, they see what they see. There is no reason to suppose that there is anything other than what they see, and there is no reason to doubt what they see. Through this wonderful stage effect Althusser claims that interpellation achieves four things.

Individuals as interpellated as subjects; subjects are subjected to the Subject; within a play of misrecognitions, the subject recognizes the Subject, recognizes other subjects, and himself as a subject. And all this is impeccably dressed as the obvious, self-evident and inescapably real, for the hapless actor.

It is this mechanism which Pecheux seeks to specify in greater detail. His general question is how interpellation works in respect to what is generally called language and meaning. His more particular question is how is it that the subject should be so convinced of the evident character of things including the subject's own identity. One major problem is that, as Paul Hirst has demonstrated, the Althusserian 'subject' is not in fact constituted by interpellation. To support the process of misrecognitions it must always already be a subject in fact and not just by conviction. Secondly, the Althusserian subject remains a unity; despite the Lacanian references the 'subject' remains a being of consciousness (Hirst 1979). At least on the second issue Pecheux had tried to reformulate the category of the subject so that the subject is not a unity; it is a 'contradictory' entity and one for which a more consistently psycho-analytic topography is appropriate. His starting point for developing this problem lies in the recognition that interpellation, although it may be experienced as recognition is really a question of identification. Individuals identify with something such that they are constituted as subjects.

Identification entails just such a 'contradictory' move. The individual identifies himself *as* a subject by identifying *with* something external. Once achieved such identification may seem to the subject no more than the recognition of what has always been so. The identify of the subject, the conviction of this identity derives then from the irruption of 'strangeness into the familiar'. Identification is made with this strangeness by which it becomes constitutive of identity. This fundamental element of interpellation corresponds, of course, to what Pecheux has already designated as the *preconstructed*. Its effect is the discursive means whereby the individual can be captivated in an identification with something external to it but which thereby becomes incorporated as the ground of its subjectivity. This 'contradiction' in the subject is the means whereby the subject can perceive itself as a unity, while being made up of difference.

This relation is exploited by certain 'childish' jokes: 'I have three brothers 'Mathew, Luke and myself.' Such jokes lift the corner of the curtain of identification to reveal, through their 'mistakes', that identity is always also an identification with something external. The same joke is at work when desires are called 'vocations'. This mechanism of the preconstructed which supports interpellation is in Pecheux's words 'an astonishing mixture of absurdity and evidentness' (107), in that the subject's identity comes from elsewhere, but in such a way that makes it appear to have sprung from the subject itself. Pecheux christens this ridiculous origin of self-evidence, the 'Munchausen effect, in honour of the great Baron who lifted himself into the air by pulling up his own hair.'

It should now be clear that the question of the evidentness of the subject is very strictly tied to the means of interpellation itself. The identification of *s* with *S*, to use Althusser's terms, is effected by the preconstructed. But the action of identification has as one of its side effects, perhaps as its elementary effect, the complete effacement of its action. The whole staging of the drama is quite hidden from the view of the subject's *ego*. All that the subject knows is what he knows and that it is he who knows it. He knows what he wants, and what he owes. Above all he says what he means (or at least he knows he can do and even if he thinks there are occasions when he should not say what he means, he has the even deeper conviction that he says no more than he means). Language is, as far as he is concerned, transparent.

It is through this tissue of the self-evidentness of the subject and the givenness of his world, through the problem of obviousness, that Pecheux attempts to deal with the question of meaning. He is concerned to avoid the problem of meaning as it appears within philosophy and linguistics. Above all he is determined to avoid conceptualizing meaning in such a way that it is continuously torn between *langue* as a system, and *parole* as a subjective exterior. For him meaning in general is not a problem; the general problem is that of ideology, the domain of significations and their effects upon subjects. It is not 'meaning' which is at stake; it is particular meaning effects upon subjects. This leads to the radical implications that one cannot speak of natural language as containing meaning at all. Meaning, for Pecheux, ceases to be a property. Meaning is neither more nor less than a particular effect upon a subject. The material character of the meaning of words and utterances lies not in the words and utterances themselves; there are no elementary lexical and syntactic units of meaning. The analysis of meaning in language should, properly speaking, be reposed as an analysis of meaning effects upon subjects within discourse. This is altogether counter-intuitive; it goes not only against conventional theories of meaning but also against the 'evidence' of daily experience that words have a meaning, and name things. But this very fact, that it flies in the face of what is evidently the case, is a token, for Pecheux, that it is on the right track. For within such arguments, as was outlined above, philosophical theories and mundane experiences are at one in Ideology in effacing the real mechanisms of determination. Pecheux proposes not simply a competing explanation, but an explanation which will explain the misrecognition by experience of what is given to experience. The self-evidentness of the subject, the 'Munchausen effect' is the hinge of this argument.

Having rejected semantics, Pecheux argues that the meaning (effects) of particular words and utterances depends not upon the words or utterances themselves but upon what he calls the 'discursive formation' in which they appear. As a consequence it follows that under certain conditions different words and utterances may have identical meaning-effects, and conversely under certain other conditions the same words and utterances can lead to different meaning effects. This is not a question of polysemy on the one hand or a question of context on the other. It is a more sweeping assertion than either of these issues; it is that there is literally *no* meaning save within a discursive formation. A discursive formation is a particular distribution of interpellations; and within discourse those interpellations are effected through *preconstruction* and *articulation*. A discursive formation achieves certain meaning effects for/upon the subject and at the same time completely conceal from that subject, the discrepancies that enter him. Subjects appear pre-eminently subjects of their own discourse. Subjects receive their reality as a system of significations (discursive formations) but they experience this as an unproblematic horizon of objects, known by their names.

This 'reality' is in fact a series of representations which not only constitute him, and press him between them but then blind him to all but himself. Subjectivity, in this account, is a *travesty*. Pecheux extends Althusser's account of the subject by calling that part of subject, in which this imaginary relation is installed, the *ego*. It is here that the blindness/self evidentness of the subject is located; it is here that the subject lacks any grasp of its subjection. This may indeed rectify part of Althusser's category the subject; the subject does not have to be a unity merely that a part of it, the *ego*, shall conceive of itself as a unity. But there are consequences of this

167

rectification. The introduction of the category of the *ego* implies that the structure of the subject is to be conceived in such a way that ties it more directly to the psychical mechanisms postulated by psycho-analysis than Althusser granted. We shall consider this problem below; for the moment it is sufficient that Pecheux uses the category of the ego to account for the appearance of the unity of the subject; the subject always and everywhere has this subject form. The *preconstructed* gives the subject the world of things, what is there and what it means. Articulation provides and sustains the subject with a relation to that meaning. Taken together they provide the subject with an experience of unity because they are repeated within the subject's own utterances as his own discourse.

Meaning effects are produced then through interpellation. The analysis of 'meaning' is therefore an analysis of effects. Within discursive formations meaning effects are produced not by language as such, but by the series of representations, with their linguistic supports. We would not expect the analysis of meaning effects to follow the same path as the analysis of meaning within semantics. It would not work at the level of lexical or syntactical analysis. It would work at the level of the relation between the representation and the subject. Although Pecheux does not detail what such an analysis would include he makes it clear that an important element is the analysis of forms of synonymy, paraphrase and substitution between elements of discourse. He introduces a distinction, to clarify this issue, between equivalence and implication. A relation of equivalence between two elements of a discursive formation means that it makes no difference whether one uses the term A or B. But in the relation of inference in which to state A→B is not equivalent to B→A; it is as if something has placed A and B in a linear sequence. Here *articulation* has intervened in a way which Pecheux designates as the *intra-discourse*, that is the relation of the discourse to itself. That is the relation of what I have said before, to what I am saying now and to what I will say afterwards. It is what constitutes the thread of my discourse, the way in which one thing 'naturally' follows another. This distinction permits Pecheux to propose another means whereby the subject 'forgets' the determination of his discourse. It is this: that the subject's identification with something is experienced not as something external to oneself but as something *already* thought or said by oneself. Articulation induces one to misrecognize exteriority for anteriority. It is yet another discursive means whereby the subject experiences himself as the subject of his discourse. It is the very ruse whereby one is blinded to the Other.

One part of Althusser's intention was clearly that a theory of Ideology should account for the way in which subjects 'work by themselves', in the sense of being subject to those representations, which in the last instance functioned to reproduce, for example, capitalist relations of production. Ideology performs this task by recruiting individuals through interpellations; it conveys to subjects whatever is functional to capital, and incarnates these functions as positions for the subject. Consequently, Althusser's proposals bring together two registers. Firstly, the question of the representations which are supposed to secure such reproduction, and secondly, the question of that part of the individual which is interpellated. Let us call this second question, the question of the subject, an issue of *psychical relations*. Althusser himself does not address the question directly, and it is left open what sort of psychical apparatus might support the action of interpellation. Only a faint Lacanian aura is left surrounding the problem. Pecheux confronts both these issues, of the action of representations and of the psyche. In this solution to the problem of the psyche, he resolves several problems which haunted Althusser's account. But in doing this he undermines the entire premiss of a theory of Ideology; that is, an account of how representations which are 'motivated' by the function of reproduction can bear upon individuals. The 'psyche' that emerges in Pecheux's argument is certainly more satisfactory from a psycho-analytic point of view; but it is very difficult to see how such a psyche can be drawn into a relation of flawless subjection to the exigencies of capitalist reproduction.

This can be seen in terms of the problem of the unconscious. Althusser had hurriedly raised the problem of the unconscious by linking it to ideology; both were without history in the sense that they were not the product of history but were the conditions of existence of social relations and subjects. Moreover, he proposed that ideology was *unconscious* in that its action was veiled from subjects. But these correspondences were developed no further; there was no consideration of the *unconscious* as a component of the psychical apparatus. As a consequence a central problem, the relation of representations to the psyche itself could not be posed. And this question must be faced if the category of interpellation is to be sustained. At the very least it must be shown how the

169

psychical apparatus can support the 'subject effect'. How do Baron Munchausen's unconscious processes work?

In his conclusion Pecheux faces these problems. We can approach them by asking what these 'representations' are which hail and interpellate subjects. Pecheux considers this from the side of the psyche rather than from the more trodden side of the question, of how socially motivated 'ideas' or 'rituals' are incorporated into the subject. If these representations work by *signifying*, what does signification entail? In answering this question Pecheux wishes at all costs, and for reasons which will be obvious by now, to avoid treating signification as any kind of communication, as the transmission of a meaning to a subject. His rejection of semantics denies that meanings can be specified prior to their effects. In this strict sense the representations from which ideologies are spun are not meanings which 'persuade' people of this or that; they do not 'socialize' people into attitudes; they do not convey 'meanings'. If they signify, they are not even signs, which represent things for subjects. If they are what interpellate individuals as subjects they are signifiers. Pecheux rigorously transposes to Ideology the terms normally reserved for conceiving of the unconscious, since it is in respect to the unconscious that the doctrine of signification he employs was developed by Lacan. He compares the representations (signifiers) to dream thoughts. 'No subject as such is their cause; quite the contrary, it is in these representations that the subject will arrive, finding themself hooked on to them, identified with them, with all the strangeness of the evident familiarity' (p. 187). Logically, these representations are prior to meaning and subjects. In signifying they are without meaning as such.

If, then, the representations of the ideological domain are to work through interpellation, they are constrained to follow the path of whatever goes to constitute the subject in its imaginary identifications. If representations are signifiers they do not represent things for subjects; they represent subjects for other signifiers. It follows that as such representations are *non-sense,* and become sense only in the moment that they become meaning effects upon individuals as subjects. Interpellation imposes sense upon representations and subjectivity upon individuals. For Pecheux 'the signifier represents nothing for the subject, but operates on the subject outside any grasp of his' (p. 190). Lacan had been captivated by the proper name as the model for this, the designation of a subject who is the slave 'of a discourse in whose universal movement his place is already inscribed at his birth if only in the form of his proper name' (Lacan 1966 p. 495). The proper name, your name, designates you without representing you. Yet you look up when your name is called. And now the circle is complete. Pecheux, in elaborating the mechanism of interpellation started from Althusser's little drama of hailing. He sees that the proper name and identification with it form a privileged example. For the proper name functions as the example of a signifier in the process of the constitution of the subject. It also functions as the elementary case of the preconstructed. The mechanisms of interpellation have been made consistent with at least a Lacanian account of the subject. But the price is ruinous in terms of any theory of Ideology as an element of the social totality.

The relation of the Subject (S) to the subject (s) in Althusser, in its very vagueness, purported to be able to cover the problem both of the way in which S was functional to the reproduction of the relations and production, *and* the mechanism of the subjection of s to S. For this to be even remotely plausible, Althusser must have covert recourse to a theory of meaning in which meanings are independent of the subject, in which meanings can be constituted by the needs of social reproduction and installed in the subject. But such a theory, or presupposition, of the nature of meaning or signification has been decisively rejected by Pecheux. His account of the subject's constitution by, and subjection to representations-as-signifiers entails that the subject can no longer be the simple bearer of 'motivated' representations whose general signifier is whatever reproduces (or indeed transforms) social relations. The signifiers through which the subject takes up his place are wildly eccentric to the task of reproducing any particular type of society. Insofar as Althusser's S has been replaced by the Lacanian Other, there is no possibility in which a psychical structure can be recruited to the task of embodying whatever is functionally required by a mode of production. This is not in any sense to pit the psyche against regular social relations, or to even assert a necessary general clash between psychical and social relations. It is simply to point out in respect to a general theory of Ideology that the Other is not reducible to a set of social functions. The Other cannot be sociologized.

For the Althusserian scheme requires, 'in the last instance', a harmonious isomorphism between social and psychical relations. Two totalities, the social and the psychical, must happily touch each other at a point, the subject, at which social functions can be realized and where psychical relations are, at least, smoothly geared to them. Pecheux's account disrupts this. The subject can no longer be induced to ensure reproduction by being the slave to commands that have originated elsewhere. If the subject's continuous performance of rituals is to be analyzed one would turn to the question of repetition rather than of reproduction. Moreover, the second problem, that of 'motivated' representations, is itself displaced. As Pecheux remarks in the conclusion, the production of humans according to certain norms, in pursuit of certain objectives in respect to behaviour does not have to be conceptualized through the category of Ideology at all. For Ideology always entails representations for a subject; the signification/subject axis is always the centre of analysis even if what is in question are rituals and behaviours. Yet there are many rituals, many social practices, which are not usefully conceived as simply forms of signification in any sense at all. It is sufficient to see that at the end of his argument, Pecheux, having sought with exemplary rigour to reformulate and extend the category of interpellation, faced the dissolution of the very category of Ideology itself.

3 Foucault

We turn now to an examination of the implications of Foucault's analyses for the discussion of ideology. To discuss them in the context of an argument devoted thus far to Althusser and Pecheux's discussion of ideology may indeed seem odd. Except for a few remarks in interviews and lectures (*Power/Knowledge*), deprecating excessive concern with the question of ideology, he studiously avoids the question. Moreover, his detailed analyses steer well away from contemporary disputes about ideology, subjectification etc. None the less, Foucault's works have profound implications for the way in which the question of ideology has been raised. His work is vast and we have discussed it in detail elsewhere, here we concentrate on the main themes which have a direct bearing on the question of ideology, and the ones we have chosen to discuss are as follows:

1) Foucault's approach to the process of subjectification;
2) techniques of individualization (*assujettisements*) characteristic of modernity;

3) the notions of the 'police' and 'bio-power';
4) reasons for revolt and the failure of power relations to
achieve their intended effect;
5) the status of illusions;
6) science and non-science.

In one of his later writings (*The Subject and Power*), looking back over his works, Foucault argues that his objective has always been to write a history of different modes by which individuals in contemporary Western societies are made subjects – that is, endowed with certain attributes and capacities, turned into objects of social practices and made fit to occupy particular positions. Generally speaking, this process of subjectification is premissed on the hypothesis that the individual inhabiting a society is not a pregiven entity on which social relations come to bear and which is seized upon by the relations of power. Among the diverse modes of subjectification he identifies three as the main concern of his case studies. The first is the emergence of discourses of man (philology, biology and economics) around the turn of the nineteenth century which assigned to humans the identities of speaking subject, the labouring subject and a living subject. The second refers to ·'dividing practices' which classified humans into the sane-mad, the healthy-sick and the law-abiding-law-breakers. And, finally, the third concerns how diverse discourses and practices came to construct the artefact 'sexuality' and endow it to humans. These envelop all of Foucault's main works and it is instructive to see how these operate in his analyses.

The loci of dividing practices to which Foucault refers are obviously the asylum, the clinic and the prison – the subject matter of three of Foucault's principal works. To begin with all three are institutions of internment – semi-enclosed domains housing special categories of individuals and governed by projects of reform, cure and correction. These three institutions in their modern form are all relatively recent: they emerged more or less simultaneously around the turn of the nineteenth century. This, Foucault would argue, has not been an accidental conjunction but an index of their intertwined genealogies. For they all developed out of the dissolution of the polymorphous regimes of succour, cure, correction and punishment which traversed pre-modern institutions of internment. From the point of view of the process of subjectification their principal feature is that they house individuals who have strayed away from the norms of reason, health or lawful conduct – they are all 'abnormals'. They are the sites of dividing practices; by separating out the 'abnormals' they cast a grid of binary classifications onto the whole population. Now, a thesis which permeates all of Foucault's work is that starting from the end of the eighteenth century reflections on adult normal humans grew out of reflections on their converse – the 'abnormals' and children. There was, as it were, a circular movement: the normal adults examined the 'abnormals' and children as special species and in time ended up using those investigations themselves as the vantage point for their own analysis. To deploy the imagery of the game of mirrors which figures so prominently in the discussion of ideology and self-consciousness, it was as if these special species formed the mirror in which normal adults came to recognise themselves. Foucault puts it thus: '. . . when one wishes to individualise the healthy, and normal and law-abiding adult, it is always by asking him how much of the child he has in him, what secret madness lies within him, what fundamental crime he has dreamt of committing' (*Discipline and Punish:* 193). And, as we shall see, he deploys a variant of the similar argument in his later *The History of Sexuality.* Now the general argument is that practices bearing on those at the margin of normal adult population and discourses on them are an important component of the disparate configuration which constitutes the process of subjectification in modern societies.

As for the third mode of subjectification singled out by Foucault, the argument is that starting from the eighteenth century there was a profusion of discourses on sexuality, initially concerned with hysteria, infantile sexuality and sexual perversions which in time furnished the conceptual grid for the examination of adult heterosexual behaviour. In the last two books published just before his death, he shifts the focus away from sexuality to the notion of the subject in discourses starting from the Greek philosophy.

It is now clear that, in a general sense, Foucault's analyses imply a critique of those theories which locate the human subject as the source of all social relations, make it the fount of meaning, knowledge and action. Thus far he could be said to share those aims which underline Althusser and Pecheux's work on ideology. This, however, is the limit of concurrence; the detailed texture of their respective arguments is marked out by fundamental differences. Rather than pose subjectification as a general problem of how humans are made subjects, Foucault simply replaces it with two specific problems: first, how has the individual become a problem for knowledge in Western culture, and, second, how are humans made subjects in Western culture? This displacement may well seem an extension of that general problem. As against general discussions of recognition and mutual recognition, detailed analyses of social relations in specific historical conjunctures open up a rich seam of possibilities for further concrete analyses. But this simply misses the point of this displacement.

First of all it may be argued that the general question of how subjects are formed itself commits one to a particular type of answer to it. For to pose such a question is to presuppose that a general account of the formation of the subject can be offered, it casts the subject in a particular mould even before it is answered. The criticisms of the Althusserian theory of ideology to which we referred earlier (15–6) rightly point this out. What Foucault says of power relations is directly relevant here. That is, they are open textured, exercised from innumerable points, prima-facie they are not limited to particular domains and they take a wide diversity of forms. *Pari passu*, there is no general structure to the processes of subjectification, they can take a wide variety of forms, the sites of relations formative of subjects are diverse and, more importantly, they do not cohere. The problem of the formation of subjects is open-ended, it does not lend itself to an exhaustive account. By itself this argument may seem empty, a licence for the proliferation of all manner and all varieties of analyses. But its purpose is to loosen the hold of the traditional schema for dealing with the question of the subject. At this stage it is instructive to trace some of the ramifications of this argument by way of a contrast.

In the analyses of subjectification such as those of Lacan, Althusser, Pecheux, or for that matter Hegel, a special privilege is accorded to signifying practices and signification. Foucault's analyses, especially his later *Discipline and Punish* and *The History of Sexuality* are marked out by their concerted attempt to steer well away from the categories of signification and ideology. It may be said that just as they devalue the importance of repression in the field of power relations, they denigrate the pertinence of signification and signifying practices in his analyses of the techniques of individualisation characteristic of modernity.

In *Discipline and Punish* and *The History of Sexuality,* Foucault conducts an analysis of what we may term technologies of persons without presuming a given human subject. That analysis is concerned with how individuals are brought under each other's control (subjected, that is) identities by which they identify themselves and others identify them. Part 2 of *Discipline and Punish* is devoted to a discussion of disciplinary techniques which, according to Foucault, came to permeate a diverse variety of institutions. Similarly, in *The History of Sexuality*, he analyses discourses and practices concerned with sexuality in terms of physical concerns with the health and the physical well-being of the individual and population (denoted by terms such as the police and bio-politics). The Foucauldian terminology of disciplinary techniques, dressage, anatomo-politics of human body and the bio-politics of the population may seem idiosyncratic and even obfuscating. But they have a precise purpose. They draw attention to the physical and the biological dimension of the relations formative of individual identities. Moreover, their implication is that those relations need not take form of representation, mediations through consciousness.

Yet another striking feature of these analyses is the absence of any recourse to the category of ideology; they simply dispense with a category forming the middle term between power relations and psyche. This is premised on a variety of reasons, which we now consider in turn. We may recall here that the notion of ideology in Althusser and later elaborated by Pecheux is a node in a web of diverse concerns. First of all it provides an answer to the question, how are social relations reproduced? Secondly, from the point of knowledge (one may qualify, scientific), although universal, it is a misrecognition, it throws a veil of illusion over subjects; and masks its mechanisms by appearing obvious. And, finally, although not coterminous with sciences it is the obverse of sciences. Sciences are not ideologies in a double sense: their relation of reality is not imaginary, and sciences, historical materialism and perhaps psychoanalysis, can tear away the mask of ideologies, or at least lift a corner of it. In a functional sense the notion of ideology is polyvalent, it is the point of intersection of philosophical, political and epistemological concerns. It is the notion of ideology, which enables one concern to be transformed into another. Thus a critique of ideology is not so much a critique of the notion itself or of its mechanisms but this configuration of concerns itself.

To take up the question of the reproduction of social relations. The insistent resort to the category of ideology in social analyses is eventually prompted by the question: why do individuals submit to prevalent social relations, especially when they are exploitative or oppressive? For Marxists the question would read, why do the exploited not rise against exploitative economic relations? Such a question cannot but lead to a heavy reliance on the category of ideology. For the exercise of force on the model of the proverbial gunman holding a gun against the head arguably plays only an indirect and relatively marginal part in the continuation of social relations. As a result, one is impelled by the question to throw the main burden of explanation on the internal acceptance by individuals themselves of social relations. Within Marxism, the question of the exercise of force leads to an analysis of the juridico-political and, in turn, the internal submission of individuals to prevalent social relations to an analysis of ideology. In thus dividing the reasons of submission, Marxists are not breaking any new ground; special terminology and the architectonic division of social relations into the economic base and political-ideological superstructure apart, they are treading a well-worn path (for an elaboration of this argument, see Cousins and Hussain: *Foucault*, 242).

Even though Foucault does not talk about submission, he has, however, something to say about its converse: resistance to the exercise of power, albeit in the form of declamations (*The History of Sexuality*, 95–6). Where there is power there is resistance, Foucault argues. Resistances to power, he goes on, are diverse in form, heterogeneous, mobile and transitory; more important, they should not be attributed to some unique locus of revolt, a spirit of resistance or revolutionary ideology. We may now contrast this perspective on resistances to the one implicit in the binary schema of submission – external enforcement by force and internal submission by individuals. Such a schema would eventually trace resistances to either the frailty of force or the lack of legitimation (the obverse of internal submission). The general argument is that if the reasons for resistance are diverse, so are the reasons for submission, which cannot be encapsulated by any general ideological mechanism.

As for the question of the veil of ideology and misrecognitions, a novel feature of Foucault's analyses of power relations is that they are conducted in terms of aims professed in discourses accompanying the exercise of power. In fact, he has often argued that power does not hide and has nothing to hide; more specifically, since the nineteenth century the bourgeoisie have followed a strategy which is absolutely conscious, reflected and there to be read in documents. For example, he does not treat the notion of the 'police' (in its old sense of the term) as a ruse; he takes literally the concern with individual and collective welfare which it expresses. This analytical strategy, one may emphasise, goes against the very grain of the analyses conducted in terms of ideology; it may seem to betray a naive faith in the transparency of aims. In contrast to Marxists, he does not regard that professed concern with welfare as a stratagem on the part of the bourgeoisie to serve their own narrow interests under the cloak of noble concern with welfare. That policies prompted by the concern with welfare have served to perpetuate capitalism, to make it more efficient, Foucault does not dispute. But, as with truth, he would argue that to treat that concern as a ruse is to elevate it; on the contrary, welfare is not outside power, or lacking in power. Concern with welfare of individuals or population is not founded in compassion or noble sentiments; it is a 'thing of this world' embedded in constraints bearing on individuals.

In more general terms, the strategy of analysis pursued by Foucault is based on the methodological postulate that there is no meaning to discourses beyond what they say; it implies a denial of the general categories of illusion or misrecognition and a refusal to conduct a discourse parallel to the proffered given over to interpretation. However, for Foucault, if things are not hidden nor masked, they are not transparent either. They may not be visible. And he would attribute that non-visibility to the fact that the field of coverage of discourses – what they say and how they say it – is limited by their very conditions of existence. Moreover, no discourse is self-subsistent; they are nodes in a network of discursive practices. Non-visibility is simply a result of this fact that all discourses are 'partial and limited'. And an analysis such as Foucault's, with its own limitations, brings the non-visible to light by a regrouping of discursive and non-practices and tracing their ramifications. In a review of *Discipline and Punish* Deleuze called Foucault a cartographer; one might say that Foucauldian analyses are more like cartography than hermeneutics.

Although Althusser has emphasised that ideology is not a converse of sciences, that a social realm free of ideology is a chimera, none the less, in his own discussion ideology cannot but ultimately figure as an error, as a discourse which is not cognizant of its conditions of existence. For Althusserian philosophy given over as it is to the defence of sciences, historical materialism, in particular, rests on a general epistemological distinction between sciences, on the one hand, and ideology on the other. Unlike Althusser, Foucault is not committed to any materialist project of rescuing sciences from the constant encroachments of ideology, and he would argue that despite all qualifications to the contrary, the very project is premissed on a general category of error. In a review of Foucault's *The Order of Things* Canguilhem remarked that there is today no philosopher less concerned with the general norms of scientificity than Foucault. His histories are not written from the point of view progress and the dissipation of errors, social as well as epistemological. In fact, in eschewing the category of progress Foucault has been profoundly influenced by Canguilhem himself, but he has taken Canguilhem's methodological protocol a great deal further. Unlike historians of sciences, he has marked out domains of analyses cutting across intellectual disciplines and discursive and non-discursive practices. They are epistemologically heterogeneous and they do not lend themselves to assessment in terms of a norm of scientificity. Rather than with their normative assessment, Foucault is concerned with their conditions of existence and genealogy. In relation to discourses, the principal question for him is not one of error but what he in his later writings terms the 'regime of truth', and the distinction between science and non-science for him as significance only in the context of the regime of truth which started to emerge at the end of the eighteenth century. Therefore there is no general problem of ideology.

Note

This paper draws heavily on Mark Cousins: 'Jokes and Their Relation to the Mode of Production', *Economy and Society*, Vol. 14, No. 1, 1985, pp. 94–12.

References

Althusser, L. (1970): *Reading Capital*, NLB, London.
Althusser, L. (1971): *Lenin and Philosophy and Other Essays*, NLB, London.
Cousins, M. and Hussain, A. (1984): *Michel Foucault*, Macmillan, London.
Foucault, M. (1970): *The Order of Things,* Tavistock, London.
Foucault, M. (1977): *Discipline and Punish,* Allen Lane, London.
Foucault, M. (1979): *The History of Sexuality,* Vol. 1, Allen Lane, London.
Foucault, M. (1980): *Power/Knowledge,* edited by C. Gordon, The Harvester Press, Brighton.
Hirst, P. (1979): *Law and Ideology,* Macmillan, London.
Lacan, J. (1966): *Ecrits,* Editions de Seuil, Paris.
Pecheux, M. (1982): *Language: Semantics and Ideology: Stating the Obvious.*

On authority and its relationship to power

Barry Barnes

Abstract

This paper suggests an alternative to the received view of the relationship between power and authority. It regards authorities as the passive agents of powers. Thus to possess authority is to possess less than to possess power in its own right. Contrast this with the received view where to possess authority is to possess more than to possess power: authority may be power plus legitimacy, or power plus consent.

The paper goes on to consider some of the implications of this alternative view, and shows how it allows an analogy between *possessing* authority in relation to actions and *being* an authority in relation to knowledge and culture.

The received view of authority within the sociological tradition is that it is power plus: power plus consent, or power plus legitimacy, or power plus institutionalisation. There is debate and controversy about what precisely must be added to power to transform it into authority, but there is wide agreement that something must be. And there is wide agreement too that the consequent transformation enhances the effectiveness of what initially is power, that it is a transformation much to the advantage of possessors of power, even essential to their continued enjoyment of their dominant position. Power holders, it is said, do well to seek legitimacy and consent as soon as they may, so that they can enjoy the enduring benefits which flow to occupants of positions of authority.[1] Against this, I shall argue here that authority should be thought of as power minus, that to possess power is more expedient and advantageous than to possess mere authority, and that consent and legitimacy are immaterial to understanding the difference between the two attributes.

Let me hasten to add that I intend no direct frontal assault on accepted wisdom. Someone who thinks of authority as power plus and someone like myself who thinks of it as power minus will find themselves referring at times to different phenomena as authority, or manifestations of authority. There will be an insufficient number of agreed external 'facts about authority' for use in deciding between them. Hence the alternative conceptualisations will have to be compared and chosen between in terms of their pragmatic value. I do not hope to refute or decisively overthrow the power plus account. I merely seek to stress what I regard as the present value and the future promise of the power minus alternative, and recommend its use as a tool of thought. Strictly speaking, this paper is concerned only with the issues which arise from the possibility of an alternative definition of 'authority'.[2]

Power

I shall say very little about power, only as much as is necessary to carry forward the argument which follows. But it is actually necessary to offer some simple image of the nature of power in society, because there is no widely accepted account or image already in the literature. Indeed it is tempting to say that there is no account at all in the literature, accepted or not, of the basic nature of power in society.[3] There is a great deal on how to define power, how to detect its presence, how to measure it through empirical indicators and visible correlates, how to identify its material effects; but there is next to nothing upon what power is, 'in itself' as it were. Sociologists have insistently proceeded as positivists in their treatment of power, where they might with benefit have been realists.

Power is often thought of as the capacity to enforce one's will, to get things done, to press through a sequence of actions, even against opposition. But what is the capacity? What does it consist in? How does an agent (or a role perhaps) with power, differ from one lacking it? It is at this point that most of the literature goes silent. I shall try to fill the gap with a crude, prototypical image. The very act of setting it down makes its fundamental deficiencies glaringly apparent, but it will have to do for present purposes of exposition.

Think first of society as nothing more than automated, routinised collective activity, simply so many patterned collectively executed routines. This is clearly wrong. Routines are stopped and started; they are pointed this way and that; they are set in combinations and used in concert. In any particular society specific agents will be charged with the task of doing the stopping and starting, the pointing, the combining.[4] Let us take a net, then, and capture all these agents. I want to say that thereby we shall have captured all the powers in the society.

We shall, however, have captured more than the powers. Some of our captured agents, those involved in changing routines, may themselves appear to be acting routinely and automatically. Perhaps they always throw a switch when they see a certain light come on. Perhaps they have a book of rules and go by the book. For the moment, let us throw back all such agents, all those who change routines routinely. Suppose we were to end up with an empty net. I should then want to say that we had found a society without powers. But in practice many agents will always remain in the net. These are agents with *discretion* in directing routines, who act not in response to predetermined external signs but on the basis of their own judgement and decision. These, I want to say, are the powers in the society.

A power directs a routine, and directs it with discretion.[5] This is the basis of power, the nature of the capacity to enforce something upon others. The routine can, as it were, be pointed at those others or away from them; and because the pointing is at discretion it can be made consequent upon what those others do: the artillery may fire, or not; the certificate may be issued, or not; the payment may be made, or not; depending. The routine controlled may be made the basis for a threat against others. Thus, as discretion over routines is extended, power is extended; as discretion over routines is lost, power is lost.[6]

Authority

Whereas a power directs a routine with discretion, an authority directs it without discretion. All those who direct routines routinely and automatically are thus to be thought of as authorities. Like powers they switch routines on and off, point them this way and that, combine them together or separate them off. But they do so in response to external indications; the basic pattern of their actions is entirely the product of external constraint. Authority, then, is power minus discretion.

Note how this conception of authority as power minus fits perfectly well with many aspects of common usage. In Britain, for example, the monarch signs Acts of Parliament into law. The monarch possesses the authority to switch on the provisions of an Act, or to hold them back. But it is open to question whether this authority represents power. And as the point is argued in common sense discourse, it is precisely the matter of discretion which is central. Never mind which side is right or wrong. If it is thought that the monarch derives power from the need for the Royal assent, then it will be said that there is discretion in the giving or withholding of the assent. If the monarch is seen as powerless in this regard, then it will be said that the assent just must be given to any properly constituted Act, and that there is no discretion. An intuitive understanding of power as authority plus discretion is clearly evident in this example.

Authority in relation to power

Authorities direct routines routinely, in response to external signs and signals. What produces these signs and signals? They may be produced automatically, by the operation of other routines. If all of them were to be produced in this way, we should have, in a certain sense, an automated society, reminiscent of a programmed device running on the basis of a determinate, isolated and unchangeable programme. But no such society exists. In all actual societies some of the relevant signs and signals are activated at discretion, by powers. And in practice powers and authorities are coupled together by chains of such signs and signals, so that discretionary acts by powers produce determinate further acts by authorities, indeed whole chains of such further acts, with the consequence that whole systems of established routines are controlled. Or so we tend to think.

This implies that authorities serve as the passive agents of powers, that they are relays, as it were, in systems of control. Again this way of thinking is close to aspects of common usage, as when an agent is *authorised* to implement a decision, to close a company, say, or sequester funds, or buy or sell so many shares.[7]

Why should an authority reliably direct routines in conformity with the indications of a power? There may of course be any number of revelant contributory factors, but in general the authority will itself be vulnerable to the power of which it is the agent. Only this will force the authority to conform even against its own inclination, and thus to operate with complete reliability. But this, of course, implies that any power must have discretion over not one but many routines, so that those authorities operating one routine may be threatened with the application of another, and every part of the system is at once sustained by threat and a source of threat. Here is a part of what sustains the typically pyramidal patterns of power and authority.

Maximising power

Maximising power is a matter of retaining as much discretion as possible over as many routines as possible. Naturally, some routines are more strategic than others, but that can be set aside for the moment: it remains the case that to accumulate discretion over additional routines is to increase in power, and vice versa. To retain discretion in a large number of routines requires delegation; to add to the range of such routines requires additional delegation. But for the maximum retained discretion over any particular routine the requirement is that authority be delegated but not power. In the sense of the terms used here, delegates should as far as is possible be authorised, but not empowered. There is no way in which the delegation of discretion, and thus power, can be guaranteed not to amount to the loss of discretion, and thus power. The problem of the power holder in this context is to create passive agents and prevent their metamorphosis into active agents, as far as their relationship to the relevant routine or routines is concerned.[8] And it is likely enough in most actual situations of this kind that authorities will take any opportunity to move the other way, to build up a sphere of discretion and to transform authority into power.

No doubt competition for power of this kind is very widespread and commonplace, although it may not be explicitly acknowledged by the parties involved. It is almost always expedient, in so far as explicit discourse is concerned, for powers to represent themselves as authorities and to deny their possession of discretion. This serves to avert suspicion and hostility from powers 'above' who might look askance at discretion accumulating 'below' them. And it is also an expedient image to proffer to those 'below', since it represents the power holder as the mere agent of something yet more formidable and more threatening; and by presenting him as lacking all discretion it discourages all attempts to persuade, pressure or otherwise influence his judgment. For these reasons even supreme powers like to represent themselves as mere authorities, whether by appeal to supernatural power, or to the constraint of rule and commandment, or to some hypostatised entity like 'the people' or 'the general will'. Although one American President did apparently work behind the legend, 'the buck stops here', the inclination not to be a terminus of this kind must surely be very strong.

Let me return however to the actual situation wherein a power holder is surrounded with agents or delegates. Imagine that the holder of power actually does succeed in sustaining a maximum level of power, that he keeps all discretion in his own hands and enforces the position of his agents as mere authorities. How will he have done this? Part of the answer must describe how he has maintained threats against all his agents, so that their conformity is enforced even against their own inclination. But the other part of the answer must describe how that conformity is specified and defined. If an authority is to act in a determinate way according to external circumstances or signals, then that determinate way must be specified and the nature of the relevant circumstances and signals made clear. The authority must *know* what is to be done, and in response to what, and the power must know what the authority knows. The system of power and authorities must also necessarily represent a *distribution of knowledge*. In many cases the knowledge may be thought of, in the first instance, as a set of instructions or rules according to which the authority is required to act. Such rules or instructions are crucial to the business of limiting the discretion of the authority.

Authorities-on

At this point I shall make a small digression, and call attention to another aspect of the common usage of the term 'authority'. It is a form of usage to which we resort when we concern ourselves directly with the distribution of knowledge in society. It helps us to allocate and maintain credibility. It is a part of the discourse through which we announce and confirm, not who may rightly require or perform an action, but who may rightly expect belief.

We often, although not invariably, use a systematically distinct idiom when we use the term 'authority' for this kind of work. Whereas one *possesses* the authority to do or to act, one typically *is* an authority *on* something or somebody. One may be an authority on the geology of the North Sea, or Hungarian folksongs; or on Aristotle or Thomas Aquinas.

What is implied by being an authority in this way? On a power plus view of authority, an authority on, say, Aristotle would be anyone generally empowered and accepted as an expositor and interpreter of Aristotle. The authority would derive his standing wholly and entirely from his society, which would empower him to expound Aristotle, and treat his expositions as legitimate versions. Any actual connection between the authority and Aristotle, or Aristotle's texts, would be contingent, essentially accidental. A community might have a fancy for authorities familiar with the texts upon which they pronounced – or it might not: either way it would appoint what 'authorities' it wished. This, of course, is counter-intuitive. We habitually regard the connection between an authority and that upon which he is an authority as a *necessary* one. We expect an authority on Aristotle to know Aristotle, and to expound him, so far as is possible, correctly.

This habitual way of thinking is perfectly compatible with a power minus notion of authority. An authority on a text must know that text, and the very fact that the text is known is presumed to restrict discretion in expounding it. Ideally, knowledge of the text eliminates all discretion in its exposition, so that the authority becomes transparent to the text: the text shines through the authority, as it were, and makes itself visible to us directly. This, at any rate, is the theory which gives the authority its credibility, its very standing as an authority. To the extent that it is thought to lack discretion an authority is credited. To the extent that it is thought to be exercising discretion an authority is distrusted. It is no longer transparent to the text. It is no longer Aristotle who is heard, but the personal voice of his expositor. As discretion enters in, Aristotle becomes more and more distant, so that at the point of full discretion there is no longer any reason to prefer the authority to any other expositor of Aristotle. An authority on Aristotle is the passive agent of Aristotle, rather as the possessor of authority is the passive agent of a power. Note that we have authorities on Aristotle in a way that we could not contemplate having powers over Aristotle.

In discussing authorities-on, in what follows, I shall confine myself to authorities on texts; but it is worth mentioning that the same analysis applies to authorities on physical phenomena. The authority on the geology of the North Sea should ideally lack discretion as much as the authority on Aristotle. The authority must know the geological phenomena, be constrained by what is known, and thus become transparent to the phenomena. The set of relevant phenomena, a part of natural reality itself, must shine through the authority, as it were, and make itself directly visible to us. This, at any rate, is the theory which most readily lends credibility to *scientific authority*. Why should we credit our scientists if they speak of reality with discretion? Note again that we may have authorities on the geology of the North Sea in a way that we could not contemplate having powers over that geology.

A central problem

In the mainstream of sociological theory, a central problem is to account for the form and stability of systems of power and authority; this is an aspect of the most fundamental problem of all, that of the nature and basis of social order.[9] In the sociology of knowledge and culture, a central problem is to account for the form and stability of systems of cognitive authority and patterns of credibility; this is an aspect of the fundamental problem of the nature and basis of cognitive order. Both problems concern the extent to which verbal rules or instructions may be used to restrict discretion, and hence the extent to which their significance and implications can be made definite, clear and unambiguous. In an important sense, therefore, there is just one central problem here, not two. Here is the point where the study of action and the study of belief meet. Here knowledge and power, culture and social structure reveal themselves not as distinct phenomena, as is generally held, but as the very same phenomena looked at from different points of view. Here too we see that the key to a general understanding of all these phenomena lies in a proper appreciation of the characteristics of verbal communications. Any account of the possibilities of such communication is also a prototypical theory of cognitive order and of social order; and vice versa.

Possible solutions

How definite and unambiguous can the significance of a text be made? How firm and clear the implications of a rule or instruction? Opinions differ markedly, sometimes violently, on these questions within the social sciences, and the differences of opinion indicate basic differences concerning the nature of social hierarchy and social and cognitive order.

It is still widely assumed that rules or instructions can readily be made clear and definite, that they may carry fixed logical implications or fixed semantic implications, which can serve to constrain the conforming action or conforming speech of those receiving them. This is the assumption which sustains the traditional perspectives of macro-sociology, and allows social order and cognitive order to be referred to routinely as objective structures. On this view powers can use rules to bind tiers of passive agents, and hierarchies of authority are straightforwardly intelligible. On this view texts can fix their own proper exposition, and cognitive authority is straightforwardly intelligible.

It is important not to overlook the merits of this traditional point of view, or the large amounts of empirical material for which it promises a satisfactory treatment. People do report experiencing constraint when conforming to rules or instructions. People do tell of constraint in their exposition of texts. It is plausible to account for the existence of such constraint or perceived constraint, by reference to the logical or semantic implications of rules or texts. At least this acknowledges the important empirical fact that rules and texts make a difference to people. Nonetheless, it has to be recognised that this is not a point of view which has emerged from the detailed study of rule use or linguistic communication, or which has been justified ex post facto by such study. It is accepted as a general account of rules and verbal formulations which fits conveniently with traditional sociological theory, but it lacks independent justification. As such the current basis of its credibility is suspect.

Where rule use and linguistic communication has been made the subject of detailed sociological study, the conclusions arrived at have tended to be very much the opposite of those assumed above. A consensus seems to have developed, in the relevant special fields, that verbal formulations have neither fixed logical implications nor fixed semantic implications. Studies of texts and written records, whether literary, philosophical, religious, historical or even scientific, have again and again tended to support this point of view. Ethnomethodological studies of rule use and the following of instructions in everyday situations have sought to vindicate it by showing how actions are successfully made out after the fact as in accordance with rules. In both fields it is agreed that there is nothing inherent in a verbal formulation to determine its implications or define its true significance. No particular implication can be assigned unproblematically to a rule or instruction, by inspection as it were, as 'the' implication of the rule; and no particular significance can be assigned to a text as 'the' significance of the text. Therefore, it is said, implications must be derived and significances imputed entirely at the discretion of the agents involved.[10]

The consequences of such a position for an understanding of power and authority are as easy to elucidate as they are hard to accept. Having turned our assumptions about linguistic communications upside down we must expect to find our understanding of social and cognitive authority turned upside-down too. Start by thinking of a potential authority as an initially free agent confronted by verbal formulations, whether to be expounded or obeyed. Verbal formulations have neither fixed logical implications or fixed semantic implications. Therefore, it would seem, their use puts no restrictions upon the freedom of the agent: he retains his complete discretion. Even though he must act [or speak] properly and correctly, he is nonetheless free to act [or speak] as he will, since he may make what he will of the formulations to which he conforms. Where the agent is expected to expound a text there will be no 'objective' exposition available to him; he will necessarily have to practise interpretation, exegesis, hermeneutic art. His 'exposition' will be an artful creation which, rather than finding meaning in the text, will construct a meaning for the text. The exposition will, to use the now all too familiar phrase, be amenable to deconstruction. Similarly, where the agent is expected to obey an instruction, there will be no 'objective' indication of what it is so to obey; he will simply have to act and then make out the act as an obedient act. His 'obedience' will be the artful creation of ex post facto accounting, a contingent accomplishment as ethnomethodologists are apt to say.

On this view agents retain their discretion and hence remain powers: there can be no authorites as I have defined them. All attempts to create and constrain authorities fail, and putative authorities remain powers in their own right. The supposed passive agents of a power actually remain unconstrained and exercise discretion as they will; the supposed authorities on a text actually expound it as they will. Here is another admirably

189

straightforward solution to the problem of the relationship between power and authority. There is no authority, only power.

A more rigorous examination of the situation, however, indicates that it is scarcely worthwhile even to refer to power in these circumstances. Consider a chain of command along which instructions pass at the instigation of a power, the power at the top as it were. If the first link of the chain must fail, if constraint cannot be established across that link, then the second link must fail for the same reasons, and the third, and so on. Each individual in the chain retains power, full discretion, but only over his own individual acts – power of a sort perhaps, but certainly not *social* power. If verbal utterances may be given any interpretation, then social order falls apart and only isolated, atomic individual actors remain. Consider similarly an authority expounding a text. If the authority is unconstrained then for the same reasons the authority is unable to constrain. If the text can never fix its own significance than neither can any interpretation or exposition of the text fix its own significance. It is not, then, that significance comes ex post facto, but that it never comes at all. What else is an exposition of a text but a text? What else is a deconstruction of a text but a text? If the first link in a chain of interpretation must fail, then all links must fail for the same reason. Nowhere in the chain is discretion pressed upon. If verbal utterances may be given any interpretation then cognitive order falls apart, and only isolated, atomic individual believers remain.

Conclusion

I have discussed two strongly contrasting accounts of verbal communication and the use of verbally formulated rules, and have shown how they inspire contrasting views of social and cognitive authority. My purpose has been to emphasise the intimate connection between the two forms of authority, and to indicate how an understanding of power and authority in society implies an understanding of the nature of linguistically mediated communication. What I have not felt able to do in this context is actually support and commend any specific theory of such communication. The alternatives I have considered above have served for purposes of illustration only: both of them have major inadequacies. Indeed it may be that a more satisfactory account will eventually emerge from reflection upon these inadequacies.

The traditional sociological account of rules and their use reflects a deep interest in the ordered character of the social activity which people produce, and indeed in the empirical characteristics of the people producing it, but a contrasting lack of interest in rules themselves as verbal formulations. The alternative account reflects a deep interest in the nature of rules as verbal formulations, but a lack of interest in the empirical characteristics of the people employing the formulations. Indeed, some proponents of the alternative account may well consider it incorrect to impute empirical characteristics to people.

The alternative account is surely correct in its characterisation of rules and verbal formulations: they do indeed lack fixed logical or semantic implications. But this is turned into a statement about human behaviour only by making a cipher out of the individual human being. He is represented as a 'free' agent who retains discretion in the face of rules or instructions without determinate implications. Now it may well be that an abstractly conceived 'free' agent, any man with just his reason and a dictionary, may indeed be pressed nowhere in particular by rules or instructions. Such an agent may only be constrained in his understanding by fixed and clear implications of rules, implications which do not and cannot exist. But what entitles us to characterise any actual human being as such an agent? The answer must surely be: nothing at all.

What is overwhelmingly clear is that actual people in actual situations find many verbal formulations clear and unproblematic, to the extent that they are able to respond to them at once, without hesitation. However much one attends to the linguistic aspects of such formulations as 'switch on the light', exposing their formal quirks and genuine ambiguities, it is nonetheless the case that they serve as a clear and definite basis for action by particular people. Nor does the fact that linguistic formulations can always be interpreted in many ways count against the more important fact that large numbers of people will all alike take them in just one way – as, for example, on the army parade ground.

Linguistic formulations must not, for sociological purposes, be considered formally in terms of their meaning for any man with a dictionary; they must be considered empirically, behaviorally, impinging on particular groups of people.[11] If they produce a fixed and definite sense for all of a group of people, a sense sufficient for action, a sense which emerges unreflectively, automatically, as a matter of course, then they may serve as the basis for systems of authority. No matter that by taking thought alternative, equally justifiable senses might be brought to mind. No matter that another group of people confronted by the same verbal formulation might unreflectively, as a matter of course, impute one of these alternative senses as 'the' sense. No matter that a 'free' agent may be pressed to no particular sense at all by them.

The concept of a free agent has an established role in speaking of choices between alternative *actions,* but it needs to be used with great care when imported into discussions of problems of intelligibility and understanding. Here, there is a certain important sense in which we are not free. We are not always free to decide our initial, immediate understanding of or response to a verbal formulation. We often find ourselves making, without reflection, unthinkingly, as a matter-of-course, one particular response. If this is the case, and if there is uniformity of such response throughout a group, that is enough. That actual response can then be talked up, ex post facto, as the implied response, the correct response, the only sensible response, and ordered communication can be established. There is no further barrier to the erection of systems of authority as far as problems of intelligibility and clear communication are concerned.

There is not a great deal to be said about why we make these initial, matter-of-course responses, or why different people should be able to agree upon them. We do not know enough about ourselves, our congenital tendencies and competences, the malleability of these tendencies and competences, to pretend to an explanation here. But we do know how to encourage the phenomena which we cannot explain: we do know how to create unhesitating responses, uniform throughout a collectivity. What is required is the procedure involved in intensive and comprehensive socialisation: repetitive practices, drill, rote, on the one hand; shared environment, shared experiences, shared overall culture on the other. What is not attainable by reason and a dictionary may be put within reach by thorough and prolonged induction into an entire form of life.

If something along these lines were to prove correct, what would it suggest about the relationship of power and authority? It would suggest that powers may indeed entertain hopes of creating authorities, passive agents without discretion in the way they interpret instructions.[12] It would suggest that rules and instructions can indeed be successfully employed in this way, but only in delimited contexts, with particular people with a particular history. The struggle to create authorities, and to prevent their metamorphosis into powers, can be no less than a global enterprise. It involves not the mere drawing-up of rules, and some system of enforcement, but the fashioning of a whole world of social experience, and its continual maintenance and reinforcement. It involves the manipulation of education, the shaping of culture, even the refashioning of the physical environment itself. And, needless to say, such a project is always and invariably to some extent a failure. The standardisation of people and of context, essential if responses to symbols are likewise to be standardised, is always too large a task to be satisfactorily accomplished even for immediate practical purposes. We may think of powers continually at work with the objective of further restricting the discretion of their agents whilst these agents continually and ubiquitously develop the scope of their sphere of discretion within the very system of rules or instructions which is conceived of as a restriction upon them.

The problems surrounding authorities-on, and the texts they expound, are of course even more complex and difficult of solution. When a verbal communication passes from a power to an authority all that matters is uniformity of initial response. If the context is such that uniform responses exist, if all in the context take the communication to imply the same act, then successful communication occurs. But a text persists whilst contexts change. At the very least it must be considered in relation to the context in which it was written and the context in which it is read. One plausible conception of an authority on a text is of someone who seeks to regenerate the context of writing in order to rediscover the original sense of the text. But it has been much commoner in practice for such authorities to expound their texts in relation to the context in which they themselves have lived and written. Indeed, perhaps the commonest task performed by such 'authorities' has been the reinterpretation of texts to suit contemporary taste and preference: all the refinements of the hermeneutic art have been used over and over again, by generation after generation of commentators, to make texts, and notably the revered ancient texts of philosophy and religion, usable and acceptable in the current circumstances, with the usable and acceptable versions served up to eager recipients as what the texts have always meant. In exegetical enterprises of this kind ignorance of the initial context of a text is a positive advantage, since it allows that context itself to become an interpretative resource: a context may be laid on for the text wherein the text clearly means what it has to mean.

It is tempting to suggest, given this, that whereas context is essential to the social use of current rules and instructions, since they fail to generate constraint when abstracted from it, loss of context is essential to the social use of inherited texts, for the same reason.

Notes

1 Although he does not himself accept it, Wrong (1979) rightly refers to 'the familiar dichotomy of "naked" versus "legitimate" or "institutionalised" power, usually called "authority", which has become such a commonplace in the sociological literature' (pp. 39–40).

2 Matters of precise verbal definition are not of great significance in the social sciences; an exaggerated importance is often attributed to them. Martin (1977) is a writer who lays great emphasis on the importance of precise definition (p. 8). He goes on to criticise a whole series of definitions of 'power'. Dahrendorf 'defines out of existence non-legitimate structural or recurrent power relations' (p. 36). Weber 'defines . . . out of existence' power as a generalised means of achieving collective goals (p. 37). 'Parsons defines out of existence the problems which have usually preoccupied sociologists of power' (p. 38). It rather sounds as though verbal acts of definition can annihilate sociological phenomena and sociological problems. But surely all they can actually do is inhibit specific ways of using particular words, and require the use of other words instead. This, at any rate, is why I regard problems of verbal definition, including that central to the present paper, as small problems, and why I see only very limited possibilities of gain from the criticism of definitions.

3 Amongst the possible exceptions here, Talcott Parsons (1967) is pre-eminent.

4 I talk of agents as the possessors of power not out of conviction, but simply as a means of dodging for the moment some important further questions about power. It remains to be considered whether power is better associated with actors or with roles, and if with actors, whether collective actors may be involved or only individual actors.

5 There is a presumption here that a routine can be treated as a stable, continuing entity available at discretion. See also note 9.

6 Needless to say, the acquisition and loss of discretion are complex social processes, not well thought of in atomistic terms. Loss of discretion often feeds on itself and multiplies, as does the accumulation of discretion. The phenomenon should perhaps be called 'the Enobarbus effect' after Shakespeare's vivid dramatisation in *Anthony and Cleopatra*.

7 I do not wish to make too much of common usage or to claim that my own favoured notions accord particularly closely with it. In common usage 'authority' is often used as a synonym for 'power', and to 'authorise' may be to delegate discretion and hence power, as when someone is authorised to negotiate, or to draw up and sign a treaty.

8 I do not wish to imply that the *best* policy for a power holder is that of maximising immediate discretion. On the contrary it will generally be wiser to settle for less discretion and to empower agents to act on the basis of their own

judgement. Policies designed to maximise power may be much more risky than less ambitious ones.

9 The discussion in this paper dodges the most basic issues involved in the problem of social order by taking the existence of routines for granted, and speaking merely of the direction of routines. Any developed account of the nature of power must provide a convincing account of routines and their stability: see Barnes (1983) for an attempt to provide the beginnings of such an account.

10 The extensive literature on rule use, following Garfinkel, and textual deconstruction, following Derrida, is widely cited, although not all those who have contributed to it take the view that verbal formulations can be interpreted with complete discretion. For an alternative line of argument which arrives at closely related conclusions, see Barnes (1982, 1984).

11 The model and exemplar for this kind of approach is L. Wittgenstein (1968); see also Bloor (1983).

12 As before (note 8), I do not wish to imply that it is natural or inevitable for powers to seek to create passive agents; I only seek to explore the possible consequences of attempts to do so.

References

Barnes, B. (1982), 'On the Extensions of Concepts and the Growth of Knowledge', *Sociological Review,* vol. 30, no. 1, pp. 23–44.

Barnes, B. (1983), 'Social Life as Bootstrapped Induction', *Sociology,* vol. 17, no. 4, pp. 524–45.

Barnes, B. (1984), 'The Conventional Component in Knowledge and Cognition', in N. Stehr and V. Meja (eds), *Society and Knowledge,* Transaction Books, New York.

Bloor, D. (1983), *Wittgenstein: A Social Theory of Knowledge,* Macmillan, London.

Martin, R. (1977), *The Sociology of Power,* Routledge & Kegan Paul, London.

Parsons, T. (1967), *Sociological Theory and Modern Society,* Free Press, New York.

Wittgenstein, L. (1968), *Philosophical Investigations,* Blackwell, Oxford.

Wrong, D. (1979), *Power, Its Forms, Bases and Uses,* Blackwell, Oxford.

Some elements of a sociology of translation: domestication of the scallops and the fishermen of St Brieuc Bay

Michel Callon

Abstract

This paper outlines a new approach to the study of power, that of the sociology of translation. Starting from three principles, those of agnosticism (impartiality between actors engaged in controversy), generalised symmetry (the commitment to explain conflicting viewpoints in the same terms) and free association (the abandonment of all a priori distinctions between the natural and the social), the paper describes a scientific and economic controversy about the causes for the decline in the population of scallops in St. Brieuc Bay and the attempts by three marine biologists to develop a conservation strategy for that population. Four 'moments' of translation are discerned in the attempts by these researchers to impose themselves and their definition of the situation on others: (a) problematisation: the researchers sought to become indispensable to other actors in the drama by defining the nature and the problems of the latter and then suggesting that these would be resolved if the actors negotiated the 'obligatory passage point' of the researchers' programme of investigation; (b) interessement: a series of processes by which the researchers sought to lock the other actors into the roles that had been proposed for them in that programme; (c) enrolment: a set of strategies in which the researchers sought to define and interrelate the various roles they had allocated to others; (d) mobilisation: a set of methods used by the researchers to ensure that supposed spokesmen for various relevant collectivities were properly able to represent those collectivities and not betrayed by the latter. In conclusion it is noted that translation is a process, never a completed accomplishment, and it may (as in the empirical case considered) fail.

1. Introduction

The object of this paper is to present an outline of what is now called sociology of translation and to show that this analytical framework is particularly well adapted to the study of the role played by science and technology in structuring power relationships.

The starting point is to recognize that sociologists, who have attempted a detailed analysis of scientific and technological contents over the last few years, find themselves in a paradoxical situation. The explanations and interpretations proposed by these social scientists are in fact marked by a conspicuous asymmetry. When it comes to acknowledging the right of the scientists and engineers that they study to debate, sociologists' tolerance knows no limits. The sociologists act impartially and refer to the different protagonists in the same terms, even if one among them succeeds in imposing his will. The sociologists attribute the actors with neither reason, scientific method, truth, nor efficiency because these terms denote the actor's success without explaining the reasons for it.[1] This perspective has been at the basis of very lively and detailed descriptions of the shaping of science.[2]

However, the liberalism of these sociologists does not extend to allow the actors studied to discuss society and its constituents in an open manner. For once they have taken the scientific and technical aspects of the controversies into account, the sociologists faithfully restore the existing points of view to their places and, in addition, they rightly abstain from taking sides. They acknowledge the existence of a plurality of descriptions of Nature without establishing any priorities or hierarchies between these descriptions. However, and this is where the paradox is revealed, within their proposed analyses, these social scientists act as if this agnosticism towards natural science and technology were not applicable towards society as well. For them Nature is uncertain but Society is not.[3]

Is it a matter of simple privilege which sociologists grant themselves through a corporatist reflex when they remove their own knowledge from public discussion? The answer is not quite that simple. This asymmetry plays a crucial role in the explanation of science and technology. Since Nature by itself is not in a position to establish a consensus between experts, then sociologists and philosophers require something which is more constraining and less equivocal, to explain the emergence, development, and eventual closure of controversies. Some relegate this superior force to the scientific method and, consequently, to the existence of social norms which guarantee its execution.[4] Others turn to existing social forces such as classes, organizations or professions.[5] When the society described by sociologists confronts nature (no matter which description they give), society always has the last word.[6] If the norms are removed, the sciences collapses. If the existence of social classes and their interests is denied or if the battle waged against scientists to increase their personal capital of credibility disappears, then science and technology comes to a halt, deprived of any outlet.

This frequently implicit privilege bestowed on social sciences concerning the manner in which science and technology are explained leads to three major difficulties.

The first and most apparent difficulty is a matter of style. Although scientists and engineers who are involved in the most technical of controversies are as suspicious of society as they are of nature, the sociologists' account generally bears no trace of the actors' discussions concerning social structures. The sociologist tends to censor selectively the actors when they speak of themselves, their allies, their adversaries, or social backgrounds. He allows them to express themselves freely only when they speak of Nature. The few rare texts in which this censorship is not imposed produce a very different literary effect.[7] This is due to the simple fact that the actors are not separated from a part of themselves. The impression of sociological reductionism too often given by the best writings on scientific content is evidently a product of this systematic and at times relentless censorship undertaken by sociologists in the name of sociology. Researchers have the right to debate in the most minute detail over solar neutrinos, coefficients of statistical association, and the shape of the brain, but the social analyses and interpretations which they propose and discuss at the same time are considered to be irrelevant, or worse, are used against them to criticize their scientific and technical choices.[8] Sometimes the effect can be so devastating that the reader has the impression of attending a trial of natural science presided over by a privileged scientific knowledge (sociology) which has been judged to be indisputable and above criticism.

The second difficulty is of a theoretical nature. As a number of authors have revealed, the controversies over sociological explanations are interminable. Sociologists only very rarely succeed in coming to any agreement among themselves. Just like the scientists they study, they are divided by continuing controversies. Consensus, when it occurs, seems even more rare and fragile than in other fields. Should one speak of social classes and interests rather than norms and institutions? The debate is as old as sociology itself and does not spare the sociology of sciences. This is because one position is defended with as much pugnacity and success as the other.[9] Is it legitimate to speak of social classes when the observations are based on only a few individuals? How can norms or rules of the game be isolated and how can their generality be determined? These are amongst the questions that divide the social sciences and show no signs of disappearing. The issue is clear: the sociological explanation of scientific and technical controversies is as debatable as the knowledge and objects which it accounts for. The theoretical difficulty is the following: from the moment one accepts that both social and natural sciences are equally uncertain, ambiguous, and disputable, it is no longer possible to have them playing different roles in the analysis. Since society is no more obvious or less controversial than Nature, sociological explanation can find no solid foundations.[10]

The third difficulty is methodological. During their elaborations, those sociologists who have studied scientific and technical innovations have realized that both the identity and the respective importance of the actors are at issue in the development of controversies. What are the convictions of Pasteur or Pouchet concerning spontaneous generation? The positions of the protagonists are never clearly defined, even retrospectively. This is because the definition of these positions is what is at issue.[11] What actually were the interests of Renault when the EDF announced that the end of the twentieth century would inevitably see extensions in the use of electric vehicles? Who could one have turned to to know what Renault really wanted?[12] Science and technology are dramatic 'stories' in which the identity of the actors is one of the issues at hand. The observer who disregards these uncertainties risks writing a slanted story which ignores the fact that the identities of actors are problematic.

One way to avoid these difficulties would be to return to the beginning and simply deny the possibility of providing a sociological definition of science and technology. Another possibility conserves and extends the recent findings of the sociology of science and technology. In this paper, we hope to show that the analysis can be carried out using a society which is considered to be uncertain and disputable. Within the controversies studied, the intervening actors develop contradictory arguments and points of view which lead them to propose different versions of the social and natural worlds. What would happen if symmetry were maintained throughout the analysis between the negotiations which deal with the natural and the social worlds? Would the result inevitably be total chaos? These are the questions which we will attempt to answer in this study.

To avoid the three difficulties presented above, we have decided to obey faithfully the following three methodological principles.

The first principle extends the agnosticism of the observer to include the social sciences as well. Not only is the observer impartial towards the scientific and technological arguments used by the protagonists of the controversy, but he also abstains from censoring the actors when they speak about themselves or the social environment. He refrains from judging the way in which the actors analyze the society which surrounds them. No point of view is privileged and no interpretation is censored. The observer does not fix the identity of the implicated actors if this identity is still being negotiated.

The second principle is one of generalized symmetry. It is similar to D. Bloor's principle of symmetry but is considerably extended.[13] The goal is not only to explain conflicting viewpoints and arguments in a scientific or technological controversy in the same terms. We know that the ingredients of controversies are a mixture of considerations concerning both Society and Nature. For this reason we require the observer to use a single repertoire when they are described. The vocabulary chosen for these descriptions and explanations can be left to the discretion of the observer. He can not simply repeat the analysis suggested by the actors he is studying. However, an infinite number of repertoires is possible.[14] It is up to the sociologist to choose the one that seems the best adapted to his task and then to convince his colleagues that he made the right choice. Having opted in this text for a vocabulary of translation we know that our narrative is no more, but no less valid, than any other. But given the principle of generalized symmetry, the rule which we must respect is not to change registers when we move from the technical to the social aspects of the problem studied. Our hope is that the translation repertoire, which is not that of the actors studied, will convince the reader.

The third principle concerns free association. The observer must abandon all a priori distinctions between natural and social events. He must reject the hypothesis of a definite boundary which separates the two. These divisions are considered to be conflictual, for they are the result of analysis rather than its point of departure. Further, the observer must consider that the repertoire of categories which he uses, the entities which are mobilized, and the relationships between these are all topics for actors' discussions. Instead of imposing a pre-established grid of analysis upon these, the observer follows the actors in order to identify the manner in which these define and associate the different elements by which they build and explain their world, whether it be social or natural.[15]

An example of the application of these principles is provided in the following text. Our goal is to show that one can question society at the same time as the actors and explain how they define their respective identities, their mutual margins of manoeuvre and the range of choices which are open to them. As we hope to prove, this story should lead to a better understanding of the establishment and the evolution of power relationships because all the fluctuations which occur are preserved. In the episode which is traced here, the capacity of certain actors to get other actors – whether they be human beings, institutions or natural entities – to comply with them depends upon a complex web of interrelations in which Society and Nature are intertwined.

II Scallops and fishermen

Highly appreciated by French consumers, scallops have only been systematically exploited for the last twenty years. Over a very short period they have become a very sought-after gourmandise to the extent that during the Christmas season, although prices are spectacularly high, sales increase considerably. They are fished in France at three locations: along the coast of Normandy, in the roadstead of Brest, and in St. Brieuc Bay. There are several different species of scallops. Certain ones, as in Brest, are coralled all year round. However, at St. Brieuc the scallops lose their coral during spring and summer. These characteristics are commercially important because, according to the convictions of the fishermen, the consumers prefer coralled scallops to those which are not.

Through the 70's, the stock at Brest progressively dwindled. This was due to the combined effects of marine predators (starfish), a series of hard winters which had lowered the general temperature of the water, and the fishermen who, wanting to

Michel Callon

satisfy the insatiable consumers, dredged the ocean floor for scallops all year round without allowing them time to reproduce. The production of St. Brieuc had also been falling off steadily during the same period, but fortunately the Bay was able to avoid the disaster. There were fewer predators and the consumers' preference for coralled scallops obliged the fishermen to stay on land for half the year. As a result of these factors, the reproduction of the stock decreased less in St. Brieuc Bay than at Brest.[16]

The object of this study is to examine the progressive development of new social relationships through the constitution of a 'scientific knowledge' that occurred during the 1970's.[17] The story starts at a conference held at Brest in 1972. Scientists and the representatives of the fishing community were assembled in order to examine the possibility of increasing the production of scallops by controlling the cultivation of these crustaceans. The discussions were grouped around the following three elements.

1) Three researchers who are members of the CNEXO[18] have discovered during a voyage to Japan that scallops are being intensively cultivated there. The technique is the following: the larvae are anchored to collectors immersed in the sea where they are sheltered from predators as they grow. When the shellfish attain a large enough size, they are 'sown' along the ocean bed where they can safely develop for two or three years before being harvested. According to the researchers' accounts of their trip, this technique made it possible to increase the level of existing stocks. All the different contributions of the conference were focused around this report.

2) There is a total lack of information concerning the mechanisms behind the development of scallops. The scientific community has never been very interested in this subject. In addition, because the intensive exploitation of scallops had begun only recently, the fishermen knew nothing about the earlier stages of scallop development. The fishermen had only seen adult scallops in their dredges.[19] At the beginning of the 1970s no direct relationship existed between larvae and fishermen. As we will see, the link was progressively established through the action of the researchers.

3) Fishing had been carried out at such intensive levels that the consequences of this exploitation were beginning to be visible in St. Brieuc Bay. Brest had practically been crossed off the map. The production at St. Brieuc had been steadily decreasing. The scallop industry of St. Brieuc had been particularly lucrative and the fishermen's representatives were beginning to worry about the

dwindling stock. The decline of the scallop population seemed inevitable and many feared that the catastrophe at Brest would also occur at St. Brieuc.

This was the chosen starting point for this paper. Ten years later, a 'scientific' knowledge was produced and certified; a social group was formed (the fishermen of St. Brieuc Bay) through the privileges that this group was able to institute and preserve; and a community of specialists was organized in order to study the scallops and promote their cultivation.[20] We will now retrace some part of this evolution and see the simultaneous production of knowledge and construction of a network of relationships in which social and natural entities mutually control who they are and what they want.

III The four moments of translation

To examine this development, we have chosen to follow an actor through his construction-deconstruction of Nature and Society. Our starting point here consists of the three researchers who have returned from their voyage to the Far East. Where they came from and why they act is of little importance at this point of the investigation. They are the primum movens of the story analyzed here. We will accompany them during their first attempt at domestication. This endeavour consists of four moments which can in reality overlap. These moments constitute the different phases of a general process called translation, during which the identity of actors, the possibility of interaction and the margins of manoeuvre are negotiated and delimited.

1 The problematization or how to become indispensable

Once they returned home, the researchers wrote a series of reports and articles in which they disclosed the impressions of their trip and the future projects they wished to launch. With their own eyes they had seen the larvae anchor themselves to collectors and grow undisturbed while sheltered from predators. Their question is simple: is this experience transposable to France and, more particularly, to the Bay of St. Brieuc? No clear answer can be given because the researchers know that the briochine species

Michel Callon

(Pecten maximus) is different from the species raised in Japanese waters (Pecten patinopecten yessoeusis). Since no one contradicts the researchers' affirmations, we consider their statements are held to be uncontestable. Thus the aquaculture of scallops at St. Brieuc raises a problem. No answer can be given to the following crucial question: does Pecten maximus anchor itself during the first moments of its existence? Other questions which are just as important accompany the first. When does the metamorphosis of the larvae occur? At what rate do the young grow? Can enough larvae be anchored to the collectors in order to justify the project of restocking the Bay?

But in their different written documents the three researchers did not limit themselves to the simple formulation of the above questions. They determined a set of actors and defined their identities in such a way as to establish themselves an an obligatory passage point in the network of relationships they were building. This double movement, which renders them indispensable in the network, is what we call problematization.

1.1 The interdefinition of the actors

The questions formed by the three researchers and the commentaries that they provide bring three other actors directly into the story:[21] the scallops (Pecten maximus), the fishermen of St. Brieuc Bay, and the scientific colleagues.[22] The definitions of these actors, as they are presented in the scientists' report, is quite rough. However it is sufficiently precise to explain how these actors are necessarily concerned by the different questions which are formulated. These definitions as given by the three researchers themselves can be synthesized in the following manner.

a) *The fishermen of St. Brieuc:* they fish scallops to the last shellfish without worrying about the stock;[23] they make large profits; if they do not slow down their zealous efforts, they will ruin themselves. However, these fishermen are considered to be aware of their long term economic interests and, consequently, seem to be interested in the project of restocking the Bay and approve of the studies which had been launched to achieve this plan. No other hypothesis is made about their identity. The three researchers make no comment about a united social group. They define an average fisherman as a base unit of a community which consists of interchangeable elements.

b) *Scientific colleagues:* participating in conferences or cited in different publications, they know nothing about scallops in general nor about those of St. Brieuc in particular. In addition, they are unable to answer the question about the way in which these shellfish anchor themselves. They are considered to be interested in advancing the knowledge which has been proposed. This strategy consists of studying the scallops in situ rather than in experimental tanks.

c) *The scallops of St. Brieuc:* a particular species (Pecten maximus) which everyone agrees is coralled only six months of the year. They have only been seen as adults, at the moment they are dredged from the sea. The question which is asked by the three researchers supposes that they can anchor themselves and will 'accept' a shelter that will enable them to proliferate and survive.[24]

Of course, and without this the problematization would lack any support, the three researchers also reveal what they themselves are and what they want. They present themselves as 'basic' researchers who, impressed by the foreign achievement, seek to advance the available knowledge concerning a species which had not been thoroughly studied before. By undertaking this investigation, these researchers hope to render the fishermen's life easier and increase the stock of scallops of St. Brieuc Bay.

This example shows that the problematization, rather than being a reduction of the investigation to a simple formulation, touches on elements, at least partially and locally, which are parts of both the social and the natural worlds. A single question – does Pecten maximus anchor? – is enough to involve a whole series of actors by establishing their identities and the links between them.[25]

1.2 The definition of obligatory passage points (OPP)

The three researchers do not limit themselves simply to identifying a few actors. They also show that the interests of these actors lie in admitting the proposed research programme. The argument which they develop in their paper is constantly repeated: if the scallops want to survive (no matter what mechanisms explain this impulse), if their scientific colleagues hope to advance knowledge on this subject (whatever their motivations may be), if the fishermen hope to preserve their long term economic interests (whatever their reasons) then they must: 1) know the answer to the question: how do scallops anchor?, and 2) recognize that their alliance around this question can benefit each of them.[26]

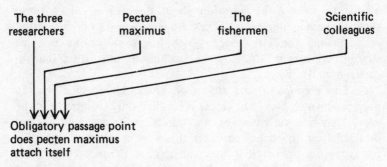

Figure 1

Figure 1 shows that the problematization possesses certain dynamic properties: it indicates the movements and detours that must be accepted as well as the alliances that must be forged. The scallops, the fishermen, and the scientific colleagues are fettered: they cannot attain what they want by themselves. Their road is blocked by a series of obstacles-problems. The future of Pecten maximus is perpetually threatened by all sorts of predators always ready to exterminate them; the fishermen, greedy for short term profits, risk their long term survival; scientific colleagues who want to develop knowledge are obliged to admit the lack of preliminary and indispensable observations of scallops in situ. As for the three researchers, their entire project turns around the question of the anchorage of Pecten maximus. For these actors the alternative is clear; either one changes direction or one recognizes the need to study and obtain results about the way in which larvae anchor themselves.[27]

As Figure 2 shows, the problematization describes a system of alliances, or associations,[28] between entities, thereby defining the identity and what they 'want'. In this case, a Holy Alliance must be formed in order to induce the scallops of St. Brieuc Bay to multiply.

2 The devices of 'interessement' or how the allies are locked into place

We have emphasized the hypothetical aspect of the problematiza-

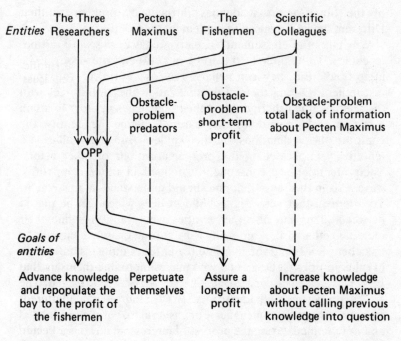

Figure 2

tion. On paper, or more exactly, in the reports and articles presented by the three researchers, the identified groups have a real existence. But reality is a process. Like a chemical body it passes through successive states.[29] At this point in our story, the entities identified and the relationships envisaged have not yet been tested. The scene is set for a series of trials of strength whose outcome will determine the solidity of our researchers problematization.

Each entity enlisted by the problematization can submit to being integrated into the initial plan, or inversely, refuse the transaction by defining its identity, its goals, projects, orientations, motivations, or interests in another manner. In fact the situation is never so clear cut. As the phase of problematization has shown, it would be absurd for the observer to describe entities as formulating their identity and goals in a totally independent manner. They are formed and are adjusted only during action.[30]

Interessement is the group of actions by which an entity (here the three researchers) attempts to impose and stabilize the identity

207

of the other actors it defines through its problematization. Different devices are used to implement these actions.

Why talk of interessement? The etymology of this word justifies its choice. To be interested is to be in between (inter-esse), to be interposed. But between what? Let us return to the three researchers. During their problematization they join forces with the scallops, the fishermen, and their colleagues in order to attain a certain goal. In so doing they carefully define the identity, the goals or the inclinations of their allies. But these allies are tentatively implicated in the problematizations of other actors. Their identities are consequently defined in other competitive ways. It is in this sense that one should understand interessement. To interest other actors is to build devices which can be placed between them and all other entities who want to define their identities otherwise. A interests B by cutting or weakening all the links between B and the invisible (or at times quite visible) group of other entities C, D, E, etc. who may want to link themselves to B.[31]

The properties and identity of B (whether it is a matter of scallops, scientific colleagues, or fishermen) are consolidated and/or redefined during the process of interessement. B is a 'result' of the association which links it to A. This link disassociates B from all the C, D, and E's (if they exist) that attempt to give it another definition. We call this elementary relationship which begins to shape and consolidate the social link the triangle of interessement.[32]

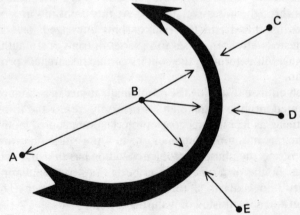

Figure 3

The range of possible strategies and mechanisms that are adopted to bring about these interruptions is unlimited. As Feyerabend says about the scientific method: anything goes. It may be pure and simple force if the links between B, C and D are firmly established. It may be seduction or a simple solicitation if B is already close to the problematization of A. Except in extremely rare cases when the shaping of B coincides perfectly with the proposed problematization, the identity and 'geometry' of the interested entities are modified all along the process of interessement.[33] We can illustrate these points by the story of the domestication of scallops.

The domestication of scallops strikingly illustrates the general interessement mechanisms. The three researchers are inspired by a technique that had been invented by the Japanese. Towlines made up of collectors are immersed in the sea. Each collector carries a fine netted bag containing a support for the anchorage of the larvae. These bags make it possible to assure the free flow of water and larvae while preventing the young scallops from escaping. The device also prevents predators from attacking the larvae. In this way the larvae are protected during the period when they have no defence: that is, when they have no shell.[34] The collectors are mounted in a series on the line. The ends of the two lines are attached to floats that are kept in place by an anchorage system.

The towline and its collectors constitute an archetype of the interessement device. The larvae are 'extracted' from their context. They are protected from predators (starfish) which want to attack and exterminate them, from currents that carry them away where they perish, and from the fisherman's dredge which damages them. They are (physically) disassociated from all the actors who threaten them.

In addition, these interessement devices extend and materialize the hypothesis made by the researchers concerning the scallops and the larvae: (1) the defenceless larvae are constantly threatened by predators, (2) the larvae can anchor, (3) the Japanese experience can be transposed to France because St. Brieuc's scallops are not fundamentally different from their Japanese cousins. The collectors would lose all effectiveness if the larvae 'refused' to anchor, to grow, to metamorphose, and to proliferate in (relative) captivity. The interessement, if successful, confirms (more or less completely) the validity of the problematiz-

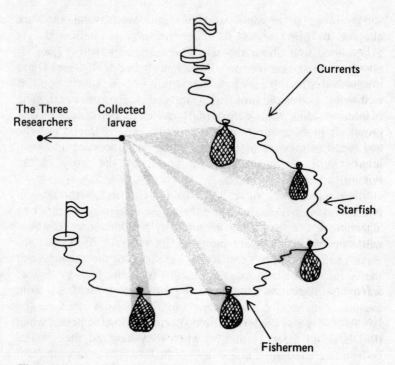

The Three Researchers

Collected larvae

Currents

Starfish

Fishermen

Figure 4

ation and the alliance it implies. In this particular case study, the problematization is eventually refuted.

Although the collectors are necessary for the interessement of the scallops and their larvae, this type of 'machination' proves to be superfluous for the interessement of the fishermen and the scientific colleagues. In addition, the three researchers do not intend to convince the first group as a whole. It is rather the representatives of professional organizations who are the targets of the researchers' solicitation. The three researchers multiply their meetings and debates in order to explain to the fishermen the reasons behind the extinction of the scallops. The researchers draw up and comment upon curves which 'indisputably' show the incredible decline of the stock of scallops in St. Brieuc Bay. They also emphatically present the 'spectacular' results of the Japanese. The scientific colleagues are solicited during conferences and through publications. The argumentation is always the same: an exhaustive review of the literature shows that nothing is known about scallops. This lack of knowledge is regrettable because the survival of a species which has increasing economic importance is at stake (in France at least).[35]

For the case of the scallops (like the fishermen and the scientific colleagues) the interessement is founded on a certain interpretation of what the yet to be enrolled actors are and want as well as what entities these actors are associated with. The devices of interessement create a favourable balance of power: for the first group, these devices are the towlines immersed in St. Brieuc Bay; and for the second group, they are texts and conversations which lure the concerned actors to follow the three researchers' project. For all the groups involved, the interessement helps corner the entities to be enrolled. In addition, it attempts to interrupt all potential competing associations and to construct a system of alliances. Social structures comprising both social and natural entities are shaped and consolidated.

3 How to define and coordinate the roles: enrolment

No matter how constraining the trapping device, no matter how convincing the argument, success is never assured. In other words, the device of interessement does not necessarily lead to alliances, that is, to actual enrolment. The issue here is to transform a question into a series of statements which are more certain: Pecten maximus does anchor; the fishermen want to restock the Bay.

Why speak of enrolment? In using this term, we are not resorting to a functionalist or culturalist sociology which defines society as an entity made up of roles and holders of roles.[36] Enrolment does not imply, nor does it exclude, pre-established roles. It designates the device by which a set of interrelated roles is defined and attributed to actors who accept them. Interessement achieves enrolment if it is successful. To describe enrolment is thus to describe the group of multilateral negotiations, trials of strength and tricks that accompany the interessements and enable them to succeed.

If the scallops are to be enrolled, they must first be willing to anchor themselves to the collectors. But this anchorage is not easy to achieve. In fact the three researchers will have to lead their longest and most difficult negotiations with the scallops. Like in a fairy tale, there are many enemy forces which attempt to thwart the researchers' project and divert the larvae before they are captured. First the currents: 'Of the six towlines that were placed,

211

four functioned correctly before different variables intervened. It clearly appears that the larvae anchor themselves better in the innermost parts of the Bay where the tidal currents are the weakest.'[37]

To negotiate with the scallops is to first negotiate with the currents because the turbulences caused by the tide are an obstacle to the anchorage. But the researchers must deal with other elements besides the currents. All sorts of parasites trouble the experiment and present obstacles to the capture of the larvae.

A large part of the variation is due to the way in which parasites are attracted. We have had many visitors who provoked accidents, displaced lines, entangled collectors. This immediately caused negative results. It seems that the scallops are extremely sensitive to all manipulations (displaced lines, collectors which rub against each other, etc.) and react by detaching themselves from their supports.[38]

The list goes on. A veritable battle is being fought. Currents and visitors are only some of the forces which are opposed to the alliances which the researchers wish to forge with the scallops.[39] In the triangle A-B-C which we spoke of earlier, C, the party to be excluded (whether it is called currents or starfish) does not surrender so easily. C (the starfish) has the possibility of interrupting the relationships between A (the researchers) and B (the larvae). C does this by also interesting B (the larvae) which are coveted by all.

The census done by the researcher also shows that the anchorages are more numerous 'between 5 meters above the sea floor and the sea floor itself. This is perhaps due to the depth as well as to the specific behaviour of the scallops when they anchor: the larvae lets itself sink and anchors itself to the first obstacle that stops its descent.'[40]

The towline, an interessement device, reveals the levels of anchorage to the observer. The hypotheses and the interpretations of the researchers are nothing but a programme of negotiations: larvae, should we search for you at the bottom of the Bay or should we wait for you on your way down in order to trap you as you sink?

This is not all. The researchers are ready to make any kind of concession in order to lure the larvae into their trap. What sort of substances do the larvae prefer to anchor themselves on? Another series of transactions is necessary to answer the question.

'It was noted that the development of the scallops was slower with collectors made of straw, broom, or vegetable horsehair. These types of supports are too compressed and prevent water from circulating correctly through the collector.'[41]

Thus a modus vivendi is progressively arranged. If all these conditions are united then the larvae will anchor themselves in a significant manner. But what does the adjective 'significant' signify? To answer this question, we must introduce, as in the tripartite Vietnam conferences held in Paris, the second actor with whom the three researchers must negotiate: scientific colleagues.

In the beginning a general consensus existed: the idea that scallops anchor was not discussed.[42] However, the first results were not accepted without preliminary negotiations. The proposition: 'Pecten maximus anchors itself in its larval state' is an affirmation which the experiments performed at St. Brieuc eventually called into question. No anchorages were observed on certain collectors and the number of larvae which anchored on the collectors never attained the Japanese levels. At what number can it be confirmed and accepted that scallops, in general, do anchor themselves? The three researchers are prepared for this objection because in their first communication they confirm that the observed anchorages did not occur accidentally: it is here that we see the importance of the negotiations which were carried out with the scallops in order to increase the interessement and of the acts of enticement which were used to retain the larvae (horsehair rather than nylon, etc.). With scientific colleagues, the transactions were simple: the discussion of the results shows that they were prepared to believe in the principle of anchorage and that they judged the experiment to be convincing. The only condition that the colleagues posed is that the existence of previous work be recognized, work that had predicted, albeit imperfectly, the scallop's capacity to anchor.[43] It is at this price that the number of anchorages claimed by the researchers will be judged as sufficient. Our three researchers accept after ironically noting that all bonafide discoveries miraculously unveil precursors who had been previously ignored.[44]

Transactions with the fishermen, or rather, with their representatives, are non-existent. They watch like amused spectators and wait for the final verdict. They are prepared simply to accept the conclusions drawn by the specialists. Their consent is obtained (in advance) without any discussion.

Therefore for the most part, the negotiation is carried out

between three parties since the fourth partner was enrolled without any resistance. This example illustrates the different possible ways in which the actors are enrolled: physical violence (against the predators), seduction, transaction, and consent without discussion. This example mainly shows that the definition and distribution of roles (the scallops which anchor themselves, the fishermen who are persuaded that the collectors could help restock the Bay, the colleagues who believe in the anchorage) are a result of multilateral negotiations during which the identity of the actors is determined and tested.

4 The mobilisation of allies: are the spokesmen representative?

Who speaks in the name of whom? Who represents whom? These crucial questions must be answered if the project led by the researchers is to succeed. This is because, as with the description of interessement and enrolment, only a few rare individuals are involved, whether these be scallops, fishermen or scientific colleagues.

Does Pecten maximus really anchor itself? Yes, according to the colleagues, the anchorages which were observed are not accidental. Yet, though everyone believes that they are not accidental they acknowledge that they are limited in number. A few larvae are considered to be the official representatives of an anonymous mass of scallops which silently and elusively lurk on the ocean floor. The three researchers negotiate the interessement of the scallops through a handful of larvae which represent all the uncountable others that evade captivity.

The masses at no time contradict the scallops which anchor themselves. That which is true for a few is true for the whole of the population. When the CBI negotiates with union delegates they consider the latter to be representatives of all the workers. This small number of individuals speaks in the name of the others. In one case, the epistemologists speak of induction, in another, political scientists use the notion of spokesman. The question however is the same. Will the masses (employers, workers, scallops) follow their representatives?[45]

Representation is also an issue in the researchers' transactions with the colleagues and fishermen. Properly speaking, it is not the scientific community which is convinced but a few colleagues who read the publications and attend the conference. It is not the fishermen but their official representatives who give the green light to the experiments and support the project of restocking the Bay. In both cases, a few individuals have been interested in the name of the masses they represent (or claim to represent).

The three researchers have formed a relationship with only a few representatives – whether they be larvae on a collector, professional delegates or scientific colleagues participating at a colloquium. However it may seem that the situations are not comparable. The delegates and colleagues speak for themselves while the larvae are silent. On the one hand, they are real spokesmen but on the other, the anchored larvae are simply representatives. However this difference disappears on closer analysis.

Let us return to the scallops. The larvae which anchored themselves on the collector are 'equal' to the scallops of St. Brieuc Bay. They themselves express nothing. However they end up having, like the fishermen, an authentic spokesman. As we have seen, the negotiations between the scallops and the researchers revolve around one question: how many larvae can be trapped? The fact that this number should be retained as a principal subject of discussion is not a result of any absolute necessity. By counting the larvae, the three researchers wish to know what they can count on in their negotiations with their colleagues and the fishermen. Their interlocutors pay particular attention to the number of anchorages: the first to be convinced of the generality of the observation; the latter to be convinced of the efficiency of the device. How many electors came forward to choose their representatives: How many larvae anchored themselves on the collectors? This is the only question of any importance in either case. The anchorage is equivalent to a vote and the counting of anchored larvae corresponds to the tallying of ballots.[46] When spokesmen for the fishing community are elected the procedure is the same. From the fishing community which is just as silent as the scallops in the Bay, a few individuals come forward to slip their votes into the ballot boxes. The votes are counted and then divided between the different candidates: the analysis of these results leads to the designation of the official spokesman. Where are the differences in the case of the larvae? The larvae anchor themselves and are counted; the three researchers register these numbers on sheets of paper, convert these figures into curves and tables which are then used in an article or paper.[47] These results are analyzed and discussed during a conference and, if they are judged to be significant, three researchers are authorized to speak legitimately for the scallops of St. Brieuc Bay: Pecten maximus does in fact go through an anchorage stage.

The symmetry is perfect. A series of intermediaries and equivalences are put into place which lead to the designation of the spokesman. In the case of the fishermen, the chain is a bit longer. This is because the professional delegates stand between the tallying of the vote and the three researchers. However, the result is the same: both the fishermen and the scallops end up being represented by the three researchers who speak and act in their name.[48] Although no vote is taken, the agreement of the scientific community is also based on the same type of general mechanism: the same cascade of intermediaries who little by little reduce the number of representative interlocutors. The few colleagues who attend the different conferences or seminars speak in the name of all the researchers involved.[49] Once the transaction is successfully accomplished, there are three individuals who, in the name of the specialists, speak in the name of the scallops and fishermen.

The schema below shows how entities as different as Pecten maximus, the fishermen of St. Brieuc and the community of specialists are constructed by interposed spokesmen.

Using the notion of spokesman for all the actors involved at different stages of the process of representation does not present any problem. To speak for others is to first silence those in whose name we speak. It is certainly very difficult to silence human beings in a definitive manner but it is more difficult to speak in the name of entities that do not possess an articulate language: this supposes the need for continuous adjustments and devices of interessement that are infinitely more sophisticated.[50]

Three men have become influential and are listened to because they have become the 'head' of several populations. They have mixed together learned experts, unpolished fishermen, and savoury crustaceans. These chains of intermediaries which result in a sole and ultimate spokesman can be described as the progressive mobilization of actors who render the following propositions credible and indisputable by forming alliances and acting as a unit of force: 'Pecten maximus anchors' and 'the fishermen want to restock the Bay'. The notion of mobilization is perfectly adapted to the mechanisms that we have described. This is because this term emphasizes all the necessary displacements. To mobilize, as the word indicates, is to render entities mobile which were not so beforehand. At first, the scallops, fishermen, and specialists were

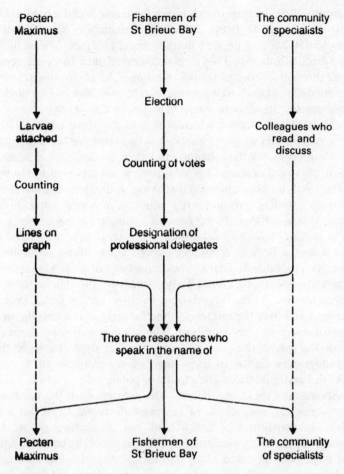

Figure 5

actually all dispersed and not easily accessible. At the end, three researchers at Brest said what these entities are and want. Through the designation of the successive spokesmen and the settlement of a series of equivalencies, all these actors are first displaced and then reassembled at a certain place at a particular time. This mobilization or concentration has a definite physical reality which is materialized through a series of displacements (Law, 1985b).

The scallops are transformed into larvae, the larvae into numbers, the numbers into tables and curves which represent easily transportable, reproducible, and diffusable sheets of paper

217

(Latour, 1985). Instead of exhibiting the larvae and the towlines to their colleagues at Brest, the three researchers show graphic representations and present mathematical analyses. The scallops have been displaced. They are transported into the conference room through a series of transformations. The choice of each new intermediary, of each new representative must also meet a double requirement: it renders each new displacement easier and it establishes equivalences which result in the designation of the three researchers as spokesmen. It is the same for the fishermen transformed into voting ballots and then professional delegates whose previously recorded points of view are reported to Brest.

The result which is obtained is striking. A handful of researchers discuss a few diagrams and a few tables with numbers in a closed room. But these discussions commit uncountable populations of silent actors: scallops, fishermen, and specialists who are all represented at Brest by a few spokesmen. These diverse populations have been mobilized. That is, they have been displaced from their homes to a conference room. They participate, through interposed representatives, in the negotiations over the anchorage of Pecten maximus and over the interests of the fishermen. The enrolment is transformed into active support. The scallops and the fishermen are on the side of the three researchers in an amphitheatre at the Oceanographic Centre of Brest one day in November 1974.

As this analysis shows, the groups or populations in whose name the spokesmen speak are elusive. The guarantor (or the referent) exists once the long chain of representatives has been put into place. It constitutes a result and not a starting point. Its consistency is strictly measured by the solidity of the equivalencies that have been put into place and the fidelity of a few rare and dispersed intermediaries who negotiate their representativity and their identity (Hennion, 1983). Of course, if the mobilization is successful, then:? Pecten maximus exists as a species which anchors itself; the fishermen want the repopulation and are ready to support the experimental project; colleagues agree that the results obtained are valid.[51] The social and natural 'reality' is a result of the generalized negotiation about the representativity of the spokesmen. If consensus is achieved, the margins of manoeuvre of each entity will then be tightly delimited. The initial problematization defined a series of negotiable hypotheses on identity, relationships and goals of the different actors. Now at the end of the four moments described, a constraining network of relationships has been built.[52] But this consensus and the alliances which it implies can be contested at any moment. Translation becomes treason.

IV Dissidence: betrayals and controversies

During recent years, sociologists have devoted numerous studies to controversies and have shown the important role they play in the dynamics of science and technology. Why and in what conditions do controversies occur? How are they ended? The proposed schema of analysis makes it possible to examine these two questions in the same way. At the same time, this schema maintains the symmetry between controversies which pertain to Nature and those which pertain to Society.

Is a spokesman or an intermediary representative? This is a practical and not a theoretical question. It is asked in the same manner for the scallops, the fishermen and the scientific colleagues. Controversy is all the manifestations by which the representativity of the spokesman is questioned, discussed, negotiated, rejected, etc.

Let us start with the scallops. The first experiment or, if we use our vocabulary, act of interressement, mobilizes them in the form of larvae anchored to collectors and in the form of diagrams discussed at Brest before a learned assembly. This group established a fact: Pecten maximus anchors itself when in the larval state. About a hundred larvae gathered in nets off the coast of St. Brieuc were enough to convince the scientists that they reflect the behaviour of an uncountable number of their invisible and elusive brothers.

But is this movement likely to last? Will the scallops continue to anchor their larvae on the collectors generation after generation? This question is of crucial importance to our three researchers. It concerns the future of the restocking of the Bay, the future of the fishermen and, in consequence, their own future. The years pass and things change. The repeated experiment results in a catastrophe. The researchers place their nets but the collectors remain hopelessly empty. In principle the larvae anchor, in practice they refuse to enter the collectors. The difficult negotiations which were successful the first time fail in the following years. Perhaps the anchorages were accidental! The multiplicity of hostile interventions (this at least is the interpretation of the researchers in their role of spokesman for the scallops), the temperature of the water layers, unexpected currents, all sorts of predators, epizooty, are used to explain why the interessement is being inefficient. The larvae detach themselves from the researchers' project and a crowd of other actors carry them away. The scallops become dissidents. The larvae which complied are betrayed by those they were thought to represent. The situation is identical to that of the rank and file which greets the results of Union negotiations with silent indignation: representivity is brought into question.[53]

This controversy over the representivity of the larvae which anchor themselves during the first year's experiments is joined by another: this time it is the fishermen. Their elected representatives had been enrolled in a long term programme aimed at restocking St. Brieuc Bay without a shadow of reservation and without a peep of doubt. In the two years following the first (and only) anchorages, the scallops hatched from the larvae 'interested' by the collectors, after being regrouped at the bottom of the bay in an area protected by a concrete belt, are shamelessly fished, one Christmas Eve, by a horde of fishermen who could no longer resist the temptation of a miraculous catch. Brutally, and without a word, they disavowed their spokesmen and their long term plans. They preferred, as in the famous aphorism of Lord Keynes, to satisfy their immediate desires rather than a hypothetical future reward.

Faced with these silent mutinies of scallops and fishermen, the strategy of the three researchers begins to wobble. Is anchorage an obligatory passage point? Even scientific colleagues get sceptical. The three researchers have now to deal with growing doubt on the part of their laboratory director and the organisations which had agreed to finance the experiment.

Not only does the state of beliefs fluctuate with a controversy but the identity and characteristics of the implicated actors change as well. (What do the fishermen really want? How does Pecten maximus behave?. . .). Nature and Society are put into place and transformed in the same movement.

By not changing the grid of analysis, the mechanisms of the closure of a controversy are now more easily understood. Closure occurs when the spokesmen are deemed to be beyond question. This result is generally obtained only after a series of negotiations of all sorts which could take quite some time. The scallops do not follow the first anchored larvae and the fishermen do not respect the commitments of their representatives; this leads the three researchers to transform the device of interessement used for the scallops and their larvae and to undertake a vast campaign to educate and inform (i.e. form) the fishermen to choose other intermediaries and other representatives. It is at this point of their story that we leave them in order to examine the lessons that can be drawn from the proposed analysis.

V Concluding remarks

Throughout this study we have respected the three principles established in the introduction.

1) To comply with the first (generalized agnosticism) principle we looked at how the three researchers considered the facts of Nature and the social contexts which they elaborated and shaped. We faithfully reported doubts about society and the alliances that could be created. We were consequently able to treat uncertainties about the properties of scallops and uncertainties about fishermen and their interests in the same way.

In addition, and this enabled us to deal with the first difficulty revealed by recent studies in sociology of science, we systematically forced ourselves to judge neither the positions taken by the actors nor to reduce them to a particular 'sociological' interpretation. For example, the three researchers' belief in the anchorage of larvae or in the existence of a homogeneous group of fishermen with the same long term interests was never presented as an illusion or an error of judgment. The existence or the non-existence of the anchorage or of this social group may only be determined at the end of the course which was followed and it is the three researchers who reveal this through their different endeavours.

2) The second principle (generalized symmetry) compelled us not to change the grid of analysis in order to study controversies in connection with Nature and those in connection with Society. We have carefully followed this requirement by using the same vocabulary throughout. Problematization, interessement, enrolment, mobilization and dissidence (controversy-betrayal) are used for fishermen, for the scallops and for scientific colleagues. These terms are applied to all the actors without discrimination.

By following this procedure, we have avoided the second difficulty mentioned in the introduction. We did not use social

factors, norms, or particular institutional or organizational con-
figurations to explain why discussions concerning the scallops or
the fishermen took place or were closed. To establish, urbi et orbi,
that larvae anchor, the complicity of the scallops is needed as
much as that of the fishermen. These three categories of actors are
all equally important. At no time can society be reduced to a
balance of power or to a series of conditions in order to explain the
growth and the closure of a controversy.

3) The third principle (free association), made it possible to follow
all the variations which affected the alliances forged by the three
researchers without locking them into fixed roles. Not only was the
identity of the scallops or the fishermen and the representatives of
their intermediaries or spokesmen (anchored larvae, professional
delegates, etc.) allowed to fluctuate, but the unpredictable
relationships between these different entities were also allowed to
take their course. This was possible because no a priori category or
relationship was used in the account. Who at the beginning of the
story could have predicted that the anchorage of the scallops
would have an influence on the fishermen? Who would have been
able to guess the channels that this influence would pass through?
These relationships become visible and plausible only after the
event.

Thus the third difficulty was circumscribed without any problem.
The story described here, although centered around the three
researchers, did not bring in any actor that they themselves did not
explicitly invoke nor did it impose any fixed definition on the
entities which intervened.

Despite what might be judged a high degree of permissiveness in
the analysis, the results were not an indescribable chaos. Certainly
the actors studied were confronted with different types of
uncertainties. The situation proposed for them here is much less
comfortable than that which is generally given by the sociology of
science. But their competences prove to be worthy of the
difficulties they encountered. They worked incessantly on society
and nature, defining and associating entities, in order to forge
alliances that were confirmed to be stable only for a certain
location at a particular time.

This methodological choice through which society is rendered as
uncertain and disputable as nature, reveals an unusual reality
which is accounted for quite faithfully by the vocabulary of
translation.

First, the notion of translation emphasizes the continuity of the displacements and transformations which occur in this story: displacements of goals and interests, and also, displacements of devices, human beings, larvae and inscriptions. Displacements occurred at every stage. Some play a more strategic role than others. Displacements during the problematization: instead of pursuing their individual short term interests, the fishermen are invited to change the focus of their preoccupations and their projects in order to follow the investigations of the researchers. Displacements during the stage of interessement: the larvae falling to the sea floor or pushed along by the currents are deflected and intercepted by the nets. Displacements during the stage of enrolment where an agreement is found through mutual concessions: the collectors are moved to a new location to capture the larvae more effectively which have also attracted the researchers to their own terrain. Displacements, and these are essential, during the stage of mobilization: the larvae anchored to the collectors, the fishermen of St. Brieuc Bay, and the colleagues dispersed throughout the world are displaced to Brest after having changed their form and state in order to support the three researchers who claim to be their spokesmen. And finally, displacement during the final stage, that of dissidence: the fishermen penetrate the barriers and, refusing to follow the researchers, devastate the fish reserve; the scallops and their larvae avoid the nets that are meant to anchor them. Because of a series of unpredictable displacements, all the processes can be described as a translation which leads all the actors concerned as a result of various metamorphoses and transformations, to pass by the three researchers and their development project.

To translate is to displace: the three untiring researchers attempt to displace their allies to make them pass by Brest and their laboratories. But to translate is also to express in one's own language what others say and want, why they act in the way they do and how they associate with each other: it is to establish oneself as a spokesman. At the end of the process, if it is successful, only voices speaking in unison will be heard. The three researchers talk in the name of the scallops, the fishermen, and the scientific community. At the beginning these three universes were separate and had no means of communication with one another. At the end a discourse of certainty has unified them, or rather, has brought them into a relationship with one another in an intelligible manner. But this would not have been possible without the different sorts of displacements and transformation presented above, the negotiations, and the adjustments that accompanied them. To designate these two inseparable mechanisms and their result, we use the word translation. The three researchers translated the fishermen, the scallops, and the scientific community.

Translation is a process before it is a result. That is why we have spoken of moments which in reality are never as distinct as they are in this paper. Each of them marks a progression in the negotiations which result in the designation of the legitimate spokesmen who, in this case study, say what the scallops want and need, and are not disavowed: the problematization, which was only a simple conjecture, was transformed into mobilization. Dissidence plays a different role since it brings into question some of the gains of the previous stages. The displacements and the spokesmen are challenged or refused. The actors implicated do not acknowledge their roles in this story nor the slow drift in which they had participated, in their opinion, wholeheartedly. As the aphorism says, traduttore-traditore, from translation to treason there is only a short step. It is this step that is taken in the last stage. New displacements take the place of the previous ones but these divert the actors from the obligatory passage points that had been imposed upon them. New spokesmen are heard that deny the representivity of the previous ones. Translation continues but the equilibrium has been modified. This is the case for the story which was presented here in which three researchers–spokesmen end up being denounced. At the same time, the description of the social and natural reality begins to fluctuate.

Translation is the mechanism by which the social and natural worlds progressively take form. The result is a situation in which certain entities control others. Understanding what sociologists generally call power relationships means describing the way in which actors are defined, associated and simultaneously obliged to remain faithful to their alliances. The repertoire of translation is not only designed to give a symmetrical and tolerant description of a complex process which constantly mixes together a variety of social and natural entities. It also permits an explanation of how a few obtain the right to express and to represent the many silent actors of the social and natural worlds they have mobilized.[54]

Notes

1 D. Bloor clearly defined the methodological principles which are now used in a growing number of social studies of science. They characterize what he calls the strong programme of sociology of science.

2 These empirical studies have concerned a wide variety of scientific fields. The most important are found in: K. Knorr, R. Krohn, R. Whitley (eds) (1980); particularly noteworthy in this book are the articles by T. Pinch and A. Pickering. Also the special issue of Social Studies of Science 11,1 (1981) was devoted to scientific controversies. See also; B. Barnes and S. Shapin (eds) (1979) and Wallis (ed.) (1979). A classic is H. M. Collins (1975). A good overview of these studies can be found in S. Shapin (1982).

3 This is affirmed most forcefully in the studies by the Edinburgh school of sociology (Barnes, 1978 and 1982; D. MacKenzie, 1978). A good overview of this sociology has been presented by J. Law and P. Lodge (1984). They demonstrate the rich relationships with the philosophy of Mary Hesse (1974). The ethnomethodologists and those who are close to them are not always directly concerned by this criticism. See for example the article by M. Lynch (1982) which explicitly admits the simultaneous construction of scientific facts and social context. His argument is used in M. Callon et al. (1984).

4 The belief in the existence of norms and their regulating role is one of the fundamental characteristics of Mertonian and post-Mertonian sociology which is itself linked to a more general functionalist or culturalist analysis of institutions (Merton, 1973). But this belief is explicitly or implicitly shared by a large number of epistemologists or philosophers of sciences. The postulate that a scientific method exists, no matter how it is characterized, leads necessarily to the idea of social or technical norms and consequently to a sociology which the sociologists themselves no longer believe in. As an example of an article in which norms are used as a determining variable, see C. Freudenthal (1984). The more one insists on the existence of scientific method, the more the sociology used is simple and out of date.

5 This is the case of Marxist inspired analysis (Yoxen, 1981).

6 Concerning the possibility of using the social sciences as a means of controlling other types of discourse, see the very critical analysis of M. Serres (Serres, 1980) and I. Stengers (Prigogine and Stengers, 1979).

7 The two major works of this type of literature remain the books of J. D. Watson (Watson, 1968) and T. Kidder (Kidder, 1982). Kidder's description is particularly interesting because even in a well identified market situation the major uncertainties are not only linked to the technical characteristics of the micro computer but also to the social relationships which are woven around it: 'They lived in a land of mists and mirrors. Mushroom management seemed to be practiced at all levels in their team. Or perhaps it was a version of Steve Walladh's ring protection system made flesh: West feeling uncertain about the team's real status upstairs; West's own managers never completely aware of all that their boss was up to; and the brand-new engineers kept almost completely ignorant of the real stakes, the politics, the intentions that lay behind what they were doing. But they proceeded headlong' (p. 105). A recent illustration of this literary style is supplied by B. Latour's analysis of Pasteur (Latour, 1984). In a field other than sociology of knowledge, L. Boltanski showed that the social

uncertainties and actor's sizes were at the heart of letters of denunciation sent to a major French evening newspaper (1984).

8 Do controversies concerning the constitution of society play as an important a role in the fundamental sciences as they do in applied or technical fields? Scientists debate the existence of solar neutrinos (T. Pinch, 1980 and 1981), charmed particles (A. Pickering, 1980) or the structure of TRF (B. Latour and S. Woolgar, 1979). Are they just as willing to call into question aspects of the social world which surrounds them? Technologists seem to have no trouble doing so (Callon, 1980; Pinch and Bijker, 1984). But what about scientists? Several answers could be given to this question. First, if the analysis of scientific controversies often seems to be confined to laboratories or scientific specialties, this is simply due to the fact that sociologists stop following their protagonists when they leave the scientific arena. Bahcall, Guillemin and Weber all have to find resources, organize teaching programmes, write manuals, create or control scientific journals if they want to succeed in their scientific activities. This activity takes place outside the laboratory but it largely determines the nature of science. It requires that researchers permanently formulate hypotheses concerning the identity and the goals of the people with whom they interact. This dimension of the social studies of science should not be ignored when seeking to explain the content of knowledge. Secondly the dynamic study of controversies shows that phases exist during which debates concern both society and knowledge (Shapin, 1979). This is notably the case when translation networks take shape and are negotiated (Callon, 1981). When these networks are consolidated the activities, roles and interests are differentiated and recognized. The controversies separate technical and scientific problems more and more frequently from their social contexts. But the separation is never totally achieved as long as the controversies continue because these imply the recruitment by the protagonists of outside and heterogeneous allies (administrators, industrialists, teachers. . .). A purely scientific controversy in which the protagonists did not undertake a 'sociological analysis' of the situation is a pure contradiction. Scientists can only agree on society if they are completely in agreement about scientific and technical issues. This can happen and in several ways: the sclerosis or total bureaucratization of a speciality (Crane, 1972); a political 'putsch' within a science which blocks technical controversies by blocking discussions about the social structure in which they develop (Lecourt, 1976).

9 This thesis is developed by Gouldner for sociology in general (Gouldner:1971). A good example of the endless controversies among sociologists about how to explain the development of science concerns the role of interests and their role in the construction and validation of knowledge. On this point see the critical analysis offered in Callon and Law (1982).

10 The classical problem of reflexivity may be posed in new terms as a result of developments in our understanding of controversy. Reflexivity is nothing more than an extension to the social sciences of the analysis that these offer for the construction of consensus within the natural sciences. Like nature, science cannot be invoked in order to explain the resolution of controversy and the construction of firm knowledge. There is no ultimate guarantee, no explanation in the last instance that cannot, in turn, be questioned. This does not mean, of course, that provisional consensus cannot be achieved. The argument that is being developed here is identical in form to that which made it possible for Popper (1934) to withdraw all logical status from induction.

11 J. Farley and G. Geison (1974).

12 Michel Callon (1981).

13 David Bloor (1976).

14 The argument developed here is similar in some respects to that advanced by Weber (1965). For Weber, the sociologist is guided by his own values (Wertbeziehung) and selects the problem to be studied and the elements of reality that seem to him to be most important. It is only once this reduction of an infinitely complex reality has been undertaken that the proper work of the sociologist can begin. The principle of generalised symmetry endows the sociologist-observer with analogous discretionary powers. In principle the choice of repertoire is entirely free. The only restriction is that it must relate both to nature and society.

15 John Law (1985b).

16 The notion of 'stock' is widely used in population demography. In the present case the stock designates the population of scallops living and reproducing in Saint-Brieuc Bay. A given stock is designated by a series of parameters that vary over time: overall number, cohorts, size, natural mortality rate, rate of reproduction, etc. Knowledge of the stock thus requires systematic measures which make it possible to forecast changes. In population dynamics mathematical models define the influence of a range of variables (e.g., intensity of fishing and the division of catch between cohorts) upon the development of the stock. Population dynamics is thus one of the essential tools for what specialists in the study of maritime fishing call the rational management of stocks.

17 For this study we had available all the articles, reports and accounts of meetings that related to the experiments at Saint-Brieuc and the domestication of scallops. About twenty interviews with leading protagonists were also undertaken.

18 CNEXO (Centre National d'Exploitation des Oceans) is a public body created at the beginning of the 1970s to undertake research designed to increase knowledge of and means of exploiting marine resources.

19 Two examples show the extent of the ignorance of both fishery professionals and fishermen. During the whole of the 1970s specialists disagreed – without ever undertaking any experiments – about whether scallops with temporary coral would conserve this feature if they were transplanted to areas where scallops have permanent coral. Again, fishermen claimed, contrary to the specialists, that scallops are able to move across the sea-bed. At the beginning of the 1980s a series of experiments was needed to resolve the first point. It was shown Scottish scallops with permanent coral retained this characteristic when moved to Saint-Brieuc Bay. On the second point, it was only with the assistance of video film that it was possible to convince the fishermen that such movement of scallops as there was was caused by currents.

20 As a result of the various alliances outlined above, in 1984 the fishermen earn about £25,000 a year (after expenses) for five hours work a week during six months of the year.

21 The term actor is used in the way that semioticians use the notion of the actant (Greimas and Courtes, 1979; Latour, 1984). For the implication of external actors in the construction of scientific knowledge or artefacts see the way in which Pinch and Bijker (1984) make use of the notion of a social group. The approach proposed here differs from this in various ways: first, as will be

suggested below, the list of actors is not restricted to social entities; but second, and most important, because the definition of groups, their identities and their wishes are all constantly negotiated during the process of translation. Therefore, these are not pregiven data, but take the form of an hypothesis (a problematisation) that is introduced by certain actors and is subsequently weakened, confirmed or transformed.

22 On the definition of constitutive unities see Latour and Strum (1985).

23 Marginal profit declines more or less rapidly as a function of the nature of stocks (dispersed or concentrated) and the demands of consumers. In the case of scallops these parameters combine to make capture of the last scallop profitable.

24 The reader should not impute anthropomorphism to these phrases! The reasons for the conduct of scallops – whether these lie in their genes, in divinely ordained schemes or anything else – matter little! The only thing that counts is the definition of their conduct by the various actors identified. The scallops are deemed to attach themselves just as fishermen are deemed to follow their short-term economic interests. They therefore act.

25 Barry Hindess (1982) has well demonstrated the negotiable character of interests. But it is necessary to go further: the identities of the actors themselves are open to question, as is the question of whether they are moved by values, interests or wishes. On this point see Michel Callon and John Law (1982).

26 For comparable analyses see Michel Callon (1981) and Bruno Latour (1984).

27 As can be discerned from its etymology, the word *problem* designates obstacles that are thrown across the path of an actor which hinder his movement. This term is thus used in a manner which differs entirely from that current in the philosophy of science and epistemology. Problems are not spontaneously generated by the state of knowledge or by the dynamics of progress in research. Rather they result from the definition and interrelation of actors that were not previously linked to one another. To problematise is simultaneously to define a series of actors and the obstacles which prevent them from attaining the goals or objectives that have been imputed to them. Problems, and the postulated equivalences between them, thus result from the interaction between a given actor and all the social and natural entities which it defines and for which it seems to become indispensable.

28 On the notion of association see Michel Callon and Bruno Latour (1981).

29 A fine example of such a change in state is to be found in Tracy Kidder (1982) where the computer can be seen taking shape in conversations which are converted into a paper computer which in turn is transformed into a network of cables and printed circuits. For a philosophical discussion of realisation and non-realisation see *Irreductions* (Latour, 1984).

30 This is without doubt the major lesson of Touraine's sociology. The actor does not exist outside the relationships which he enters. His identity fluctuates in parallel with them (Touraine:1974). In this he differs from Pierre Bourdieu (1972 and 1975) where the actor – whom he calls the agent – is defined in terms of certain fundamental properties.

31 Serres (1983) uses the notion of interest in a similar manner but the conclusions which he draws are entirely different. For him, interests sterilise knowledge because they come between the latter and its object. The apologue that he uses is magnificent (Alexander coming between Diogenes and his sun), but his

interpretation is false, as recent developments in the sociology of science have shown.

32 No hypothesis is offered here about the nature or size of A, B, C, D, E, . . . They may be social classes which mutually define one another (Touraine, 1974), father and son who tie their Oedipus complex, the elementary mechanisms of mimetic desire (Girard, 1982), or . . . scallops which are interested by researchers.

33 On the analysis of this process see L. Thevenot (1984) and his concept of investment in forms.

34 When the shell is formed it constitutes an effective shield against certain predators such as starfish.

35 Numerous analyses have made it clear that scientific argument may be seen as a device for interessement. See, amongst others, Michel Callon *et al.* (1983, 1984) Michel Callon, John Law and Arie Rip (eds) (1985), John Law (1983), John Law and Rob Williams (1982) and Bruno Latour (1984). Since this point is well established, details of the rhetorical mechanisms by which academics and fishermen were interested are not described in the present article.

36 For a systematic and penetrating outline of this style of analysis see Nadel (1970).

37 D. Buestel, J.-C. Dao, A. Muller-Fuega, 'Resultats preliminaires de l'experience de collecte de naissains de coquilles Saint-Jacques en rade de Brest et en baie de Saint-Brieuc' in Colloque sur l'aquaculture, Brest, Octobre 1973, *Actes de Coloque,* 1, (1974), CNEXO (ed.).

38 *Ibid.*

39 The description adopted here is not deliberately anthropomorphic in character. Just because currents intervene to thwart the experiments of researchers does not mean that we endow them with particular motives. Researchers sometimes use a vocabulary which suggests that starfish, climatic changes and currents have motives and intentions of their own. But it is precisely here that one sees the distance that separates the observer from the actor and the neutrality of the former with respect to the point of view of the latter. The vocabulary adopted, that of interessement and enrolment, makes it possible to follow the researchers in their struggles with those forces that oppose them without taking any view about the nature of the latter.

40 *Op. cit.,* note 37.

41 *Ibid.*

42 The discussions were recorded in reports which were made available.

43 One participant in the discussion, commenting on the report of Dao *et al.,* noted: 'At a theoretical level we must not minimise what we know already about scallops . . . It is important to remember that the biology of *pecten* was somewhat better known than you suggested.'

44 Dao: 'Obviously this is a very interesting observation. Our experience suggests that in general it is when the work has been done that tongues are loosened and we start to get information. For example, the fishermen had never seen scallops attached by a byssus. But since we have revealed that they are fixed in this way, they know where these are to be revealed, that they are fixed in this way, they know where these are to be found and they know where they were before. I believe that much the same thing is true for scientific information.' (*Ibid.*) On discussions about precursors and on the way in which credit is attributed to them, see in particular A. Brannigan (1979).

45 This is only a particular example of the general problem of induction.
46 Furthermore, right at the beginning of the experiments, the three researchers gathered the Saint Brieuc collectors together and transported them to their laboratory at Brest. Only after their arrival in Brest and in the presence of attentive colleagues, were the larvae extracted from the collectors, arrayed on a pallet somewhere near the Spanish Bridge, and counted. There is no difference between this and what happens after the polling stations close and the ballot-boxes are sealed. These are only reopened under the vigilant gaze of the scrutineers gathered round the tables upon which they are to be counted.
47 It needs to be shown in detail how to vote, that is to say an enumeration, whether this be of larvae or fishermen, can be transformed into an enrolment and relations of force. To do this would be to throw light upon the fundamental reasons for which (whether in politics or science) arithmetic plays a central role. This question will be further discussed in a future paper.
48 This general definition of representation throws light upon the notion of mental representation as this is used in cognitive psychology.
49 In the course of discussion the researcher whose opinions were constantly sought by the participants made this judgement: 'Let me underline the fact that this very remarkable communication marks an important date in our knowledge of the growth of Pecten maximus.'
50 This does not imply that all fishermen actively subscribe to the position adopted by their delegates. Rather it simply signifies that they do not interrupt the negotiations that those delegates undertake with the scientists and the larvae. As what subsequently happened reveals, interruption can occur without the fishermen explaining themselves publicly.
51 Following L. Thevenot (1984) one could there talk of 'investments of form'.
52 To describe the network of constraints and resources that results from a series of operations of translation I have proposed the concept of the actor-network (Callon:1985).
53 It is no surprise that the controversy or dispute was not explicitly voiced. Even electors sometimes 'vote with their feet'.
54 This point links with the notion of the political economy of power proposed by Michel Foucault (1976).

References

Barnes, Barry (1977), *Interests and the Growth of Knowledge*, Routledge & Kegan Paul, London.

Barnes, Barry (1982), *T.S. Kuhn and Social Science*, Macmillan, London.

Barnes, Barry and Shapin, S. (eds) (1979), *Natural Order: Historical Studies of Scientific Culture*, London and Beverly Hills, Sage Publications.

Bauin, Serge, Callon, M., Courtial, J.-P., *Le développement de l'aquaculture: analyse d'un système social complexe*, mimeo, CSI, 300p.

Bijker, Weibe, Pinch, T. and Hughes, T.P. (1986), *New Directions in the Social Study of Technology*, Cambridge, Mass., MIT Press.

Bloor, David (1976), *Knowledge and Social Imagery*, Routledge & Kegan Paul, London.

Boltanski, Luc (1984), 'La Dénonciation', *Actes de la Recherche en Sciences Sociales*, 51, 3–40.

Bourdieu, Pierre (1972), *Esquisse d'une théorie de la pratique*, Droz, Genève.

Bourdieu, Pierre (1975), 'The specificity of the scientific field and the social conditions of the progress of reason', *Social Science Information*, 14, 19–47.

Brannigan, A. (1979), 'The reification of Mendel', *Social Studies of Science*, 9, 423–54.

Callon, Michel (1980), 'Struggles and negotiations to define what is problematic and what is not; the socio-logic of translation', in K. D. Knorr and A. Cicourel (eds), *The Social Process of Scientific Investigation. Sociology of the Sciences Yearbook, Vol. 4*, D. Reidel Publishing Company.

Callon, Michel (1981), 'Pour une sociologie des controverses technologiques', *Fundamenta Scientiae*, 2, 381–399.

Callon, Michel (1985), 'The sociology of an actor-network', in: M. Callon, J. Law, A. Rip (eds).

Callon, Michel and Latour, Bruno (1981) 'Unscrewing the Big Leviathan: how actors macrostructure reality and how sociologists help them to do so', in K. Knorr Cetina and A. Cicourel (eds), *Advances in Social Theory and Methodology: Toward an Integration of Micro and Macro-Sociologies*, London, Routledge & Kegan Paul.

Callon, Michel and Law, John (1982), 'On interests and their transformation: enrolment and counter-enrolment', *Social Studies of Science*, 12, 615–625.

Callon, Michel, Courtial, J.-P., Turner, W. and Bauin, S. (1983), 'From translation to problematic networks: an introduction to co-word analysis', *Social Science Information*, 22, 191–235.

Callon, Michel, Bastide, F., Bauin, S., Courtial, J.-P. and Turner, W. (1984) 'Les mécanismes d'intéressement dans les textes scientifiques', *Cahiers STS-CNRS*, 4, 88–105.

Callon, Michel, Law, J. and Rip, A.(eds) (1985), *Texts and their Powers: Mapping the Dynamics of Science and Technology*, Macmillan, London.

Collins, H.M. (1975), 'The seven sexes: a study in the sociology of a phenomenon, or the replication of experiments in physics', *Sociology*, 9, 205–224.

Crane, Diana (1972), *Invisible Colleges*, Chicago, University of Chicago Press.

Farley, John and Geison, Gerald (1974), 'Science, politics and spontaneous generation in nineteenth-century France: the Pasteur-Pouchet Debate', *Bulletin of History of Medicine*, 48, 161–198.

Foucault, Michel (1976), *Surveiller et punir, Naissance de la Prison*, Gallimard, Paris.

Freudenthal, Gad (1984), 'The role of shared knowledge and science: the failure of the constructivist programme in the sociology of science', *Social Studies of Science*, 14, 285–95.

Girard, René (1961), *Mensonge romantique et vérité romanesque*, Grasset, Paris.

Girard, René (1982), *Le bouc émissaire*, Grasset, Paris.

Gouldner, A.W. (1971), *The Coming Crisis of Western Sociology*, Heinemann, London.

Greimas, A.J. and Courtes, J. (1979), *Sémiotique: dictionnaire raisonné de la théorie du langage*, Hachette, Paris.

Hennion, Antoine (1983), 'Une sociologie de l'intermédiaire: le cas du directeur artistique de variétés', *Sociologie du Travail*, 4, 435–453.

Hesse, Mary B. (1974), *The Structure of Scientific Inference*, Macmillan, London.

Hindess, Barry (1982), 'Power, interests and the outcomes of struggles', *Sociology*, 16, 498–511.

Kidder, Tracy (1982), *The Soul of a New Machine*, Penguin Books.

Knorr, K.D., Krohn, R., Whitley, R. (eds) (1980), *Sociology of the Sciences Yearbook 4: the social process of scientific investigation*, Dordrecht, London and Boston, Mass, Reidel.

Latour, Bruno (1984), *Les microbes, guerre et paix, followed by Irréductions*, A. M. Métailié, Paris.

Latour, Bruno (1985), 'Visualisation and Cognition', H. Kuclick (ed.), *Sociology of Knowledge, Science and Art*, forthcoming.

Latour, Bruno and Strum, S. (1985), 'Human social origins: please tell us another origin story', *Journal of Biological and Social Structure*, in press.

Latour, Bruno and Woolgar, S. (1979), *Laboratory Life: the Social Construction of Scientific facts*, London and Beverly Hills, Sage.

Law, John (1983), 'Enrôlement et contre-enrôlement: les luttes pour la publication d'un article scientifique', *Social Science Information*, 22, 237–251.

Law, John (1985a), 'Technology, closure and heterogeneous engineering: the case of the Portuguese expansion', in Bijker, W., Pinch, T. and Hughes, T.P.

Law, John (1985b), 'On the methods of long distance control: vessels, navigation, and the Portuguese route to India', this volume.

Law, John and Lodge, P. (1984), *Science for Social Scientists*, London, Macmillan.

Law, John and Williams, R. (1982), 'Putting facts together: a study in scientific persuasion', *Social Studies of Science*, 12, 535–558.

Lecourt, D. (1976), *Lyssenko, Histoire réelle d'une 'Science prolétarienne'*, Maspero, Paris.

Lynch, M. (1982), 'Technical work and critical inquiry: investigations in a scientific laboratory', *Social Studies of Science*, 12, 499–534.

MacKenzie, D. (1978), 'Statistical theory and social interests: a case study', *Social Studies of Science*, 8, 35–83.

Merton, Robert K. (1973), *The Sociology of Science, Theoretical and Empirical Investigations*, The University of Chicago Press, Chicago.

Nadel, Sigfried F. (1970), *La théorie de la structure sociale*, Editions de Minuit, Paris.

Pickering, A. (1980), 'The role of interests in high-energy physics: the choice between charm and colour', in K. D. Knorr, R. Krohn and R. Whitley (eds) (1980).

Pinch, Trevor J. (1980), 'Theoreticians and the production of experimental anomaly: the case of solar neutrinos', in K. D. Knorr, R. Krohn and R. Whitley (eds) (1980).

Pinch, T.J. (1981), 'The Sun-set: the presentation of certainty', *Social Studies of Science*, 11, 131–158.

Pinch, T.J. and Bijker, W. (1984), 'The social construction of facts and artefacts: or how the sociology of science and the sociology of technology might benefit each other', *Social Studies of Science*, 14, 399–441.

Popper, K. (1934), *Logik der Forschung*, Springer, Vienna.

Prigogine, I. and Stengers, I. (1979), *La nouvelle alliance*, Gallimard, Paris.

Serres, Michel (1980), *Hermes V: Le passage du Nord-Ouest*, Editions de Minuit, Paris.

Serres, Michel (1983), *Détachement*, Flammarion, Paris.

Shapin, S. (1979), 'The politics of observation: cerebral anatomy and social interests in the Edinburgh phrenology disputes', in R. Wallis (ed.).

Shapin, S. (1982), 'History of science and its sociological reconstructions', *History* of Science, 20, 157–211.

Touraine, A. (1974), *Production de la Société*, Seuil, Paris.

Thevenot, A. (1984), 'Rules and implements: investment in forms', *Social Science Information*, 23, 1–45.

Wallis, R. (ed.) (1979), *On the Margins of Science: the Social Construction of Rejected Knowledge*, Keele, University of Keele (Sociological Review Monograph 27).

Watson, James D. (1968), *The Double Helix*, Mentor Book, N.Y.

Weber, M. (1965), *Essais sur la théorie de la science*, Plon, Paris.

Young, Robert and Levidov, L. (eds) (1981), *Science, Technology and the Labour Process*, CSE Books, London.

Yoxen, E. (1981), 'Life as a productive force: capitalising the science and technology of molecular biology', in Young, R. and Levidov, L. (1981).

On the methods of long-distance control: vessels, navigation and the Portuguese route to India

John Law

Abstract

It is argued that long-distance control depends upon the creation of a network of passive agents (both human and non-human) which makes it possible for emissaries to circulate from the centre to the periphery in a way that maintains their durability, forcefulness and fidelity. This argument is exemplified by the empirical case of the fifteenth and sixteenth century Portuguese expansion and the reconstruction of the navigational context undertaken by the Portuguese in order to secure the global mobility and durability of their vessels. It is also suggested that three classes of emissaries – documents, devices and drilled people – have, together and separately, been particularly important for long-distance control, and that the dominance of the West since the sixteenth century may be partly explained in terms of crucial innovations in the methods by which passive agents of these three types are produced and interrelated.

(1) The problem

Columbus's discovery of the New World in 1492, when taken with the arrival of heavily armed Portuguese vessels in the Indian Ocean in 1498, clearly marks an important turning point in the balance of power between Europe and the rest of the world. From that moment onwards until the very recent past the rest of the world has been under European control and domination.

Given the importance of these episodes, it is unsurprising that historians have written extensively about the Iberian expansion. Thus historians of Portuguese imperialism have written in great detail about the political and military strategies adopted by commanders in the field and in Lisbon (Diffie and Winius 1977, Boxer 1969) and about the vital techniques of buying, selling and the raising of capital (Magalhaes-Godinho 1969). Such accounts are necessarily a central resource for any student of the Portuguese expansion. However, much of the serious work on ships, on methods of navigation and on the development of cannon has been left to specialists in maritime history (Cotter 1968; Landstrom 1978; Taylor 1956; Waters 1958). This work often displays a high degree of sensitivity to economic and social considerations (e.g. Lane 1934). However, the number of historians who have seriously attempted to integrate what might be called the technology of Portuguese expansion into more general accounts of the latter is relatively limited – Chaunu (1979) being, perhaps, the most notable exception.[1]

In this paper I want to argue that it is not possible to understand this expansion unless the technological, the economic, the political, the social and the natural are all seen as being interrelated. My argument is that the Portuguese effort involved the mobilisation and combination of elements from each of these categories. Of course kings and merchants appear in the story. But so too do sailors and astronomers, navigators and soldiers of fortune, astrolabes and astronomical tables, vessels and ports of call, and last but not least, the winds and currents that lay between Lisbon and Calicut.

Thus the problem for the Portuguese was not just one of social control, though this was important. It was rather, or in addition, one of how to manage long distance control *in all its aspects*. It was how to arrange matters so that a small number of people in Lisbon might influence events half-way round the world, and thereby reap a fabulous reward. And it is also my argument that if these attempts at long-distance control are to be understood then it is not only necessary to develop a form of analysis capable of handling the social, the technological, the natural and the rest with equal facility, though this is essential. It is also necessary that the approach should be capable of making sense of the way in which these are fitted together.

This, then, is the first purpose of the present paper: to make a contribution to a general analysis of long-distance social control. There is a small body of recent work in which an attempt has been made to develop a systematic vocabulary that would make this possible[2] and this paper is therefore intended as a contribution to that literature. It is also, however, intended as a contribution

235

towards the sociological treatment of technology. As I have implied above, the idea that artefacts may be treated in isolation from, or at best as a function of, social factors seems to me to be fundamentally mistaken. The second purpose of this paper is thus to argue that though artefacts form an important part of systems of long-distance control they do not, so to speak, stand apart as means or tools to be directed by social interests. Rather they should be seen as forming an integral part of such systems, interwoven with the social, the economic and the rest, and their form is thus a function of the way in which they absorb within themselves aspects their seemingly non-technological environments.

My third aim is to make some kind of a contribution towards an understanding of the means of long-distance control involved in the growth of imperialism. How was it, in other words, that Christian Europe, at the turn of the fifteenth century, hemmed in in the East by predatory muslim powers, succeeded so dramatically in turning in tables? I cannot, of course, answer this question, but I am certain that that when an answer comes it will not be reducible to the economic, the political, the social or the technological alone. Hence this paper is also intended, if somewhat indirectly, as a tribute to the *Annales* school of interdisciplinary history and in particular to the work of Fernand Braudel.[3]

(2) On Portuguese vessels and imperial power

How, then, were the Portuguese able to bombard the Samorin of Calicut, to fight and win a naval victory against a powerful combined Gujerati and Egyptian fleet at Diu in 1509 (Parry 1963: 143) and obtain a stranglehold on the vital Indian Ocean spice trade that had previously been monopolised by muslim sailors? In short, how were they able to exercise long distance control? A full answer would require the description of a structure composed of all the people and elements mentioned in the Introduction. However, for reasons of space I concentrate here on the vessels of the Portuguese and suggest two things. The first is that, when seen in the context of the *Carreira de India*, these display certain properties that are crucial to all systems of long-distance control. The second is that their shape and form as technological objects cannot be understood unless they are seen as forming part of that system. My argument is thus that, if their structure is to be understood, they must not be reified simply because they can be seen as physical artefacts.

The mediaeval European sailing vessel was unable to operate with any degree of safety or certainty beyond European waters. Its range and endurance were limited, its carrying capacity small, its ability to handle adverse weather conditions was restricted and its ability to find its way out of sight of land or soundings was doubtful. This is not to say that it functioned badly in the context of the short journeys, the small volumes of goods, and the seasonal nature of mediaeval trade. Within this social, economic and geographical 'envelope' the single-masted sailing vessel was a relatively satisfactory means of transport, permitting (for example) Hanseatic long-distance control of all Baltic trade. However, the scope of the envelope within which its mobility and integrity was ensured was limited to a European scale. To control the Indian Ocean spice trade a structure with a larger envelope of mobility and integrity was essential. For unless vessels could travel safely from the Tagus to Goa there was obviously no possibility of controlling events in the latter. And to do this it was in turn necessary to control, direct, and maintain the integrity of the vessels sent out from Lisbon. Mobility and (which amounts to the same thing) the creation of an environment within which vessels might operate with integrity – these were the first requirements for imperial control.

In their explorations the Portuguese used a range of vessels. However, for reasons of space I here consider only the mainstay of the *Carreira*, the carrack. This has been described as the 'perfected transport ship' (Chaunu 1979:242). The hull was broad, heavily built and powerful, made in the carvel manner (Chaunu 1979:242; Parry 1963:64). There were large castles, both fore and aft, which formed an integral part of the structure of the hull. The forecastle was topped off by a large pointed platform which projected forward of the bows (Parry 1963:64–5; Chaunu 1979:242) and was used for raising and lowering anchors.[4] The castles, which in certain large ships – for instance the early sixteenth century Portuguese *Santa Catarina de Monte Sinai*, (Landstrom 1978:94) – became very high and towering, were used for defence and cabin accommodation. Most depictions of these craft show them as stepping three or sometimes four masts – a small foremast, often with a square sail, a main mast with a large square sail, sometimes topped by a top mast with a further small square sail, and a mizzen mast usually with the traditional lateen sail. If there was a fourth mast this would be a bonaventure mizzen. Sometimes vessels also carried a small spritsail beneath the bow (Chaunu 1979:242; Landstrom 1978:93–9).

These bulky ships were able to carry a great deal of cargo. They were, accordingly, used from the early fifteenth century onwards to transport bulky and heavy goods on well established trading routes. By the sixteenth century the carrack was not the latest word in naval architecture. More manoeuvrable vessels were available for a variety of purposes. Nevertheless, it embodied a range of elements which, when placed in the context of the *Carreira*, rendered it both mobile and able to act with relative impunity in the face of normal circumstances. Let me, then, note some of the features of these vessels that, when taken in context with other aspects of the Portuguese system, generated an envelope of mobility and durability appropriate to the Eastern trade.

1 First, they were virtually impregnable to attack by boarding from small craft. This was one of the normal hazards of the Eastern trade (Parry:1963:118). In the face of such attack commanders battened down the hatches, and subjected boarders to lethal cross-fire from the castles. Here, then, size and the otherwise antiquated castles counted as a positive advantage. These, together with an appropriately disciplined crew and their small-arms, ensured that this peculiarly Eastern military environment did not destroy the mobility and durability of the carrack. Another way of putting this would be to say that the castles incorporated that environment in a way that was favourable to the Portuguese and therefore extended the envelope of mobility and durability available to the vessels.

2 As I indicated above, by the standards of the age the carracks carried a great deal of cargo. This not only meant that profitable trade was possible, although this is true. It also meant that they did not have to make frequent stops *en route* and could steer the most efficient course, one which routinely took them thousands of miles from land. Once again, then, they were relatively independent of their surroundings. One might say that their architecture incorporated and appropriately handled the paucity of appropriate ports of call. It also, however, incorporated the trader's need for a relatively speedy passage between Goa and Lisbon. Here again the envelope of mobility and durability in the face of a range of environments

was extended by a combination of technological artefact and human resources.

3 The combination of square and (triangular) lateen sails characteristic of the carrack and other contemporary vessels marks a successful attempt to obtain versatility in the face of a range of different wind conditions.[5] Large square sails provided the main propulsive force, but might rapidly be reduced in area in case of storm. The smaller sails at bow and stern rendered the craft more manoeuvrable than would otherwise have been the case and the lateen sails, in combination with the bowline attached to the weather leech of the main squaresail, made it possible for the vessel to steer a course across the wind. In this way it might sail before the North East Trades from Lisbon to Madeira on the outward journey, before crossing the area of variable winds to reach across the South East Trades into the giant circle to the Cape. Thus, by means of appropriate rigging, pilotage and manpower, the Portuguese incorporated these trade winds within the *Carreira* on their own terms and thereby increased the size of the envelope within which the vessel might move and maintain its integrity.

4 The carrack was more independent of its environment than earlier types of vessel in yet another way. This arose from the fact that the handling of large lateen sails is both difficult and labour-intensive (see, e.g., Gille 1970:196).[6] Since the lateen sails of the carrack were relatively small the size of the crew was correspondingly reduced. This increased the envelope of mobility and durability of the vessels in a variety of ways. They could be sailed with relatively small crews, something that was particularly important given the high degree of mortality on the long voyages of the *Carreira da India* (Rego 1964:45). In addition, it was possible to reduce the number of stops along the way, or even to eliminate these altogether.[7] Again, then, the scope of independent action for these vessels was increased by incorporating features of their environment within their design and pilotage on terms favourable to the Portuguese.

The Portuguese vessels were not only part of a structure of heterogeneous elements that provided them with an appropriate envelope within which they might maintain their mobility and durability. They were also, and this is in some respects another way of saying the same thing, in an enhanced position to *to control or exert force upon other, non-artefactual, elements of that structure*. This capacity of extract compliance from the environment is most vividly exemplified for the case of naval battles or bombardments where unfortunate Muslims or Hindus found themselves at the wrong end of the superior Portuguese cannonfire (see, e.g., Diffie and Winius 1977:240ff). In this instance European methods of cannon-founding contributed very directly to long distance control (Cipolla 1965:102; Parry 1963:118). But so, too did the innovations in shipbuilding mentioned above. Without these there would have been no possibility of sending such floating gun-platforms half way across the globe.

However, the Portuguese not only exerted force on their sworn enemies in order to bring them into line. Their whole effort depended, from top to bottom, on the capacity to extract compliance. Seamen, merchants, masters, envoys, it was necessary to keep all of these in line and to make use of their efforts if the *Carreira da India* was to work and the vessels were to sail reliably with their loads of spices for the European markets. And such compliance was not only required from the human components of the system. It was also expected from its inanimate parts – from the hulls and sails that made up the vessels and the environments in which those vessels sailed. Thus, the improvements in methods of rigging described above can be seen as novel ways of borrowing the power of the wind, converting it, and using it to exert force upon the sea. As I have suggested, they made it possible to use the winds in ways that had not earlier been possible by transforming those that might previously have been dangerous, or simply adverse, into forces that contributed to the projects of the Portuguese by driving their vesels towards their destinations.[8] Currents were likewise transformed, this time by geographical knowledge and navigational competence, into forces that speeded rather than hindered the voyage. The metaphor, that of struggle with, attempts to extract compliance from, and making use of, potentially hostile elements, is one that works equally well for the human and the inanimate.

Finally, and partly as a function of their mobility, durability and capacity to exert force, Portuguese vessels also had the *capacity to return* to their point of origin. They were able to set sail from the Tagus and return months or even years later from Goa or Calicut in a relatively predictable manner. This was, of course, a *sine qua non* if the spice trade was to be monopolised. It was also vital if other types of control were to be maintained at the periphery, if the periphery was to belong, in any sense at all, to the centre.[9] The ability to return depended on seaworthy vessels such as the carracks mentioned above. It also depended on trained seamen and masters, the capacity to carry the necessary provisions and a host of other factors. At least as important as any of these, however, was an ability to find their way about the ocean and arrive at the desired destination. For, as I have indicated, the course followed by the *Carreira da India* did not hug the African shoreline. This would have been impossible for vessels as large as the carrack. In addition, with adverse winds and currents it would have taken far too long. Instead the Portuguese charted out a path that in places took them thousands of miles from land and required novel methods of navigation.

In the next sections I consider the late fifteenth century Portuguese development of astronomical navigation. However, before doing so I want to suggest that the features that I have described above in the context of the development of Portuguese imperialism may be seen as general characteristics of long distance control. Mobility, durability, capacity to exert force, ability to return – these seem to be indispensable if remote control is to be attempted. Indeed, they may be seen as specifications of a yet more general requirement: that there be no degeneration in communication between centre and periphery. No noise must be introduced into the circuit. Periphery must respond, as it were mechanically, to the behest of centre. Envoys must not be distorted by their passage, and interaction must be arranged such that they are able to exert influence without in turn being influenced. Finally, they must have the capacity to return, again unscathed, in order to report to centre.[10] If we except the case of the Chinese, then it was the Portuguese and the Spanish who, for the first time in history, developed the technical capacity for relatively undistorted communication at a global level.

(3) Mediaeval navigation and the Portuguese problem

In the middle ages there were two worlds of European navigation, one in the Mediterranean and the other in north-west Europe. The approaches adopted by navigators in these two worlds, though they shared certain features – for instance the magnetic compass

and the pilot book or rutter – were very different. The Mediterranean navigator used his[11] rutter in combination with a *portolan*
or plain (plane) chart to determine an appropriate magnetic
compass course.[12] This was made possible by the fact that the chart
was laid out around wind roses and rhumb lines of constant
magnetic bearing. The navigator thus determined the bearing of
his course by looking for an appropriate rhumb line coming from a
convenient wind-rose. If no wind-rose was suitably located, he
used a ruler and dividers to relate the line of his desired course to a
nearby rhumb line (Taylor 1956:111). He determined the distance
to be run by measuring this off the chart and/or by consulting his
pilot book (Waters 1958:62). He then used the magnetic compass
to steer the determined bearing, and dead reckoning, plus
landmarks mentioned in his pilot-book, to calculate distance run.
If tacking was necessary, then progress was measured by means of
a set of *marteloio* tables (Taylor 1956:112; 117–20; Diffie and
Winius 1977:130). *Portolan* charts, usually drawn on a single
sheepskin with the neck to the west, covered the Mediterranean,
the Black Sea and by the end of the thirteenth century, the
Atlantic some way south down the coast of what is now Morocco
and north to the English Channel, the Wash and Flanders (Taylor
1965:113; Waters 1958:62). Even so, they were intimately linked
with the Mediterranean world of navigation and only extended as
far as the Venetian and Genoese trade routes.

The north-west European mediaeval school of navigation
developed very differently and depended hardly at all upon charts
but instead made use of the magnetic compass and the rutter
together with the lead and line. This was popular for a number of
reasons. First, the rise and fall of the tide (which was, of course,
unknown in the Mediterranean) made it essential for the seaman
to know how much water lay under his keel (Waters 1958:18).
Second, again in contrast with the Mediterranean, the waters of
the north Atlantic were opaque and direct observation of the sea-
bottom was not usually possible. Third, (think again of the
Mediterranean) the seaman of the Atlantic frequently had to
contend with adverse visibility. He could not be certain that he
would be able to observe landmarks from any great distance. This
was no impediment to the use of the lead and line as these were
not dependent on good visibility. And finally, unlike the steeply
shelving Mediterranean, much of the north-west Atlantic was less
than 100 fathoms deep (Waters 1958:18). For all these reasons,
not only was the lead and line an aid to Atlantic navigation. It was

one of the fundamental tools around which navigational practice was organised.

That this was the case is witnessed by the surviving rutters. The earliest known example in English which is dated 1408 (Waters 1958:11) and which gives directions for the circumnavigation of the British Isles, gives names of landmarks and the magnetic compass bearings between them, has data on the direction of tidal flows, a section on the establishment of ports[13] and much information (consisting of about a third of the whole) on soundings and the nature of the sea bed. Thus even in very poor visibility the master of a vessel was able to move his way from point to point with some degree of success by using his compass, his rutter and by taking periodic soundings which also allowed him to determine the nature of the sea bed.

These systems of navigation served their purpose very well. The limitations detected in them by later commentators (which related particularly to an ignorance of, or an inability to cope with, the magnetic variation) were scarcely relevant to the practice of seafarers in the middle ages. So long as the established trading routes were followed few difficulties arose and regular communication was possible. This is witnessed both by the regular trading activities of the Venetians and Genoese who sailed from the Black Sea and the Holy Land at one end of Christendom to England and Flanders at its other and those of the Hanseatic masters and their British, French and Basque counterparts who navigated from the Baltic to Palestine. However, the Mediterranean system and that of the North-West Europeans had one feature in common: they were only effective over certain (though admittedly quite extensive and important) geographical areas. The vessel that strayed out of these areas, or indeed, off the charted routes within them, was liable to lose its way and risk disaster.

What was the case for the carrack is true again here. The vessels were physically mobile, forceful and durable only while they stayed *within* the envelope generated by rutters and charts. Or, to put it somewhat differently, they were undisturbed by their external environment only so long as they were able to transfer that environment inside themselves in the form of charts, rutters and the rest. But this transferred context imposed some fairly strict limits, at least for certain purposes. For an independent check on distance and direction run, navigation was dependent upon observable geographical features. For, with the influence of winds, tides and currents, and the difficulties involved in attempting to measure the speed of the vessel in the water, no master was happy to depend exclusively upon dead-reckoning and his compass course in order to determine location. The pilot books offered sometimes erroneous but nevertheless independent data that made it possible to check position under most conditions.[14] But the features noted in the rutters had two important and related characteristics. First, in order to act as the kind of check needed they had to be observable. Shorelines were visible from a distance of a few leagues, at least under favourable circumstances. Depths might be sounded and the characteristics of the sea-bed determined in waters of up to 100 fathoms. And second, their description varied in nature or quality as a function of position. It was this very characteristic that made them useful as independent checks of position. Where shorelines were not visible or depths were too great (or where, of course, neither had been observed) these methods of navigation were of no assistance. The mariner had travelled outside the envelope described by his rutter into the unknown, and at once the durability, the mobility, the strength and the capacity of his vessel to return were all were put at risk.

This, then, was the Portuguese problem. In the fifteenth century their explorations were beginning to take them beyond the charts and rutters of their time. And it was not simply that no-one had been there to observe and report back before (though this was true). It was also, and more fundamentally, that their journeys to Madeira and the Azores took them deep into the north Atlantic, far from the coastline and the limits of sounding. Compass courses and dead reckoning were useful allies in the Mediterranean where it was impossible to get very far from shore and they might be checked against written descriptions of important landmarks en route. But they no longer contributed their quantum of force when the destination was a small and isolated island which might easily be missed by a few leagues. Under such circumstances, description of (the rare) landmarks, though necessary, did not provide a context appropriate to environmental independence and the vessel no longer contained, within itself, the environment necessary to ensure such independence.

To summarise: vessels may move to and fro with relative freedom. Like faithful servants they may thus be seen as candidate means for those who wish to exercise long-distance control. However, before they can be so used, they have themselves to be controlled. They have to be able to retain their integrity under a range of circumstances. Their structure, but also their means of navigation – these are two of the features that define the envelope within which they come and go like faithful servants. In this section I have suggested that independence with respect to a *particular* context may be achieved, but that this depends upon embodying features of that context in a system of heterogeneous elements that describes an appropriate envelope of physical durability. Seen in this light then, the Portuguese problem was to build a new navigational context for their vessels that was less dependent upon European geography, one that would render their vessels independent of a broader geographical environment, and hence make possible an undistorted system of global communication and control.[15] It was to this that they turned their minds.

(4) The Portuguese solution

Every year, from the turn of the sixteenth century, the great carracks left the Tagus in March or at the latest early April. They needed to pass the Cape of Good Hope in July in order to catch the south-east monsoon, and could expect to be in Goa by the end of August or the beginning of September. To catch the monsoon for the return journey it was best to leave India in December though January would do. Then, depending on the passage, vessels could expect to be back in Lisbon again between mid June and mid September (Magalhaes-Godinho 1969:665–8; Rego 1964: 39–40). Despite losses due to the sea and, towards the end to Dutch and English privateering, the *Carreira da India* functioned, as Magalhaes-Godinho notes 'avec des resultats tres satisfaisants pendant plus de quatre-vingts ans' (1969:670).

The Portuguese solved many of the navigational problems involved in this journey between the 1460s and the 1480s. During this period, they continued the exploration of the African coast started under the direction of Henry 'the Navigator' in the 1430s. As the Mediterranean method of navigation with plain chart, compass, rutter and distance run became steadily more inadequate, they sought additional navigational aids. Perhaps as early as the 1460s they started to make systematic observations of the angular altitude of the Pole Star, *Stella Maris*, above the northern horizon.[16] By the later 1480s their mariners were using not only the Pole Star (which could be used only in the northern hemisphere) but also measuring the *altura* of the Sun and the Southern Cross as an aid to navigation. These methods, and the instruments and tables of data used in their practice, though not novel in scientific terms, nevertheless mark a major breakthrough in methods of navigation and the construction of a system within which global mobility and communication might be ensured.

Mediaeval astronomers were committed to the Ptolemaic conception of the Universe. As is well known, this considered the Universe to consist of a set of concentric spheres, with the earth at its centre. The approach, and the careful observations of the heavens that it sustained, offered well-developed explanations for the behaviour of celestial objects as observed from the earth. Furthermore, these theories had predictive value. Tables of Ephemerides which predicted the times of astronomical events of particular importance were calculated and circulated. Thus not only was there a theoretical explanation for the daily variation in the declination of the sun but the value of the latter was also routinely predicted. That there was a relationship between the observed location of heavenly bodies in the celestial sphere and the position of the observer on earth was also well understood. Ptolemy's *Geography* (which became available in Latin translation in 1409 (Taylor 1956:151)) showed how every point on the surface of the sphere of the earth might be described by a unique latitude and longitude. Accordingly, explanations for the altitude and bearing of astronomical objects were posed in terms of terrestrial latitude and longitude, while the idea that the latter might be determined by observing the former was also generally accepted.

Mediaeval astronomers and astrologers not only had a cosmological theory. They also had a range of instruments available to them. The most important for our purposes were the planispheric astrolable and the quadrant. The former, which has been described as a 'compendium of instruments' (Cotter 1968:60, citing Gunther), might, in combination with the Ephemerides, be used in a wide variety of ways. Most of these were concerned with depicting positions of heavenly bodies at a given moment in time. Thus, given a time, it was possible to display the positions of the sun and selected stars. This was important, for instance, in casting horoscopes. Contrariwise, given a star or sun sight, it was possible to tell the time. The same was also true for the quadrant, another specialist instrument of astronomers and astrologers, that had many of the same qualities. However, in addition to their properties as analogue computers, they were also built to allow measurements of the altitude of astronomical (or other) objects. In the case of the astrolabe, which was shaped in the form of a disc, this was suspended by a ring. A swivelling sight called the alidade was then turned until the object being sighted was simultaneously visible through two pin-holes. Its altitude was then determined by looking at the point where the alidade crossed a scale inscribed around its circumference. This was graduated from 0° (horizontal) to 90° (vertical). The quadrant, which was shaped like a quarter circle, was suspended from its corner and swivelled about this until one of the radii was in line with the object to be sighted. The altitude of the latter was measured by a plumb-line which fell from its corner to cross a scale marked along its circumference.

It was widely believed in the early modern period that the earth was, indeed, a sphere, and mariners, who were used to telling the time by observing the Pole Star and its surrounding stars, were well aware that the latter sank towards the horizon in the northern sky as they sailed south. However, Ptolemaic astronomy and the instruments associated with its practice, were opaque to the layman (Taylor 1956:158). Thus, though it is possible in retrospect to see how mediaeval astronomy might have been adapted to solve the problem of global navigation, we should beware of assuming that such a transfer was either easy, obvious, or an excessively long time in coming. There is controversy about the exact moment when this took place[17] but since this does not directly affect the argument that I am trying to make, I will pass over the disputed period of the 1460s and 1470s and instead discuss the progress that most historians concede occurred in the 1480s.

In 1484 King John II convened a small commission and charged it with the task of finding a method for navigating outside European waters. The commission appears to have had at least four members. There was the Royal Physician, Master Rodrigo. There was Diego Ortiz, who had been Professor of Astrology at the University of Salamanca before being forced to flee abroad, and who subsequently became, in succession, the Bishop of Tangier, Ceuta and Viseu. It is known that he liked to mix science with politics and had good connections with astronomers (Beaujouan 1966:74–6). There was Martin Behaim, a geographer, originally from Nuremberg, who was to use up-to-date Portuguese cartographic data for the magnificent globe which was made in 1492 and which bears his name (Bagrow and Skelton 1964:106–7; and Tooley and Bricker 1976:152–3).[18] And perhaps most important there was Jose Vizinho, a Jewish doctor, who had been a disciple of the astronomer Abraham Zacuto of Salamanca (Chaunu 1979:257). These four men, and probably in particular

Vizinho, were responsible for one of the earliest successful practical applications of scientific knowledge to practice: the *Regimento do Astrolabio et do Quadrante.* A printed copy, dated 1509, exists, and Taylor suggests not only that there was an earlier 1495 printed edition, but that handwritten copies would have been prepared in the 1480s for selected pilots (Taylor 1956:162).[19] Whatever the exact date, its importance is beyond question for it not only fulfilled the expectations of the king but it also laid the foundations of modern astronomical navigation.

The new navigation proposed by the commission hinged around the determination of the latitude by means of solar or stellar observation,[20] a method particularly appropriate for journeys that were mainly in a northerly or southerly direction, such as those undertaken by the Portuguese in the Atlantic and, to some extent, the Indian Ocean. This was because it depended upon sailing north or south until the vessel reached the same latitude as its destination. Then the master could steer east or west as appropriate, in the certain knowledge that he would make an appropriate landfall.

The success of the commission in putting this method into practice rested on three elements. First, it made available greatly simplified versions of the astrolabe and the quadrant. All the machinery for calculating the relationship between time and astronomical position was swept away. In the case of the astrolabe what had previously been on its back – the alidade and the scale for reading off the altitude (or zenith) – was all that was left (Waters 1976:42).[21] The quadrant was similarly reduced to its altitude-measuring essentials. Second, it made available a range of astronomical and geographical data that were essential if crude measurements of the altitude of the sun were to be converted into data about the latitude. As background reading, so to speak, it included a Portuguese translation of Sacrobosco's *Sphaera Mundi,* an elementary text written in about 1250 (Cotter 1968:21) on the spherical nature of the earth. However, the most important directly relevant data concerned the sun's declination on different days of the (leap) year. As I have indicated, these had been regularly calculated by astronomers, but the significance of the work of the commission was to make them available in a form which, like that of the astrolabe and quadrant, might be used with some hope of success by the literate but relatively untutored mariner.[22] In addition to the tables of declination, and a calendar, there were also geographical data necessary for navigational decision making. Thus the earliest known version of the *Regimento* includes observations of the *altura* for significant points on the coast from Lisbon southwards to the equator (Taylor:1956:163), a list that was further extended in subsequent years. Such data was obviously important in providing a context for the latitudes discovered by the navigator on board ship.

Third, and perhaps most important, were three sets of rules telling the mariner how he should use the instruments and data provided to determine the latitude.[23] First there was a Regiment of the North, which told how to measure the altitude of the Pole Star and then convert this into the latitude. Second, there was a Rule for Raising the Pole, which told the navigator how far he had to sail on any course in order to raise one degree, and how far east or west he had sailed in doing so. This rule was the product of what we would now call elementary trigonometry. And third there was the Regiment of the Sun, which tackled the difficult problem of guiding the navigator through a solar fix to a determination of the latitude. This was complicated, or at least it was more complicated than the analogous Regiment of the North, because of the daily variation of the declination of the sun and the consequent necessity to consult tables in order to determine the latter.

These rules were, as I have indicated above, written on the reasonable assumption that most navigators had little grasp of the principles of astronomy. They were, accordingly, rather literal in nature. Consider, for instance, the Regiment of the Sun. This starts by telling the observer to find the height of the sun 'and this must be at midday when the Sun is at its greatest elevation' (Taylor 1956:165). After writing this down (probably on a slate) he is instructed to enter the table for the month and the day.

> Take out the declination, and if the Sun is in a northern Sign,
> and if the shadow is falling to your north, then subtract the
> altitude that you found from ninety, and add the declination.
> The sum will be the number of degrees you are north of the
> equinoctial. (Taylor 1956:165)

This, however, is only one of the cases, and the rules proceed to describe the other possible combinations of declination and direction of fall of shadow, and conclude by considering those instances where the resultant calculation ends up with a figure of 90°. Given the anticipated competence of the mariner, the authors of the rule had to be sure that they covered all possible cases. Taylor makes the point in this way:

> To teach the rule of the Sun to the novice must have been a matter of great difficulty for an astronomer. The would-be pilot must learn how to 'enter' the calendar and pick out the figures, he must memorize the dates of the equinoxes and know which are the northern and which are the southern Signs. For according as the Sun's shadow falls north or south, and according as it is in the same or the opposite hemisphere to himself, the figures are to be manipulated differently. In fact he has eight rules to learn, apart from the special case when his ship is on the 'line' precisely at one of the equinoxes.
> (1956:165)

In fact, the new navigation did not depend upon the mariner being able to 'pick it up' by himself. The simple rules, the simple data and the simple instruments were supplemented by systematic training, at least from the turn of the sixteenth century. The Portuguese set up the Casa de Guinea e India at Lisbon which, writes Waters:

> included an organization equivalent to a modern hydrographic office at whose head was a cosmographer-in-chief. He was assisted by cosmographers whose business it was to draw and correct charts and to compile books of sailing directions and, no doubt, as in the similar Spanish organization of the sixteenth century, to assist in the instruction of pilots. (1958:62).

This training was thorough, at least in the early years of the sixteenth century. Though it later became somewhat lax (Rego (1964:40) goes so far as to say that this was the root cause of later marine decadence of the Portuguese) there is no doubt that the method and the training on which this depended made an indispensable contribution to the long-lived Portuguese mastery of the Indian ocean.

We started by saying that long-distance social control depended upon creating a structure of elements, both human and natural, capable of generating an envelope of durable mobility for vessels. We then noted that those vessels embodied a part of that structure in their form and were, in turn, both able to exert force upon other parts of that structure and then return to base. We then suggested that some such kind of relatively undistorted communication was a necessary adjunct to long-distance control. However, since no vessel was an island unto itself, if it was to be relatively mobile on a global scale then it was necessary to create and incorporate within itself a different, astronomical, context: one that would extend the envelope of its mobility and durability. In this section we have seen how the Portuguese faced this problem in an acute form as they pushed further south in the course of the fifteenth century, and have briefly considered the solution to which they came. Of course, they did not do without rutters and charts. These continued to be vital components of their navigational context, essential allies in routefinding. But through the activities of the commission they rebuilt that context to include the very heavens, heavens that stayed with the navigator wherever he might go. And this borrowing from the heavens was achieved by means of a judicious juxtaposition of data, instruments and rules for the guidance of mariners which in turn, had the individual and collective property that they were relatively mobile, durable and forceful.[24]

(5) The materials of long-distance control

If the Portuguese were successful in their efforts to build a navigational envelope for their vessels that made mobility and undistorted communication between Lisbon and India possible, is there any more general lesson to be learned about the way in which this success was achieved? To answer this question we need to look again at the *types* of elements that they brought together in their system.

Consider first, then, the *Regimento* itself. The Rule of the North Star, the Regiment of the Sun, the Rule for Raising the Pole, the tables of solar declination, the latitude of possible points of destination, all of these took the form of *written or printed inscriptions*. Within the envelope of the vessel (of which, in a more general sense, they formed a part) these were mobile, durable, yet also capable of exerting force upon that environment. In other words, they were endowed with the same set of properties as the carracks discussed above. But whence came that force? Part of the answer is that it came from the way in which they were juxtaposed with the right kinds of people and instruments. It came, in other words, from a specially constructed and relatively stable structure.

251

However, it also came in part from their contents, from the very inscriptions that made them up.

Consider one case, that of the table of solar declination. This represented the distillation, as it were, of many years of astronomical expertise, of thousands and thousands of calculations, of correspondence, of argument and of innovation. When it created a table the commission was therefore creating a kind of surrogate astronomer. It was not necessary to take along Jose Vizinho or Abraham Zacuto in person. Their force, and the work of their predecessors, was being borrowed, converted into a highly transportable and indefinitely reproducible form, and being put to work on every ship. The production of tables of solar declination for the purpose of navigation may thus be seen as a way of reducing the relevant aspects of a weighty astronomical tradition to a form that, in the context of the vessel, was more mobile and durable than the original. It seems, if I may mix metaphors, to have been a way of capitalising on generations of astronomical work by converting this into a nicely simplified black box that might be carried anywhere within the Portuguese system of long distance control and which would contribute to this when posed the right questions.

But the *Regimento* was not sufficient by itself. Navigation also demanded astrolabes or quadrants. In short, it demanded instruments. Like the *Regimento* itself, these were transportable and relatively durable on board ship. Indeed, much of the effort of the commission and those who followed it was devoted to devising instruments that were more mobile and versatile. When the Portuguese first started using astrolabes these appear to have been enormous wooden instruments which were taken ashore and set up, presumably on a tripod. They were quite unsuitable for observations from on board ship. Even the brass disc of the classical planispheric astrolabe offered so much wind resistance that observation was very difficult. In the course of the sixteenth century the nautical astrolabe took on a different form. It became a small, open, brass ring which, while still difficult to use from the deck of a vessel, was at least an improvement on its predecessors.

However, if the astrolabe was relatively durable within its structured envelope then it was also potentially forceful with respect to that structure. As with the *Regimento,* this force came from two sources. First, it was borrowed from the navigational context that had been specially constructed by the commission. But second, it also represented the relevant distillation of generations of work in astronomy and instrument-making. This may be a little less obvious than it was for the case of tables of declination. Perhaps this is because we tend to assume that devices have a natural solidity which is absent in the case of inscriptions. Nevertheless, the argument made there is equally applicable here. Work and discussion went into the many generations of the astrolabe, into decisions about what to fit and how to fit it together. Indeed, I mentioned a little of that work earlier: the commission, or its close Portuguese predecessors, decided that most of the components of the astronomical astrolabe were simply irrelevant to the problems of navigation and swept them away. Just as with the tables, the final mariner's astrolabe may be seen as a physical manifestation of previous work, a kind of nicely simplified black box which, if placed within the apppropriate envelope of other elements, was capable of generating the kind of answers that were needed to sustain that structure.

But documents and devices were not all. There were also the navigators themselves. In short, there were people. These are, as we all know, relatively mobile and somewhat durable. Properly clothed, sheltered, and given a means of transport, they become yet more mobile and durable. Thus the Portuguese sailors were passing through places and arriving at destinations undreamed of by previous generations. And they were also forceful, forceful for the same two reasons: first because of the structured envelope in which they were placed, and second because they themselves embodied a great deal of previous effort. The structure of which they formed a part was, of course, all-important. The Portuguese mariner, on a vessel with a cannon, was indeed powerful. The same mariner, shipwrecked on a beach, was pathetically weak. This is why the commission spent so much time designing an appropriate context for its fledgeling navigators. The latter could not afford to be mystified by a stereographic projection of the heavens. This was removed from the astrolabe. They could not afford to be confused about how to sight the Pole Star. So they were told to aim at it like crossbowmen. They could not afford to misunderstand the tables of declination and draw their data from the wrong section. So they were given a recipe which dealt with all the possible combinations of season and hemisphere. They could not afford to get their arithmetic wrong. So they were given worked examples to follow. They could not be left to do trigonometry by themselves. So they were given the Rule for Raising the Pole. The care with which the commission attended to the context of the navigator is notable, for they knew that it was only in this way that he would not go astray, that he would successfully borrow the forces that lay in the tables and the instruments. Even so, the navigator was only able to do this because of his past. He could read, he could count, he knew how to hold an astrolabe. He was, in other words, the embodiment of previous effort, both that of other people and his own. And in order to function as a navigator he had to be persuaded to select and borrow from that work. From the standpoint of successful navigation he too, then, was a black box. Placed in the right circumstances, and fed the right inputs, he produced a simple latitude.

Documents, devices and drilled people: I want to argue that it was this combination that was the key to the success of the commission. For documents, devices and people have in common that, placed in the right structure, they are potentially mobile, durable and able (though this may sound odd to those brought up in the traditions of interpretive sociology or theoretical humanism) to act upon that structure. Of course, they do not retain these characteristics under all circumstances. They may lose their force and their capacity to move if things go wrong. Nevertheless, when the commission scratched its head and considered what *kinds* of elements it could hope to put on a vessel which would subsequently retain their shape and power, the answer, though it would not have been posed in these terms, must have been obvious. It was documents, devices and drilled people. They would hold their form. They would act as they should at a distance so long as they were properly chosen and placed at the right location within an appropriately designed structure. For they could not be chosen randomly and thrown together. The right documents, the right devices, the right people properly drilled – put together they would create a structured envelope for one another that ensured their durability and fidelity.

(6) Conclusion

I have argued that the Portuguese made good use of documents, devices and drilled people and that these were obvious resources to be used by anyone who wanted to exercise long-distance control. Other work, for instance on the way in which laboratory scientists succeed in influencing their fellows, their research directors, the agencies that give them their grants and the process of industrial manufacture, also points in the same direction (Callon 1985a; Callon, Law and Rip 1985b; Latour 1984b; Law 1985a). Texts of all sorts, machines or other physical objects, and people, sometimes separately but more frequently in combination, these seem to be the obvious raw materials for the actor who seeks to control others at a distance. Of course this remains an hypothesis of an empirically testable kind. Are these the means that are generally used by those who wish to exert power at a distance, or are there others? Are there particular combinations of the three that characterise different major institutions? These are questions that take us beyond the scope of the present essay. However, I want to conclude by making a few comments that relate to the problem which I originally posed about the sources of western long-distance control.

To what extent, then, are major disparities in the creation of envelopes of undistorted communication and long-distance control explicable in terms of revolutions in methods for the creation of durable and mobile documents, devices and people? To what extent, in other words, may the hegemony of the west be explained in terms of a few basic innovations in the production of the means of control? These are questions to which it is possible to give only speculative answers. Nevertheless, there is a range of recent sociological, anthropological and historical work that bears upon them. The argument is clearest for the case of documents and texts. Goody, in rejecting the notion that there is a difference between the mind of the savage and that of his domesticated neighbour, argues that literacy and in particular the act of making lists should be seen as potent methods of domestication (Goody 1977). This argument has been extended by Latour (1985a) who cites Eisenstein's (1979) monumental study of the importance of the printing press for western social change. Thus Latour, who argues that power is a function of the capacity to muster a large number of allies at one spot, suggests that inscription, and in particular its printed reproduction, makes possible the concentration of a far wider range of allies than had previously been possible. On the one hand, then, my argument about the force of the tables of declination is consistent with and indeed follows Latour's line of reasoning. The tables can be seen as ways of allying generations of astronomical observations with a new structural envelope that rendered these durable, mobile and forceful on a global scale. On the other hand, the significance of Latour's analysis of the role of the printing press is that its invention may be seen as a revolutionary improvement in the textual means of long-distance control, one that goes some way to explaining both the hegemony of the west and the 'great divide' between primitive and modern.

Similar arguments may be made about people. In this case the primary problem for long distance control may not necessarily have to do with mobility, nor even forcefulness. It may rather be concerned with a special aspect of durability, that of fidelity. This is because it is no good sending out agents who promptly become double-agents, fail to exert the proper force, and do not report back. As we have seen for the case of Portuguese navigational methods, fidelity may be increased if the agent is placed in a well-designed structural envelope. It may also be increased if he or she is properly prepared, primed, as it were, with the appropriate range of allies, before being sent out. The question then, is whether the west has been able to exert particularly effective long-distance control via people as a result of an innovation analogous to that of the printing press. Has it, in other words, found a special way of keeping people faithful? The answer to these questions would appear to be yes. It is only recently that the implications of the invention and diffusion of military drill have come under scrutiny. Nevertheless, arguments by Foucault (1979) and McNeill (1982) suggest that its importance for social control both on and off the battlefield has been immense. Drilled armies were able to march faster and in better order than their predecessors and militarily they were much more effective. Furthermore, individual soldiers fought more reliably in battle. This was because drill broke actions down and then reassembled them into a prescribed, regular and observable structure. Previously unreliable actions were converted into ranks of dependable gestures. As is well known, the argument has been deployed by Foucault on a much broader front. The 'model' worker was one who had been drilled, who was a reliable automaton, and who accordingly offered a more convenient way of exercising power.

The argument may also be made with respect to devices and machines. It is a commonplace that the technological history of western Europe reveals the way in which devices displayed an increasing capacity to harness natural forces. Methods of milling, of agricultural work, of military technology and of ocean navigation, all of these (to name but four) developed in such a way that wind, water, animal and to a lesser extent human power were more fully harnessed, and harnessed in a more flexible manner. The result was increasing forcefulness, increasing durability and, in the case of the means of transport, increasing mobility. With respect to overseas imperialist domination, a good case can be made that the 'nautical revolution' of the fifteenth century with its invention of the three-masted, mixed rigged, seagoing sailing vessel played a crucial role. However, if there is a single innovation which had an impact with respect to devices and machines comparable with that of drill and the invention of printing on people and texts, it must surely be the development of manufacture. This, as is well known, brought together an unprecedented range of natural and human forces by taking processes that had previously been geographically dispersed and relatively undifferentiated, and breaking them down into separate but physically adjacent components. With the harnessing of steam-power the process of social control has been the subject of extensive analysis in the Marxist tradition. However, it is important to underline the way in which this occurred, not only in the workplace and to those who worked there, but also to those who never saw a factory in their lives. For it was not simply that goods of a standard quality became common. It was also that reliable machines and devices became widely available to those who wished to enhance their ability to act at a distance. These might be sent into mines (Lankton 1983), into homes (Hughes 1979; Pinch and Bijker 1984; Schwartz-Cowan 1984), into vessels and power stations (Constant 1978) and into military arsenals (MacKenzie 1984). Indeed, novel devices have been integrated with new contexts to such an extent that the moon itself is no longer the limit. It is possible to sit in a control-room in Houston and influence events at the other end of the solar system.

The empirical analysis of revolutionary development in the means of long-distance control remains, in most cases, work to be done. Equally I would not like to leave the reader with the idea that the document/device/drilled person trinity is necessarily sacrosanct. There may well be other ways of creating the structured envelope/hardened envoy duo that is so crucial to long-distance control. However, I believe the theoretical claim – that the undistorted communication necessary for long-distance control depends upon the generation of a structure of heterogeneous elements containing envoys which are mobile, durable, forceful and able to return – to be well founded. This, as I have shown above, has profound implications for the conduct of a sociology of artefacts and devices. In addition I hope that, notwithstanding the deeply held sociological prejudice in favour of privileging the status of human beings, the present essay will have demonstrated that if one wishes to understand the nature of long-distance control, then it is not only possible but also desirable to talk of people, texts and devices in the same analytical terms.

Notes

1 Cipolla (1975) is a *tour de force* on vessels, firepower and imperialism in general. Parry (1963) and Penrose (1952) are also honourable exceptions, particularly Parry whose account nevertheless falls into two parts: first the social and technological means, and second the process of expansion itself. See also Lane (1950).

2 See, in particular, Callon 1985a; 1985b; Callon and Latour 1981; Callon, Law and Rip 1985b; Latour 1983; 1984a; 1984b; 1985b; Law 1984; 1985a; 1985b.

3 Even if I had the ability and the inclination (and I have neither), in an essay of this length there would be no space to create the kind of global historical panoramas favoured by Braudel (1975; 1979) or Wallerstein (1974).

4 Each ship was equipped with six to eight anchors, which is an indication of their relative inefficiency at holding a ship of these dimensions, and also of their relative fragility (Chaunu 1979:242).

5 In a following wind, and in storm conditions, the square sail is much more suitable than the lateen (Lane 1934:38; Parry 1963:59; Gille 1966:172). It is also easier to alter its size under way, and its maximum dimensions are not subject to the strict limits imposed on the lateen by the length of its yard. By contrast the lateen is much better adapted for sailing close to the wind (Landstrom 1978:51; Parry 1963:58) and in general is more adaptable to a range of wind conditions.

6 Parry estimates that the average crew for the lateen-rigged Mediterranean vessel must have consisted of fifty men (Parry 1963:60) while a comparable square-rigged Atlantic vessel perhaps required only twenty men and twelve apprentices (see also Lane 1973:123).

7 One widely used port of call, Mocambique, was widely and rightly seen as a Portuguese graveyard. It was reported that men, dying of scurvy and other diseases, would flock ashore when the vessels arrived, but those that survived would be equally glad to be back on board after a few days in order to escape the nightmare of tropical disease. See Rego 1964:46.

8 For further discussion on this see Law 1985b.

9 For a discussion of the importance of communications for the maintenance of empire see Braudel 1975:371ff. Note, however, that the Portuguese also made use of delegation. They wisely worked on the assumption that undistorted communication was possible for strategy but not for tactics. See Wallerstein 1974:327.

10 For an analysis of parasitism in communication see Serres 1980.

11 I use 'his' throughout since, so far as I know, all mediaeval and early modern mariners were men.

12 Taylor notes that the first known Mediterranean rutter dates from 1296

(Taylor:1956:104) and the first *portolan* chart, the Carta Pisana, from about 1275 (109).

13 The latter related high or low tide of a port to the position in the sky of the new or full moon. From these data it was possible to calculate the approximate times of high or low tides at any time in the month.

14 Sailing directions 'were copied, mislaid, collected together again, and perhaps bound up to form a little leather book of ill-arranged, often conflicting information. Nevertheless, the rutter was the ship's master's *vade mecum'*, Waters 1958:12.

15 The similar notion that the development of devices should be interpreted within an analysis of the struggles and growth of systems or networks is one that has received some attention in the history and sociology of technology. See, in particular, Callon 1980; Hughes 1979; 1983.

16 Taylor (1956:159ff) takes the view that this was started in 1456–7. Beaujouan (1966:71; and Poulle 1957:114) and Chaunu (1979:254) put the date nearer 1485.

17 Whether, as Cortesao (1966:59) insists, the *idea* of astronomical navigation developed in Portugal in the early fifteenth century seems to me to be somewhat doubtful. Taylor's (1956:159) suggestion that Portuguese vessels may sometimes have carried professional astronomers in the middle of the century, though not unreasonable, is also without much proof. Again, there is historical controversy over the extent to which the Portuguese made use of astronomical navigation in the 1460s. Taylor (1956:159–60), without, I think it must be said, very much evidence, implies that this was the case. He is, however, in agreement with Waters (1958:47) and Cotter (1968:130) when they argue that regular measurements of the altitude were being made from points along the African coast – an activity which, while necessary data for astronomical navigation, none the less has to be distinguished from it. However, even this is open to dispute. See the sceptical views of Beaujouan 1966:71, Beaujouan and Poulle 1957:114 and Chaunu 1979:255.

18 It has been argued that he was the first person to suggest that the astrolabe might be used in navigation, though this is claimed by others, improbably in the view of most, for Majorcan pilots at the end of the thirteenth century. See Cotter 1968:22; 62.

19 Once again there is a dissenter. Chaunu (1979:258) takes the view that the *Regimento* postdates the great voyages of discovery. However, Beaujouan (1966:73) and Diffie and Winius (1977:140–1) side with Taylor.

20 Determination of the longitude was a very much more difficult problem which did not achieve successful solution until the development of accurate portable timepieces in the eighteenth century.

21 At first these were discs of brass or wood, but later they were made of a solid, heavy, ring of brass, which was less disturbed by the wind. Waters 1958:55.

22 It appears that the data for the sun's declinations were taken from tables calculated by Abraham Zacuto. See Taylor 1956:165.

23 Full details of the contents of the *Regimento* are to be found in Taylor 1956:162–6; Waters 1958:52–3.

24 This was because they too were located within a relatively stable context that included vessels and training schools. I have emphasised the interrelatedness of elements in the Portuguese effort elsewhere. See Law 1985b.

John Law

Acknowledgments

The research that led to this paper was undertaken at the Centre de Sociologie de l'Innovation of the Ecole Nationale Supérieure des Mines in Paris. I am grateful to the Fondation Fyssen, the Leverhulme Foundation, the Ecole Nationale Supérieure des Mines, the University of Keele and the C.N.R.S. who made it possible to spend a period of leave at the Centre. I am particularly grateful to Michel Callon, Bruno Latour and Arie Rip for commenting on an earlier version of this paper.

References

Bagrow, Leo and Skelton, R.A. (1964), *History of Cartography*, London, C.A. Watts.

Beaujouan, Guy (1966), 'Science Livresque et Art nautique au XVe siecle', Mollat and Adam (1966), 61–85.

Beaujouan, Guy and Poulle, Emmanuel (1957), 'Les Origines de la Navigation aux XV³ et XVIe siecles', Mollat (1957), 103–16.

Bijker, Wiebe, Pinch, Trevor and Hughes, Thomas (eds) (1985), *New Directions in the Social Study of Technology*, Cambridge, Mass., M.I.T. Press, forthcoming.

Boxer, C.R. (1969), *The Portuguese Seaborne Empire, 1415–1825*, London, Hutchinson.

Braudel, Fernand (1975), *The Mediterranean and the Mediterranean World in the Age of Phillip II*, translated by Sian Reynolds, London, Fontana/Collins.

Braudel, Fernand (1979), *Civilisation Materielle, Economie et Capitalisme, XVe-XVIIIe siecle*, three vols, Paris, Armand Colin.

Callon, Michel (1980), 'Struggles and Negotiations to Define What is Problematic and What is Not: the Sociologic of Translation', in Knorr, Krohn and Whitley (1980), 197–219.

Callon, Michel (1985a), 'Domestication of the Scallops and the Fishermen of St. Brieuc Bay: Some Elements of the Sociology of Translation', this volume.

Callon, Michel (1985b), 'The Electric Vehicle: No Mystery', Chapter 2 in Callon, Law and Rip (1985a), forthcoming.

Callon, Michel and Latour, Bruno (1981), 'Unscrewing the Big Leviathan: How Actors Macrostructure Reality and How Sociologists help them to do so', in Knorr and Cicourel (1981;, 277–303.

Callon, Michel, Law, John and Rip, Arie (eds) (1985a), *Studies in the Dynamics of Science*, London, Macmillan.

Callon, Michel, Law, John and Rip, Arie (1985b), 'Introduction', Chapter 1 in Callon, Law and Rip (1985a).

Chaunu, Pierre (1979), *European Expansion in the Later Middle Ages*, translated by Katherine Bertram, Amsterdam, New York, Oxford, North-Holland.

Cipolla, Carlo M. (1965), *Guns and Sails in the Early Phase of European Expansion, 1400–1700*, London, Collins.

Constant, Edward (1978), 'On the Diversity and Co-Evolution of Tec:.nological

Multiples: Steam Turbines and Pelton Water Wheels', *Social Studies of Science*, 8, 183–210.

Cortelazzo, Manlio (ed.) (1970), *Mediterranée et Ocean Indien, Travaux du Sixième Colloque International d'Histoire Maritime*, Venise, 20–24 Sept. 1962, Paris, S.E.V.P.E.N.

Cortesao, Armando (1966), 'Note sur les Origines de la Navigation Astronomique au Portugal', Mollat and Adam (1966), 137–47.

Cotter, Charles H. (1968), *A History of Nautical Astronomy*, Hollis & Carter, London.

Diffie, Bailey W. and Winius, George D. (1977), *Foundations of the Portuguese Empire, 1415–1580*, Minneapolis, University of Minnesota Press.

Eisenstein, Elizabeth L. (1979), *The Printing Press as an Agent of Social Change: Communications and Cultural Transformations in Early-Modern Europe*, Cambridge, Cambridge University Press.

Foucault, Michel (1979), *Discipline and Punish: the Birth of the Prison*, Harmondsworth, Penguin.

Gille, Paul (1966), 'Navires lourds et Navires Rapides avant et après les Caravelles', Mollat and Adam (1966), 171–8.

Gille, Paul (1970), 'Les Navires des Deux Routes des Indes (Venise et Portugal): Evolution des Types. Resultats Economiques', Cortelazzo (1970), 193–201.

Goody, Jack (1977), *The Domestication of the Savage Mind*, Cambridge, Cambridge University Press.

Hughes, Thomas P. (1979), 'The Electrification of America: the System Builders', *Technology and Culture*, 20, 124–61.

Hughes, Thomas P. (1983), *Networks of Power: Electrification in Western Society, 1880–1930*, Baltimore, Johns Hopkins University Press.

Knorr, Karin D. and Cicourel, Aaron V. (eds) (1981), *Advances in Social Theory and Methodology: Toward an Integration of Micro and Macro Sociologies*, London, Routledge & Kegan Paul.

Knorr, Karin D., Krohn, Roger and Whitley, Richard D. (eds) (1980), *The Social Process of Scientific Investigation, Sociology of the Sciences*, 4, Reidel, Dordrecht & Boston.

Knorr-Cetina, Karin D. and Mulkay, Michael J. (eds) (1983), *Science Observed; Perspectives on the Social Study of Science*, London and Beverly Hills, Sage.

Landstrom, Bjorn (1978), *Sailing Ships in Words and Pictures from Papyrus Boats to Full-Riggers*, London, George Allen & Unwin.

Lane, Frederic C. (1934), *Venetian Ships and Shipbuilders of the Renaissance*, Baltimore, Johns Hopkins University Press.

Lane, Frederic C. (1950), 'Force and Enterprise in the Creation of Oceanic Commerce', supplement to *Journal of Economic History*, 10, 19–31; reprinted in Lane (1966), 399–411.

Lane, Frederic C. (1966), *Venice and History, The Collected Papers of Frederic C. Lane,* edited by a committee of former students, Baltimore, Maryland, Johns Hopkins University Press.

Lane, Frederic C. (1973), *Venice, A Maritime Republic,* Baltimore, Maryland, Johns Hopkins Press.

Lankton, Larry D. (1983), 'The Machine Under the Garden, Rock Drills arrive at the Lake Superior Copper Mines, 1868–1883', *Technology and Culture*, 24, 1–37.

Latour, Bruno (1983), 'Give me a Laboratory and I will raise the Word', in Knorr-Cetina and Mulkay (1983), 141–70.

Latour, Bruno (1984a), *Les Microbes, Guerre et Paix* followed by *Irreductions*, Paris, Metailie.

Latour, Bruno (1984b), 'A Simple Model for Treating Technoscience Evolution', paper presented to conference on New Developments in the Social Studies of Technology at Twente University, Enschede, the Netherlands, 5–7 July.

Latour, Bruno (1985a), 'Visualisation and Cognition', *Knowledge and Society*, 6, forthcoming.

Latour, Bruno (1985b), 'The Meanings of Social', this volume.

Law, John (1984), 'A propos des Tactiques du Controle Social: une Introduction a la Theorie de l'Acteur-Reseau', *La Legitimite Scientifique, Cahiers Science, Technologie, Société*, 4, Paris, C.N.R.S.

Law, John (1985a), 'On Texts and Other Allies', *Culture, Technique*, forthcoming.

Law, John (1985b), 'Technology, Closure and Heterogeneous Engineering: the Case of the Portuguese expansion', in Bijker and Pinch, (1985), forthcoming.

MacKenzie, Donald (1984), 'Technology, the State and the Strategic Missile', paper presented at the Workshop of New Developments in the Social Studies of Technology, Twente University, Enschede, the Netherlands, 5–7 July.

McNeill, William H. (1982), *The Pursuit of Power: Technology, Armed Force and Society since A.D. 1000*, Oxford, Blackwell.

Magalhaes-Godinho, Vitorino (1969), *L'Economie de l'Empire Portugais aux XVe et XVI Siècles*, Paris, S.E.V.P.E.N.

Mollat, Michel (ed.) (1957), *Le Navire et l'Economie Maritime du XVe au XVIII Siècle, Travaux du Colloque d'Histoire Maritime 17 Mai, 1956, Academie de la Marine*, Paris S.E.V.P.E.N.

Mollat, Michel and Adam, Paul (eds) (1966), *Actes du Cinquième Colloque International d'Histoire Maritime, Les Aspects International d'Histoire Maritime au XVe et XVIe Siècles*, Lisbonne, 14–6 Sept., Paris, S.E.V.P.E.N.

Ocean Indien (1964), *Ocean Indien et Mediterranée, Travaux du Sixième Colloque International d'Histoire Maritime et du Deuxième Congrès de l'Association Historique Internationale de l'Ocean Indien*, Lorenco Marques, 13–15 Aug. 1962, Paris, S.E.V.P.E.N.

Parry, J.H. (1963), *The Age of Reconnaissance*, London, Weidenfeld & Nicolson.

Penrose, Boies (1952), *Travel and Discovery in the Renaissance, 1420–1620*, Cambridge, Mass., Harvard University Press.

Pinch, Trevor J. and Bijker, Wiebe E. (1984), 'The Social Construction of Facts and Artefacts: or How the Sociology of Science and the Sociology of Technology might Benefit Each Other', *Social Studies of Science*, 14, 399–441.

Rego, A. da Silva (1964), 'Quelques Problemes de l'Histoire Maritime de l'Ocean Indien', *Ocean Indien*, 37–48.

Schwartz Cowan, Ruth (1984), 'The "Consumption Junction": Historical and Sociological Analyses of Technological Trajectories', paper presented to the Workshop on New Developments in the Social Studies of Technology, Twente University of Technology, Enschede, the Netherlands, 5–7 July.

Serres, Michel (1980), *Le Parasite*, Paris, Grasset.

Taylor, E.R.G. (1956), *The Haven-Finding Art: A History of Navigation from Odyesseus to Captain Cook*, London, Hollis & Carter.

Tooley, R.V. and Bricker, Charles (1976), *Landmarks of Mapmaking; An Illustrated Survey of Maps and Mapmakers*, Oxford, Phaidon.

Wallerstein, Immanuel (1974), *The Modern World System, I; Capitalist Agriculture and the Origins of the European World-Economy in the Sixteenth Century*, New York, Academic Press.

Waters, David W. (1958). *The Art of Navigation in England in Elizabethan and Early Stuart Times*, London, Hollis & Carter.

Waters, David W. (1976), *The Planispheric Astrolabe*, Greenwich National Maritime Museum.

The powers of association

Bruno Latour

Abstract

This article starts with a paradox: when an actor simply *has* power nothing happens and s/he is powerless; when, on the other hand, an actor *exerts* power it is others who perform the action. It appears that power is not something one can possess – indeed it must be treated as a consequence rather than as a cause of action. In order to explore this paradox a diffusion model of power in which a successful command moves under an impetus given it from a central source is contrasted with a translation model in which such a command, if it is successful, results from the actions of a chain of agents each of whom 'translates' it in accordance with his/her own projects. Since, in the translation model, power is composed here and now by enrolling many actors in a given political and social scheme, and is not something that can be stored up and given to the powerful by a pre-existing 'society', it follows that debates about the origins of society, the nature of its components, and their relationships become crucial data for the sociologist. It also follows that the nature of society is negotiable, a practical and revisable matter (performative), and not something that can be determined once and for all by the sociologist who attempts to stand outside it (ostensive). The sociologist should, accordingly, seek to analyse the way in which people are associated together, and should, in particular, pay attention to the material and extrasomatic resources (including inscriptions) that offer ways of linking people that may last longer than any given interaction. In the translation model the study of society therefore moves from the study of the social as this is usually conceived, to a study of methods of association.

The problem of power may be encapsulated in the following paradox: when you simply *have* power – *in potentia* – nothing happens and you are powerless; when you *exert* power – *in actu* – *others* are performing the action and not you. To take an example, Amin Gemayel in his palace officially has power over the Lebanon, but since very few people act when he orders things, he is powerless in practice. Power is not something you may possess and hoard. Either you have it in practice and *you* do not have it – others have – or you simply have it in theory and you do not have it.

What makes the difference between power 'in potentia' and power 'in actu'? The actions of others. Power over something or someone is a *composition* made by many people – I will call this the 'primary mechanism' – and *attributed* to one of them – this will be called the 'secondary mechanism'.[1] The amount of power exercised varies not according to the power someone has, but to the number of other people who enter into the composition. This is why the notion of power becomes less and less useful when power increases or decreases. Progressive 'gain' or 'loss' is not usually part of the concept of power. History is full of people who, because they believed social scientists and deemed power to be something you can possess and capitalise, gave orders no one obeyed!

In spite of this essential paradox the notion of power is often used something happens. A dictator is obeyed, we say, because 'he has got' power; a manager is able to move his headquarters because, as we like to say, 'he is powerful'; a dominant female monkey is able to grab the best feeding sites because 'she holds' a powerful rank. These explanations are as tautological as the 'dormitive virtue of the opium poppy' dear to Molière's physicians. The exercise of power is no more the cause of anything than the 'dormitive virtue' is the cause of the deep sleep of patients who have smoked opium. Power is, on the contrary, what has to be explained by the action of the others who obey the dictator, the manager, or the dominant female. If the notion of 'power' may be used as a convenient way to *summarise* the consequence of a collective action, it cannot also *explain* what holds the collective action in place. It may be used as an effect, but never as a cause. The job that was done by the Cartesians when they criticised the 'occult qualities' like that of 'dormitive virtue' must now be done on this other 'occult quality' (since the notion of power has the same lenitive effect on the critical stamina of many social scientists as that of the poppy on the opium-taker).

If there were any way of getting rid of the notion of power this point would be obvious. But it is so useful as a stop gap solution to cover our ignorance, to explain (away) hierarchy, obedience or hegemony, that it is, at first sight, hard to see how to do without this pliable and empty term. In this article I explore a few alternative possibilities that would allow social scientists to treat the exercise of power as an effect rather than as a cause.

(1) From diffusion to translation

What makes the notion of power both so useful and so empty is a philosophical argument about the nature of collective action. This argument should be dealt with first if we want to do away with the 'powerful virtue' of power.

To explain the spread in time and space of an order, of a claim, of an artefact, there are two possibilities. The first is to endow the order, the claim, or the artefact – let us call it a token – with an inner force similar to that of inertia in physics. According to the inertia principle the token will move in the same direction as long as there is no obstacle. In such a model – let us call it the diffusion model – the displacement of a token through time and space does not have to be explained. What is in need of explanation is the slowing down or the acceleration of the token which results from the action or reaction of other people. For instance, scientific progress is easily understood within the diffusion model. It is not the spread of accurate facts about nature that has to be explained, but only its slowing down or its distortion caused by backward minds, countries or cultures. To take another example, technical progress is mostly (though not always) interpreted from the standpoint of the diffusion model: steam engines, electricity or computers are endowed with inertia such that they can hardly be stopped except by the most reactionary interest groups or nations; their inertial force is not what has to be explained, but rather the ability of some groups to slow them down – those that are said to be 'closed' to progress – or to accelerate them – those that are 'open' to progress. Other examples should show that fashion, ideas, gadgets, goods and life styles are also granted enough inertia to spread through society which is seen as a *medium* with various degrees of resistance.

The model of diffusion thus defines three important elements in the spread of a token through time and space: the initial force that triggers the movements and which constitutes its only energy; the inertia that conserves this energy; and the medium through which the token circulates. Clearly, when it is used as a cause to explain collective action, the notion of power is considered in terms of the diffusion model: what counts is the initial force of those who *have* power; this force is then transmitted in its entirety; finally, the medium through which power is exerted may diminish the power because of frictions and resistances (lack of communication, ill will, opposition of interest groups, indifference). In such a model, when we see that an order given by a manager has been executed by two hundred people we conclude that the force that displaced the latter should be placed in the hands of the manager. To be sure, the order as it is executed is not quite the order that was given, but such distortions may be attributed to frictions and resistances which deflected and slowed down the pace of the original force. The advantage of such a model is that everything may be explained either by talking about the initial force or by pointing to the resisting medium: when an order is faithfully executed, one simply says that the masters had a lot of power; when it is not, one merely argues that the masters' power met with a lot of resistance. Stalin thus had a great deal of clout while Amin Gemayel has many enemies.

This model of diffusion may be contrasted with another, that of the model of translation. According to the latter, the spread in time and space of anything – claims, orders, artefacts, goods – is in the hands of people; each of these people may act in many different ways, letting the token drop, or modifying it, or deflecting it, or betraying it, or adding to it, or appropriating it. The faithful transmission of, for instance, an order by a large number of people is a rarity in such a model and if it occurs it requires explanation. In other words, there is no inertia to account for the spread of a token. When no one is there to take up the statement or the token then it simply stops.

More importantly, displacement is not caused by the initial impetus since the token has no impetus whatsoever; rather it is the consequence of the energy given to the token by everyone in the chain who does something with it, as in the case of rugby players and a rugby ball. The initial force of the first in the chain is no more important than that of the second, or the fortieth, or of the four hundredth person. Consequently, it is clear that the energy cannot be hoarded or capitalised; if you want the token to move on you have to find fresh sources of energy all the time; you can never rest on what you did before, no more than rugby players can rest for the whole game after the *first* player has given the ball its *first kick*.

The third aspect of the translation model is the most important. Each of the people in the chain is not simply resisting a force or transmitting it in the way they would in the diffusion model; rather, they are doing something essential for the existence and maintenance of the token. In other words, the chain is made of *actors* – not of patients – and since the token is in everyone's hands in turn, everyone shapes it according to their different projects. This is why it is called the model of translation. The token changes as its moves from hand to hand and the faithful transmission of a statement becomes a single and unusual case among many, more likely, others.

In the two models the elements to be considered are utterly different: in the translation approach the initial force does not count for more than any other; force is never transmitted in its entirety and no matter what happened earlier, it can stop at any time depending on the action of the person next along the chain; again, instead of a passive medium through which the force is exerted, there are active members shaping and changing the token as it is moved. Instead of the *transmission* of the same token – simply deflected or slowed down by friction – you get, in the second model, the continuous *transformation* of the token. When, as a result of unusual circumstances, it is made to stay the same, this is what requires an explanation.

Clearly, the notion of power would look entirely different if it were considered in terms of the translation model. The obedience to an order given by someone would require the alignment of all the people concerned by it, who would all assent to it faithfully, without adding or subtracting anything. Such a situation is highly improbable. The chances are that the order has been modified and composed by many different people who slowly turned it into something completely different as they sought to achieve *their* own goals. How can we be so sure of this? Simply because if it were not the case, then the order would not have been 'obeyed' in the first place, and the person who gave the order would be said to be powerless! 'Power' is always the illusion people get when they are obeyed; thinking in terms of the diffusion model, they imagine that others behave because of the masters' clout without ever suspecting the many different reasons others have for obeying and doing something else; more exactly, people who are 'obeyed' discover what their power is really made of when they start to lose it. They realise, but too late, that it was 'made of' the wills of all the others.

A shift from the diffusion to the translation model is thus the first move that will allow social scientists to understand power as a consequence and not as a cause of collective action.

(2) From a past to a present-day origin for society

If we wish to transform the 'occult quality of power' into something the social scientist can study we have to make use of the translation model. This, however, is not easy for we are obliged to modify, so to speak, the *timing* of the origins of society.

Since Durkheim, social scientists have considered political philosophy to be the prehistory of their science. Sociology had become a positive science only once it stopped bickering about the origins of society and instead *started with* the notion of an all-embracing society that could then be used to explain various phenomena of interest. The question of its origins thus became one of those obsolete problems better left to philosophers. Viewed in such a framework, the notion of power becomes convenient for sociologists. There is always enough already accumulated energy to explain, say, the spread of the multinationals, Pinochet's dictatorship, male domination in black ghettos, the division of labour in factories, and so on. You start with so many inequalities that their origins seem to be irrelevant. It thus seems unproblematic to say that Reagan, Napoleon, the City of London, or capitalism 'have got power' – unproblematic, that is, so long as you are able to draw on the big reservoir of energy provided by an ever present and overarching society.

If you apply the translation model, this reservoir dries up immediately. You no longer have any stored-up energy to explain why a President is obeyed and a multinational grows since these effects are a consequence of the actions of multitudes. You are thus faced with multitudes that wonder how to act as one. This problem is typical of the kind of question raised by political philosophers since the time of Aristotle. Power is *not yet* there as it is in the social sciences. It is composed *first,* as for instance in Hobbes' or Rousseau's theories of contract. This position raises problems for sociologists since it means moving backwards and reopening the question of the origins of society that they thought they had exorcised once and for all when they became respectable scientists. It might mean going back to prehistory. . .

Fortunately the drift is not that big. When we apply the translation model we simply have to understand that the origins of society are still with us today and that debates about how it all began are still shaping our behaviour here and now. If we make such a hypothesis, then all the debates about what holds society together stop being endless and fruitless; instead they themselves become *one of the ways* of holding society together and enrolling enough people to constitute power. Elsewhere I have argued that ·debates about the origins of society do not occur at random but turn about a small number of items:[2] (a) the *units* in terms of which each person defines the society (family, genes, classes, kin, individuals, cities); (b) the *qualities* these units are endowed with (foresight, social skills, greed, blind force, selfishness); (c) the *form* the relations between units take (exchange, calculation, parasitism, exploitation, asymmetry) and when it is appropriate (d) the *currency* with which the relations are calculated (money, number of offspring, energy, pleasure and pain, power) as well as (e) the *time-delay* with which these calculations take place (a day, a year, a generation, a million years) and (f) the *degree of reciprocity* deemed acceptable (one to one barter, potlach, personal balance, market or generalised exchange).

When these questions are considered, a new order emerges from the continuous debates about what it is that holds us all together. The order obtained is a function of the options selected from the above 'questionnaire' and the composition of society that results accordingly differs radically. Any modification, no matter how small or how scientific, to each of the answers might have enormous consequences. Sociobiology is a good case in point: a shift from group to kin selection, for instance, leads the costs and benefits of all the actors in society to be modified.[3] To take another example, to trace the division of labour between men and women a few thousand years earlier (or later) entails a complete change in what women can and cannot do today.[4] Establish the drives of social actors on the basis of natural instead of divine laws, and the legitimation of all the powers in society changes signs.[5]

The origins of society are no longer behind us, and the task is not the discovery of the 'real' units, the 'real' qualities, the 'real' currency, and the 'real' time delay that make up society. The task before us is rather to use the screams and furies of the entire range of groups dissatisfied with the genealogy of their positions, because each of these fierce debates – whether in the political or the scientific arena – are deciding on the composition of society *now,* before our very eyes. It is clear, for instance, that if the units are two classes engaged in a constant struggle whose form is defined and counted in terms of the use of labour value then society is made to move in one direction: some members will be defined by others as parasitic exploiters who hold great power.[6] If, to take another example, the units are kin clans whose qualities are good self control, the form of their relations that of obedience and the currencies those of honour and shame, then *another* society will be defined.[7] A third is constructed if the units are genes that stop at nothing to propagate replicas of themselves and which make this calculation in terms of the number of offspring on a thousand-year timescale. In the latter case completely different lists of winners and losers, exploiters and exploited, the powerful and the powerless, and the selfish and the altruistic are proposed.

Either power is something provided by the prior existence of society, or it is something that has to be obtained by enrolling many actors. If the former is the case, then neither power nor society have to be explained. Rather they are what provide the explanation for the behaviour of everything else. If the latter is the case, neither power nor society are used as explanations. These arise out of the modifications that are made to the developing definition of what society is about. The sources of power are in the hands of those who are able to shift around the answers to the questionnaire outlined above. Clearly, if this is accepted then the notion of power becomes a consequence and the translation model may be easily used.

(3) From an ostensive to a performative definition of the social link

So far I have argued that in order to speak reasonably about power this notion has to be turned upside down and should be treated as a consequence instead of a cause of collective action.[8] However, to do this I was obliged to propose a shift from a diffusion to a translation model. This led us into a difficulty: in order to make this shift possible we had to modify the chronology of society: its origins were not in a remote past. Rather they were ever-present and constantly open to question in scientific or political debates. This position in turn opens another difficulty: if society is made before our eyes then it cannot *explain* our behaviour but is rather shaped by our collective action. It is no more a cause of the latter than power itself. Does this mean that we have to deny the existence of an overarching society in order to do away with the notion of power? Not exactly, but we have to shift from an ostensive to a performative definition of society. In this way we will understand why each definition of society, each debate about what it is made of, each new science that aims at discovering its function, each new genealogy of man's past, has such an enormous influence over us all. The critique of the notion of power entails a critique of the most cherished notion – that of society. To make this point clear, let me list the basic principles of the ostensive and performative definitions:

Ostensive definition

1 *In principle* it is possible to discover properties which are typical of life in society and could explain the social link and its evolution, though *in practice* they might be difficult to detect.

2 Social actors, whatever their size, are in the society defined above; even if they are active, as their name indicates, their activity is restricted since they are only parts of a larger society.

3 The actors in society are *useful informants* for those who seek the principles that hold society together (see 1), but since they are simply parts of society (see 2), actors are *only informants* and should not be relied upon too much because they never see the whole picture.

4 With the proper methodology, social scientists can sort out the actors' opinions, beliefs, illusions and behaviour to discover the properties typical of life in society (see 1) and piece together the whole picture.

Within such a framework, all controversies including those about the origins of society are only *practical difficulties* that will be eliminated with more data, a better methodology and better insulation of the social scientists' endeavour from ideology and amateurism. Uncertainties, controversies about what the society is, these are only momentary problems hiding a picture of society that can be the object of an ostensive definition.

Performative definition

1 It is impossible *in principle* to define the list of properties that would be typical of life in society although *in practice* it is possible to do so.

2 Actors, whatever their size, define in practice what society is, what it is made of, what is the whole and what are the parts – both for themselves and for others.

3 No assumption is necessary about whether or not any actor knows more or less than any other actor. The 'whole picture' is what is at stake in the practical definitions made by actors.

4 Social scientists raise the *same questions* as any other actors (see 2) and find different *practical* ways of enforcing their definition of what society is about.

In this framework, controversies on what society is about cannot be eliminated to let the scientists unfold the whole picture. No matter what their scale and intensity, controversies are part and parcel of the very definition of the social bond. The question: 'What links us together?' is not answerable in principle, but in practice, every time someone raises it a new association is made that does indeed link us together. Society is not the referent of an ostensive definition discovered by social scientists despite the ignorance of their informants. Rather it is performed through everyone's efforts to define it.[9] Those who are powerful are not those who 'hold' power in principle, but those who practically define or redefine what 'holds' everyone together. This shift *from principle to practice* allows us to treat the vague notion of power not as a cause of people's behaviour but as the consequence of an intense activity of enrolling, convincing and enlisting. When the second framework is chosen instead of the first the practical resources necessary to perform society appear clearly. We have to study them if we wish to do away with the notion of power.

(4) From matters of principle to practical resources

If power is not something you can hoard and possess, it is something that has to be *made*. Who will make it? *Others*, by definition (see Section 1). These others, the only ones who are really powerful (*in actu*), therefore have to attribute their action to one amongst them who becomes powerful *in potentia*. This means that a constant debate will rage about who obeys and who is obeyed (Section 2). In these continuous struggles there will be as many definitions of 'the whole picture' as there are actors striving to enrol and/or to be enrolled. 'Society' can explain these struggles no more than can 'power'. On the contrary, they are the provisional outcome of many definitions: society is what you perform for as long as you are able to perform it (see Section 3). Does this mean that we are led into utter chaos, society being made and unmade constantly? There is no answer to this question in principle. We may or may not be led into chaos. This depends *only* on the practical resources one may mobilise in order to make a definition hold over time. The whole burden of making society firm has shifted from the society itself (which has become a consequence) to the many material tasks that may enforce or reinforce the provisional bonds made by the actors.[10]

To make this point clear, I will give one example taken from the sociologist who is most far removed from this point of view. Durkheim is the epitome of what I call the ostensive definition of the social link and nowhere is this more clear than in *The Elementary Forms of the Religious Life*.[11] In Book II, Chapters III, V and VII he acknowledges, however, that the clan structure is not tight enough to hold the clan together. These are the only places in the whole book where the overarching society, used elsewhere as a cause to explain everything, is deemed insufficient. Where does Durkheim turn in order to make the clan hold together? To material resources that reinforce the bond:

> But if the movements by which these sentiments are expressed are connected with something that endures, the sentiments themselves become more durable. (p. 231)

These resources (flags, names, scarifications, colours, tattoos) are not, he says, simply labels: 'attached to representations already made, in order to make them more manageable: they are an integral part of them' (idem.). And two pages later, these 'integral parts' of the bond have become their cause:

> A clan is essentially a reunion of individuals who bear the same name and rally round the same sign. Take away the name and the sign which materialises it, and the clan is no longer representable. Since the group is possible only on this condition, both the institution of the emblem and the part it takes in the life of the group are thus explained. (344)

Very soon after this passage Durkheim goes back to his usual framework and explains collective behaviour by the existence of society, but for a few pages, and for the vague notion of the clan at least, resources have taken the most important role and have become what ties the clan together. The main point he made during this short lapse is that the *durability* of the definition of the clan depends upon the *duration* of the resources used to make it hold together.[12] The claim is a weak and short-lived notion, and it becomes longer lasting and stronger with tattoos, flags, names and scarifications. This means that in defining society we need *a longer* list that includes, of course, the notion of clan, but *also* includes flags, colours, names and tattoos. To put it differently: society is not made up of social elements, but of a list that mixes up social and non-social elements.

This becomes clearer when we express its opposite: when a society is made of social elements alone it does not have a stable structure. To find such a situation one has to study not human but animal societies. Elsewhere, with Shirley Strum, I have shown how baboon societies, for instance, manage their intense social lives without the use of what we call extrasomatic resources.[13] They build the collective body with their own bodies alone, using no resources beyond these. This leads to the extreme *complexity* of their social skills, since they have no way of transforming a weak bond into a stronger one other than by using *more* social skills. The result of such an active redefinition of their society is that there is no stable structure, but rather social skills to repair constantly a decaying social order. As they make use of no extrasomatic resources to do this repair we may half-jokingly picture the baboons as the ideal 'competent member' as defined in ethnomethodology.

For human society, however, the baboon model works no better than the ethnomethodological one, since what counts in holding the society together is mostly extrasomatic. Each performative definition of what society is about is reinforced, underlined and stabilised, by bringing in new and non-human resources. The same social skills applied among non-human primates to other bodies, are now applied in human societies to things that hold bodies in place.[14] The notion of power is emptied of all its potential at this point. 'Power' is now transferred to the many resources used to strengthen the bonds. The power of the manager may now be obtained by a long series of telephone calls, record-keeping, walls, clothes and machines, just as the clan depends upon the use of new items such as tattoos and scarifications to perform its definitions. The exact composition of the list is not important for the present argument. What counts is that *it is open ended*, that the so-called social elements are simply *items among* many others in a much longer list; that they cannot be used to *replace* all the other elements; or even used as their headings.

Yet if social elements are of so little use, something must have gone wrong somewhere in the definition of the social. I have to tackle this final point in order to empty the notion of power of its powers of fascination.

(5) Conclusion: from the study of society to that of associations

The argument above may be summarised in one sentence: society is not what holds us together, it is what is held together. Social scientists have mistaken the effect for the cause, the passive for the active, what is glued for the glue. Appealing to a reserve of energy, be it 'capital'[15] or 'power', to explain the obedient behaviour of the multitudes, is thus meaningless. This reservoir is full only as long as you do not need it, that is as long as others dutifully fill it. It is empty when you need it, that is when the others are no longer filling it. There is no way out of this paradox. No matter how much power one appears to accumulate, it is always necessary to obtain it from the others who are doing the action – this is what I called the shift from diffusion to translation. Thus it is always necessary to redefine who is acting, why it is necessary to act together, what are the boundaries of the collective, how responsibility should be allocated, what are the best metalanguages to define collective action – this is what I call maintaining the origins of society in the present. The result of such a continuous definition and redefinition of what collective action is about is to transform society from something that exists and is in principle knowable into something which is built equally, so to speak, by every actor and that is in principle unknowable – it involves shifting from an ostensive to a performative definition. From where do inequalities between the definitions of society performed by each actor come if it is not from a stable society? From a miscellaneous list of extrasomatic resources mobilised by actors to enforce their definition – this is what I called shifting from matters of principle to practices.[16] Stable states of society can be achieved, but not with social elements alone. As long as it is simply social skills that are brought in, one does not get a society more stable and more technically developed than that of the baboons or the chimpanzees.[17] The only way to understand how power is locally exerted is thus to take into account everything that has been put to one side – that is, essentially, techniques.[18]

All the above shifts then lead to a slight but necessary redefinition of what sociology is about. As a science of society, it cannot go very far since, following what I have argued above, it will always treat effects as causes. It will use notions of 'power' and 'capital' when these have to be locally *composed;* it will talk of 'classes', 'ranks' and 'values' when these are the outcome of a continuous debate on how to classify, to rank and to evaluate; it will try to make society hang together with 'hierarchies', 'professions', 'institutions' or 'organisations' whereas the practical details that make it possible for these entities to last for more than a minute will escape attention; finally, despairing of finding something strong enough to tie us together, sociology will invent notions like 'legitimacy', 'authority', 'roles', 'culture', or 'Zeitgeist', even though such notions are efficient only when everything else is solidly tied together. Making society hang together with social elements alone is like trying to make a mayonnaise with neither eggs nor oil – that is, out of hot air alone.

An alternative way of defining sociology is to make it the study of *associations* rather than of those few ties that we call social. If this new definition is accepted, another type of explanation becomes available to the analyst. He or she can use all the forces that have been mobilised in our human world to explain why it is that we are linked together and that some orders are faithfully obeyed while others are not. These forces are heterogeneous in character: they may include atoms, words, lianas or tattoos. They are also, themselves, bound together to create machines and machinations that keep us all in place.

This paper has presented a negative argument: it has suggested that the notion of power should be abandoned. Now study of the stuff of which society is made may begin in earnest. In the false start made by sociology something was forgotten, something that at first seemed unimportant: the glue strong enough to hold us together, the glue that takes the form of all the sciences and technologies.

Notes

This paper is a personal rendering of ideas that have often been discussed with Michel Callon and Shirley Strum. I thank John Law for his help in bringing it to the light of day.

1 The most complete study of this problem is that of Tolstoy in *War and Peace* (1957). The primary mechanism is that of the half million soldiers in the Great Army, each of them doing more or less what they want – fleeing, killing, dying. The secondary mechanism gives a solution to what the collective is doing at any moment: Napoleon leads the great army and is the cause of its moves.
2 See Latour and Strum (1985): among the origin stories studied in this article are those of Sigmund Freud, Richard Dawkin, René Girard, Thomas Hobbes, Richard Leakey, Karl Marx and Jean-Jacques Rousseau.
3 This is the major revolution introduced by sociobiology in the calculation of all social links. To get an idea of this shift, compare E. O. Wilson's book on insects (1971) which uses a traditional group selection political philosophy with his *Sociobiology* (1975) which uses kin selection.
4 See, for instance Hardy (1981). The notion of genealogy is useful to map all these debates; each new position on the past modifies the genealogy (and thus the rights and duties) of every group in present society.
5 This is, for instance, the change made by Hobbes, in his *Leviathan* (1981).
6 It is never sufficiently emphasised that Marxism is in effect a mode of calculating all the exchanges practised in a society. If labour value is used as a standard, then the same capitalist who appeared to pay for everything at its price when counted in exchange value, appears as an exploiter. The indignation of the exploited is maintained as long as the accounting system is enforced. If all the exchanges in a society are now counted in *kilocalories* a quite different list of the exploited and parasites is drawn up.
7 No difference is to be made at this point between so called traditional and so called modern societies. Potlatch, for instance, is simply obtained by giving different answers to the same questionnaire (Mauss: 1923; 1967).
8 This is again what Tolstoy does in his book: Napoleon's moves, his genius, his competence, his inefficiency – none of these explain what happened to the Great Army. For an historical and philosophical commentary see Latour (1984).
9 The shift is analogous to that in physics between prerelativism (where it is necessary to have a referent to make good measurements) and relativism where it is necessary *not* to have any referent to make good and compatible measurements. See Callon and Latour (1985) and Strum and Latour (1984).

10 See the work of Elihu Gerson and his colleagues on 'tasks'.
11 Durkheim (1915).
12 In French, 'durée' and 'dureté'. On this point see Lâtour (1984), second part.
13 See Strum and Latour (1984); among the most relevant work on baboon societies see Strum (1982; 1983a; 1983b; and Westein, 1982).
14 This implies a different way of considering technology and its relations with society. On this see Callon and Latour (1981).
15 The critique made here of power could be addressed to the notion of 'capital' which is so popular, for instance, in Pierre Bourdieu's sociology. France is full of firms and banks that, because they held vast amounts of capital, thought that this was enough to exist and hold sway for ever. The factories are now closed and the banks bankrupt. For a critique of capital see Thevenot (1984).
16 This is what John Law calls 'heterogeneous engineering'. See Law (1985) and this volume.
17 Technical development is inversely proportional to that of social skills, so that, paradoxically, we are led to consider non-human primate societies as more complex than human ones. See Strum and Latour (1984).
18 This is in effect the same result as that obtained by Michel Foucault (1977) when he dissolved the notion of a power held by the powerful in favour of micro-powers diffused through the many technologies to discipline and keep in line. It is simply an expansion of Foucault's notion to the many techniques employed in machines and the hard sciences.

References

Callon, Michel and Latour, Bruno (1981), 'Unscrewing the Big Leviathan, or How Actors Macrostructure Reality and How Sociologists help them to do so', pp. 277–303 in Karin Knorr-Cetina and Aaron Cicourel (eds), *Advances in Social Theory and Methodology: Toward an Integration of Micro and Macro Sociologies,* London, Routledge & Kegan Paul.

Callon, Michel and Latour, Bruno (1985), 'Pour une Sociologie Relativement Exacte', mimeo, Paris, Ecole Nationale Supérieure des Mines.

Durkheim, Emile (1915), *The Elementary Forms of the Religious Life,* London, George Allen & Unwin.

Foucault, Michel (1977), *Discipline and Punish: The Birth of the Prison,* Harmondsworth, Penguin.

Hobbes, Thomas (1651; 1981), *The Leviathan,* New York, Pelican.

Hrdy, Sarah B. (1981), *The Woman that Never Evolved,* Cambridge, Mass., Harvard University Press.

Latour, Bruno (1984), *Les Microbes, Guerre et Paix,* followed by *Irréductions,* Paris, Anne-Marie Metailié.

Latour, Bruno and Strum, Shirley (1985), 'Human Social Origins: Oh Please Tell Us Another Origin Story', *Journal of Biological and Social Structure,* forthcoming.

Law, John (1985), 'Technology, Closure and Heterogeneous Engineering: the Case of the Portuguese Expansion', in Wiebe Bijker, Trevor Pinch and Thomas Hughes (eds), *New Directions in the Social Study of Technology,* Cambridge, Mass., M.I.T. Press, forthcoming.

Mauss, Marcel (1923; 1967), *The Gift: Forms and Functions of Exchange in Archaic Society,* New York, Norton & Co.

Strum, Shirley and Latour, Bruno (1984), 'The Meanings of Social', paper presented to International Primatology Society Meeting, Nairobi.

Strum, Shirley (1982), 'Agonistic Dominance among Baboons: An Alternative View', *International Journal of Primatology*, 3, 175–202.

Strum, Shirley (1983a), 'Use of Females by Male Olive Baboons', *American Journal of Primatology*, 5, 93–109.

Strum, Shirley (1983b), 'Why Males use Infants', in D.M. Taub (ed.), *Primate Paternalism*, New York, Van Nostrand Reinhold, 145–85.

Strum, Shirley and Western, Jonah (1982), 'Variations in Fecundity with Age and Environment in Olive Baboons', *American Journal of Primatology*, 3, 61–76.

Thevenot, Laurent (1984), 'Les Investissements de Forme', paper presented to Centre de Sociologie d'Innovation, Ecole Nationale Supérieure des Mines, Paris.

Tolstoy, Leo (1957), *War and Peace,* Harmondsworth, Penguin.

Wilson, Edward O. (1971), *The Insect Societies,* Cambridge, Mass., Harvard U.P.

Wilson, Edward O. (1975), *Sociobiology: The New Synthesis,* Cambridge, Mass., Harvard U.P.